Computers and Learning

Computers and Learning

Helping children acquire thinking skills

Jean D. M. Underwood
and
Geoffrey Underwood

Basil Blackwell

Copyright © Jean D. M. Underwood and Geoffrey Underwood 1990

First published 1990

Basil Blackwell Ltd.
108 Cowley Road, Oxford, OX4 1JF, UK

Basil Blackwell, Inc.
3 Cambridge Center
Cambridge, Massachusetts 02142, USA

British Library Cataloguing in Publication Data

A CIP catalogue record for this book is available from the British Library.

Library of Congress Cataloging in Publication Data

Underwood, Jean D. M.
  Computers and learning / Jean D. M. Underwood and Geoffrey Underwood
      p.   cm.
  Includes bibliographical references (p.   ).
  ISBN 0-631-15807-3—ISBN 0-631-15808-1
    1. Education—Great Britain—Data processing.   2. Computers and
children.   3. Cognition in children.   I. Underwood Geoffrey.
II. Title.
  LB1028.42.U53   1990   89-49282
  372.13'34—dc20   CIP

Typeset in 10 on 12 pt Palatino
by Graphicraft Typesetters Ltd., Hong Kong.
Printed in Great Britain by Billing and Sons Ltd, Worcester

Contents

Preface

Computers can be successfully integrated into the classroom, and our aim is to demonstrate some of the opportunities offered by this educational innovation. We shall also discuss some of the theoretical and practical questions which arise when we introduce this powerful machine.

There are a number of assumptions underlying the assertion that computers can be used for educational benefit. The first is that educationalists, parents, and society in general would like to see the effective use of new technology in the classroom. Although many people are apprehensive about computers they are also interested in the machine and acknowledge its power. The second assumption is that not all classroom use of new technology is beneficial, often because of the paucity of training for new and serving teachers in the more fruitful uses of the machine. This is a problem addressed directly by this book. Thirdly we would argue that by using the computer as a tool it becomes both an amplifier of human capabilities and a catalyst to intellectual development. These views of the computer lead to more productive outcomes in the classroom than do those uses which turn the machine into a surrogate teacher. But these uses may require new social organisations in the classroom, which in turn may lead teachers to question the purpose and mode of pupil evaluation. Briefly here we will expand on these points.

Whether we are travel agents, engineers, air traffic controllers, school children or policemen, one of our key roles is that of the information processor. We collect, interpret and then make decisions upon a vast array of data. We are George Miller's *informavores*, having developed an advanced society through our ability to make use of information gathered by earlier generations and by distant colleagues. This is not a new role, but the quantity and the quality of data now available to us is increasing exponentially. This is due in no little part

to the new technologies. We need help in handling all this new information. There is a long tradition of using aids such as books and pens
to supplement and amplify our own mental powers and the computer
is the latest addition to this range of tools. As such it is important for
all educated members of society to acquire basic computer-use skills –
skills other than computer programming, it should be stressed – in
the same way as we expect people to acquire basic literacy or indeed,
to learn to drive a car.

As well as being an amplifier of our own limited mental abilities –
an artificial aid to our memories, and a means of producing fast
answers to arithmetic questions, for instance – the classroom computer should be seen as a catalyst. It provides us with the means of
producing changes in the quality of thinking in children, and part of
our discussion is taken with demonstrations of tool-like software
involving databases, word processors and programming that can be
seen to have effects upon children's intellectual development. We
shall be reviewing the uses that teachers are currently making of their
classroom computers, by considering surveys of usage, and by presenting examples of class work that encourage this view of computers
as tools.

The supply of hardware and software to our schools is now sufficient, with careful slection, for our educational needs. Hardware is
largely a matter of funding, and is beyond the scope of our
discussions. We have a plethora of software from which to choose,
although there are shortages in some specific content areas. We want
to stress that these shortages do not pose a problem, because our
main focus should be upon general tools which will be useful across
the curriculum. There are a number of evaluations of tool-like packages now available, and we shall be reviewing some of them here.

Deciding upon a program is not the end of it. Once the software is
introduced into the classroom the teacher is faced with decisions
about the social organisation around the computer, and with decisions about the evaluation of children's work. Some of these decisions are present with non-computer work of course, but when the
computer is introduced they are unavoidable. With only one computer in the classroom we might expect to see children waiting in
line for their five minutes at the keyboard, but more likely we would
see a change in the pattern of working, with group work replacing
intensive individual work. The organisation of these groups is critically important, and has gender implications. Girls tend to become
disillusioned when working in competitive groups, and their education suffers. When children work co-operatively, with responsibility
for their own learning and for their collaborators, their own learning

and understanding benefits. Children working in these groups become autonomous and effective learners. When children do not work in this way their performance declines, but particularly affected are the girls. Despite the stereotyped view, there are no gender differences in competence and interest in computer-based work. It is not the nature of the work which causes problems for girls here, so much as the social organisation of that work. If we are to have children working in groups around the computer, and there are excellent reasons for this recommendation, then the group must be organised co-operatively otherwise we could be jeopardising girls' education.

Once children are working in co-operative groups we have the problem of evaluating the single final product. What grade should be assigned to each child in the group if the final product is, for example, a class newspaper? The problem becomes even more difficult when we add the changing role of teacher as co-learner. The computer often invites co-learning by taking the role of problem-setter, and when there is no closed answer to a task the teacher is as much a contributor as any of the children in the group. A third problem of evaluation here is a product of the non-linearity of computer-based work. With word processed writing, in particular, we are presented with the opportunity of continuous revision. When a piece of work has been written, it can still be developed, and this raises the question of when should it be evaluated.

These are some of the issues that emerge when we consider using the classroom computer. There are considerable educational gains to be made by taking the route offered by educational computing, as shown by the examples presented here. They are not problems to discourage us, for they compel us to consider our educational assumptions, clarify our own thinking and review our classroom practice.

Evaluation is a tricky word in education. How should we investigate an educational treatment? There are those who argue against experiments in classroom settings, on the basis of the highly specified conditions under which educational changes are observed. And there are others who argue against the single-learner case study, on the basis of lack of generalisation to other learners. There are advantages to both methods, of course. The classroom experiment, while specifying the conditions under which a treatment will have an effect, does exactly that – it tells us the optimal conditions for a treatment to be used to our advantage. The case study, while restricting its conclusions to an individual learner, also shows what can be achieved under these circumstances and gives a deeper understanding of process. In our evaluations of databases, word processing, and LOGO programming, we shall be drawing upon whatever evidence is available. No evidence has been rejected or omitted here on the grounds of its investigational stable. Evidence is invaluable in that it allows us to replace our hunches with reason. Decisions are only as good as the information that they are based upon, and we should be prepared to evaluate the soundness of the evidence case-by-case.

We would like to express our thanks to all those teachers, students and children who collaborated on the computer-based learning projects which we are able to describe. Their ideas have been invaluable and have provoked many of the discussions presented here.

Jean Underwood
Geoffrey Underwood

1 Issues in the use of educational computers

Classroom computers are now commonplace, but will any good come of it? Is it naive 'techno-romanticism' to believe that the introduction of computers into the school classroom will have a positive effect upon children's cognitive development? Does their use add a new dimension to the learning environment or does it simply parallel established classroom practice? In this book we shall be discussing the effectiveness of the computer as an aid to classroom learning, and looking at the potential of computer-based activities which are currently available. The critic might argue that putting microcomputers into our classrooms is a misguided romance with new technology, and that there will be no educational effects or merit. Our purpose is to point to the educational gains that can be better achieved with classroom computers, or achieved only with this medium. What *have been* the effects of information technology (IT) upon society in general – from the introduction of the printed book to global digital information communication – and *why* should we expect IT in the classroom to have any effects upon education?

Extending human capabilities and shrinking the world

The perception of a shrinking world is brought about largely by technological change. Although it is not a new phenomenon, the accelerating rate of change in the latter half of the twentieth century has increased this feeling of a shrinking world. Distance is less often measured in kilometres or miles today, but rather we talk of travel time. Technology has brought about the Global Village.

This dramatic shift in our perceptions of space, where Moscow is more familiar than Cheltenham or Charleston, is a result of the richness of the information we receive. Information pours into our homes from across the world and children can now talk cogently about African famine relief, the plight of the whale and the hole in the ozone layer, while being unaware of the loss of native plants, or of the poverty in their own cities. Environmental problems down the street and around the block in their own neighbourhoods do not appear on prime-time television news.

Caught in this information deluge from around the world, we must look to new tools to help us to cope. We need bigger memory stores, faster and more accurate retrieval systems and, above all, the ability to sift and sort the information before we drown in it. The computer is the tool we have designed to extend our over-stretched human capabilities, and IT or Informatics is the name we give to the science or art of processing information by machine.

At one time in history we could memorise all the information we needed, and the oral story carried the wisdom of the age. As the quantity of information grew we invented artificial memory stores for that information which was beyond the capacity of our personal memories. Books satisfied this requirement for centuries. Books are now giving way to computers as storage systems partly because they allow the reader to organise the information in store, and partly because they allow more efficient retrieval. Retrievals from these systems are fast, and can be customised for the individual reader, or user, as we generally describe the person who accesses information stored in a computer. The speed of access is a key factor in the usability of computer storage systems. Questions are not forgotten while answers are being found, as they can be when initiating a conventional library search. This speed of processing together with the vast storage capacity in even the simplest of machines combine to give considerable processing power. This enables us to transcend a basic human limitation – the limit to the number of things we can think of at once. The processing power of artificial storage systems is also flexible. It allows us to create a simulated world which can look like a book or a movie film or a battle scene or a chessboard or any number of things. This power is available through the microcomputers which are being installed in our classrooms and is available as a tool with which children can learn to think. It is this use of computers as tools that can have an impact on children's minds that is the central concern of this book.

This chapter reviews current computer use in our schools and addresses the general question of what it is that we want from educational computing. In considering the alternative uses of this technology we will discuss both current practice and future possibilities, and reflect on the way both our educational philosophies and our perceptions of the human/computer relationship can affect the uses we make of machines.

Since the first computers were introduced into our classrooms, when they were used mainly for teaching programming languages, there has been a huge growth in the activities which can now be supported. Some of these activities are still essentially concerned with programming, for there is an active group of educationalists who argue that learning to program is an ideal way of learning to think. One of our goals is to evaluate the evidence for this proposition. Programming is a popular classroom activity, for all ages of children, but it is by no means the only activity these days. Software can be described along a continuum of open-endedness, with programs at one end which can be used for one and only one task. At this end of the continuum we find the electronic worksheet, the drill-and-practice program and many simulations. At the other end of our continuum are the open tools such as word processors (and programming languages), with which any number of different products can be achieved. Another way of describing this continuum is in terms of the computer as a 'teacher' or as a tool. The closed packages have a known goal or a well-defined product, whereas the open packages are more like pencils and bicycles in that they are not the goal in themselves so much as tools with which other goals can be reached. With the closed packages there is a clearly identified 'correct' answer, and at the other end 'correctness' depends upon the capacities of the user. This raises the thorny issue of evaluation in education, and as we shall see, the use of educational computers does nothing to side-step the issue.

One of the questions to be raised in this book concerns the educational goals which are inherent in the use of these different software packages. If we are content to use computers as 'teaching' machines, or more accurately, automated practice and testing machines, then we will be identifying ourselves with the content-oriented curriculum, and with the notion that education is about knowing things. This approach will require us to select programs which will help children to acquire the facts that we, as teachers, consider worth knowing. There is strong support for this view in certain influential educational circles, and whereas the merits of the approach are apparent in the body of knowledge that will be maintained by the society, we recognise dangers in only knowing *what* at the expense of knowing *how*, and incline in the direction of an approach which also recognises the importance of knowing what to do with one's body of facts. There is little merit in educating children to become walking encyclopedias, for our society needs problem-solvers who have access both to the information relevant to a problem and to the routines for solving it. Machines can remember facts better than people can, and so we should rely upon the machines for the storage of facts, and rely upon people for problem-solving. More than with any other educational innovation, the microcomputer is useful here. This approach advocates the view of the computer as a tool with a variety of purposes which have the common characteristic of developing a flexibility of thought. Of course, to make use of a tool one has to know *what* as well as *how*, and the ideal philosophy is somewhere between the two extremes. Before we select the software we need to ask ourselves about our educational philosophy.

The computer is a powerful instrument which may be used to stimulate and support a number of educational goals – but which one should we choose? This is a critical question, for the choices we make about the use of the computer may have profound effects, not only upon the development of children's minds, but also upon the nature of education itself. The computer is not a passive addition to the classroom; it is not a neutral black box. It is versatile, and because of its ability to support many educational philosophies it forces us to reflect actively upon which form of education we want for our children. After all, we have never asked whether or not a blackboard or a book will replace the teacher, but we do ask that question about computers. At intellectual, social, economic and pragmatic levels, computers are a challenge to current educational practice.

What's the use of classroom computers?

This book is not about 'doing computers' in that we shall not be discussing the growth and relevance of computer awareness or computer studies courses in schools. The issues discussed here are all concerned with the use of the computer as an instructional tool within the broadest school curriculum. To some extent this is a fuzzy distinction. Often activities in the classroom which appear to be concentrating on using the computer as an instructional tool are in reality geared to giving children hands-on experience with the computer. Attempts to persuade primary schools to change the organisation of computer use from the 'one-day-a-week-for-each-class' format to block usage often founder on the belief that parents will not accept such a reorganisation. Teachers argue that parents value their children's contact with the computer and feel that it is necessary for them to have the opportunity of five minutes of regular keyboard experience as though it were a panacea for a number of ills, particularly that of unemployment! Classroom computers are currently being used to support a variety of aims, and we shall mention a number of them before discussing their potential uses as educational catalysts.

Although computers entered our schools in the 1960s, their use was restricted to a small group of dedicated teachers and selected children. Computing in those days was an offshoot of mathematics, and its general application was unrecognised. Not until the late 1970s did the use of classroom computers begin to spread. The computer was initially the object of study in its own right, either through 'awareness' and 'literacy' courses or through computer studies courses, or as an instructional tool in mathematics. Computers have now spread through a range of curricula areas, and it is general classroom computing which is our concern.

The rise of 'computer studies' as a school curriculum subject is no trivial matter, of course, for it can have profound effects on education. The place of such studies on the timetable has been justified in a number of ways. In particular, two well-worn arguments have been put forward; one concerning the needs of society and one concerning the need to foster the development of children's minds.

The first argument is the need for societal and vocational relevance, a theme in the minds of politicians. Computers play an increasing role in our everyday lives, and our children should be educated in their use and in their principles of operation, in preparation for their encounters with them in the workplace and elsewhere. This is a very limited view of the educational use of computers, even though the parental lobby gives it regular voice. This is the lobby which views hands-on keyboard experience as the most important measure of computer use. But if keyboard experience was all that mattered then we might as well replace our lessons with computer games. Games freaks are generally very knowledgeable about the general principles of computer operation – input/output interfaces, memory media, operating system constraints etc. – and so it may be the point has some force. There are some concerns about the transferability of skills from such experiences, however. What would be lost by encouraging little more than keyboard experience would be the opportunity to develop children's powers of thinking, and this is where the second argument takes over.

The second argument revolves round the teaching of programming. Here it is asserted that introducing children to programming will result in a new way of thinking, and that the child will become a

LOGO

formal reasoner of some power, solving problems through heuristics, and being placed in a position that encourages a recognition of the flaws within any suggested solutions. This is the same argument as has been put forward for the relevance of Classics in the education of Whitehall mandarins. Programming, it can be argued, is the new Latin, but both programming and Latin will only be of use outside of their own restricted domains if there is transfer of skill to other more general domains. It is one of our purposes to evaluate the claims that have been made for a 'transfer of training' from the acquisition of programming skills to thinking about non-programming problems.

These arguments highlight the dilemmas of the school curriculum. The introduction of any new subject results in pressure on all other curricula areas. If a high value is placed on one area, through the allocation of resources for materials and staff training, then pupils will gravitate to those subjects and other areas may be starved of time, resources and the most able students. In this way the average or less gifted student may be unable to gain access to prestigious knowledge, and other subject areas may be unable to gain access to resources. Somewhat paradoxically, the growth of computer studies has resulted in a stifling of computer use across the curriculum, and currently many secondary school pupils, having been keen computer users in their primary schools, have no access to the machine in their new schools. In the UK, the Department of Education and Science National Curriculum *should* place IT firmly in the curriculum for all children, for it will require each child to show competence in the use of tools such as the word processor and the data base, plus basic skills in the operation of hardware and software.

The impression is that 'awareness' goals are seen as being important. Teachers declare that an important use of classroom computers is in introducing children to the technology and in giving them an awareness of what computers can do. This was confirmed by an analysis of British teachers' declared aims for using the computer, and which was outlined in a survey reported elsewhere (Underwood, 1988). Further evidence comes from the Ontario provincial government's 'Microcomputers in the Classroom' project conducted in eight elementary schools (Eaton and Olson, 1986). Although not all the teachers used the computer for 'awareness', those that did argued that it was important to prepare children for the computer society of the future. Their method of preparing their students was to get the children to use the computer frequently but for short periods of time. As the teacher would be conducting the 'normal' class activities at the same time, the computer children, usually two at a time, had to be independent and make no demands on the teacher. The teachers therefore selected small stand-alone programs often of drill-and-practice format, but which were childproof and 'user-friendly'. The use of programming language packages such as LOGO was not seen as practicable. There is now a shift in focus. In our discussions with teachers about their use of computers, we often receive the apologetic reply 'We're only using it for word processing ...', as though this is a failure on their part rather than an important step forward. Indeed, we shall be arguing that one of the most productive uses for a classroom computer is as a word processor – the key here being that a word processor is an open-ended tool which transcends human limitations and which can be used to help develop thinking.

The Canadian study recorded a second finding which many of us can readily confirm, that the computer was used as a reward. Well-behaved children were given extra time on the machine but those who misbehaved lost their turn in the rota. In this way the computer can be reduced to an extrinsic reward, the up-to-date version of the gold stars or bars of chocolate which are still visible in many schools today.

At the outset, then, it should be noted that teachers' statements that they are using the computer to develop language or mathematics skills may hide a range of other educational goals. Eaton and Olson's teachers in Ontario, although initially aiming to provide experience of the machine, developed new goals related to motivation and a desire to change the social structure of the classroom. Observation of classroom activities can help us to identify the goals which lie behind any one activity. These teachers used programs in standard curricula areas but their articulated goals were to give keyboard practice and reduce negative feelings toward the machine through familiarity.

Our intended uses of educational computing range from primitive rewards, to awareness and vocational preparation goals, to the development of children's ability to think. It is the use as a catalyst for cognitive development that we shall focus on here.

A technology bandwagon or an educational opportunity?

Patrick Suppes predicted that developments in educational technology, and specifically in computer usage, would change the face of education in a very short space of time. This prophecy was made in 1966, and was based on his perceptions of the unique capabilities of the computer. He saw it as a tool which can be used interactively, presenting materials in novel ways not easily available through other media, and with the flexibility to adapt to different learning and teaching styles. The second prophet, Seymour Papert, also expresses ambitious aims for classroom computers, suggesting that we can abandon the worksheet curriculum and confidently allow children's minds to develop through the exploration of computer-simulated 'microworlds' (Papert, 1981). These are not the views of some computer hacker thinking that his interests should be everyone's interests, for there is a widely held view that microcomputers are providing us with the means for an educational revolution. In making his predictions Suppes was drawing on a long history of educational innovation. What is the evidence, twenty years after the prediction, that the face of education has been redesigned?

There is evidence of a significant impact of micro-technology in some areas of our educational system, but the prophecy does not look close to fulfilment. Certainly, the computer plays an important part in communication in many higher educational establishments, through the use of text and information-processing packages, as well as through electronic mailing systems. Academic researchers in both the Arts and the Sciences have responded to the benefits that micro-technology can bring: word processors, data analysis, the on-line control of experiments, and the computer modelling of systems, are all evidence of the acceptance of the new tools. The school system is not immune to the march of technology, either. It has its own international communication system – The Times Network System (TTNS) which is part of Campus 2000 – and there is considerable use of word processing and computer-based learning packages. The full potential has yet to be reached, however, and there is some risk that classroom computers may become very familiar instruments by which only our old goals are achieved, perhaps with greater efficiency. This is very different from the goal of changing not only the process of education but also the nature of the end product. We can change the ways in which children think through the use of computers, but this is not the same as giving keyboard familiarity and IT awareness.

The least that we can say is that children often see computers being used in their classrooms. The active acquisition of hardware has gained momentum with the help of both national and local government funding, and by the beginning of 1984 no less than 80 per cent of UK secondary schools had some level of computing provision (Wood, 1984). Provision in the primary sector has also moved on apace. It is claimed that in 1980 only thirty primary schools in England were using computers (Jones, 1980). In a survey of Hertford-shire schools conducted four years later it was found that 56 per cent of establishments had at least one computer and a further 24 per cent were waiting for a machine to arrive (Jackson, Fletcher and Messer, 1986). By 1985 this had increased to 94 per cent of schools with at least one machine, according to Bleach's representative sample of UK primary schools (1986). These are promising figures, and show that the equipment is available, if only we knew how to use it to maximise the beneficial effects upon children's minds.

Paula Bleach found that more than half of the primary schools had purchased only one computer, and of those that had done so the vast majority had taken advantage of the UK government's subsidised purchase scheme. The ratio of children to computers varied enormously. At its worst, one school shared a computer between 450 pupils, but over 65 per cent of schools had one computer for every 150 pupils or less, and in 21 per cent of establishments this ratio was 1 to 50 or less. This pattern of extremely broad penetration, but without a concentration of resources, is paralleled in the United States (Goor, Melmed and Ferris, 1981) and Canada (Eaton and Olson, 1986).

More disturbing than the overall machine-to-school or machine-to-pupil ratios was Bleach's discovery of the lack of peripherals for machines. Only 25 per cent of schools had a printer and only 9 per cent had purchased a 'concept keyboard'. This is a replacement for the standard 'qwerty' keyboard which uses touch-sensitive pads to detect pressure on drawings and pictures, for example. With the concept keyboard a response to the computer can be as simple as a choice between two pictures. Many people consider this to be a vital piece of equipment for effective work with young or less able children. The lack of printers is not surprising, and is the product of the UK government's funding policy. Perhaps this is a result of decisions by the Department of Trade and Industry rather than by the Department of Education – it was a commercial initiative (and applied only to hardware produced in the UK) rather than having anything to with educational policies. Those responsible for funding did not see the relevance of printing equipment in primary schools, yet a survey of children's opinions of educational software found that the use of word processing systems was almost universally popular (Smith and Keep, 1986). The children found the experience of developing, manipulating and reproducing text to a professional standard to be very satisfying. Government and, perhaps more importantly, the local education authorities in the UK, have now reversed the initial funding policy and have recognised the need for a wide variety of peripherals at all levels of education. Printers are now part of the computer installation in our primary schools.

Despite the massive injection of resources the impact of the technology appears to be minimal. Education appears to have changed very little. This lack of change is underscored by Bleach's report (1986). She found that, in general, computers were under-used. For 58 per cent of her survey schools the machines were in operation for less than 60 per cent of available time. For a significant minority, 20 per cent of schools, this costly resource was used for less than 20 per cent of the available time. This would suggest that the computer is in far less demand than that other technological innovation in the classroom, the television!

Although Jackson's team presented a generally healthy picture of enthusiastic teachers willing to use the new technology, they too report a very low level of impact (Jackson, Fletcher and Messer, 1986). The main change reported by their teachers, following the introduction of the computer into their classroom, was the need to rearrange the furniture to accommodate the machine! Only 25 per cent reported changes in their style of teaching when the computer was in use and 28 per cent reported a change in timetabling.

We should not be too critical of these teachers because the organisational problems of computer usage are very real. The computer may be seen as enriching the learning environment, but at the same time it is a scarce resource which teachers must allocate with care. Allocation is often on a principle of natural justice ('fair-shares-for-all') unless the child behaves in such a way as to warrant withdrawal of the privilege, even if that prevents the use of exciting materials such as those available through LOGO programming. Teachers must also decide on how much of their time can be spent on supporting computer activities and at what cost to other curricula areas. Eaton and Olson's teachers in Canada decided that the cost must be minimal, although they did articulate the need for guidelines from their school inspectorate (1986). Teachers in the UK are being given firm directives to use IT by the National Curriculum, although guidance as to how to meet goals is less forthcoming.

It is the lack of good software that is frequently cited by teachers as a reason for their reluctance to incorporate computer-based learning (CBL) techniques into their own classroom practice. One reason for this is the difficulty that teachers face in reviewing potentially useful software. Many software houses, unlike book publishers, are extremely reluctant to send out review copies of their products, and only a few program producers have tried to resolve the problem by giving small exemplar programs to allow teachers to understand what the complete program can offer. Teachers are also disappointed because they cannot find software to meet a specific curriculum goal. For example, some of our current students have been fixated on their failure to find a good program to teach the concepts of time and clock-time to 7- and 8-year-olds. The alternative to this search is to reject software which does not fit into the curriculum or which involves an uncomfortable teaching style, for example explorative problem-solving programs in a factual and didactic classroom setting. Software may also be rejected because teachers feel they can do the job just as well by conventional means without all the effort associated with organising a technological classroom. The assumption that CBL is no more effective than traditional teaching is one that can be challenged effectively with research. These concerns about software often hide an inherent conservatism in the teaching profession. Teachers need a great deal of support if they are to explore the potential of software for the new education envisaged by Suppes and by Papert.

Now that many of the initial technical and economic problems of computers in education have been resolved with the advent of cheaper and increasingly reliable microcomputer systems, this emphasis on software is understandable. However, the questions arising out of the spread of new technologies into the classroom are not just those of how to put traditional lessons onto the machine in an efficient and economical manner, even though much of the current research is directed towards that end. Even powerful tools such as word processors can be used in a fossilised education if they are viewed as 'neat' typewriters rather than as text manipulation and information-handling packages which allow us to explore our own thoughts. If we are to achieve the potential which led Patrick Suppes to anticipate an educational revolution, and for Seymour Papert to imagine how it might be achieved through simulated microworlds, then we will need to do more than create computer-based versions of our existing lessons. Computers are invading our classrooms, but to achieve their potential we need a revolution in educational practice.

The selection of software will, to a large part, be determined by the role that we see for the computer in the classroom. Is it to be the equivalent of an electronic book, to be consulted like an oracle, or the equivalent of an electronic taskmaster perhaps, to be used for the development of a specific sub-skill? Or perhaps it will be used as a tool with which we can come to understand the world, to find ways of understanding the world, and to express our ideas about it? The role that we give the computer will determine the limits of our achievement with it.

Our relationships with the computer

> Computers call up strong feelings, even for those who are not
> in direct contact with them. People sense the presence of some-
> thing new and exciting. But they fear the machine as powerful
> and threatening. (Turkle, 1984, p. 3)

Sherry Turkle's claim may seem extravagant. Why does the computer generate such powerful feelings and expectations? Our environments – the home, the workplace and the school – already contain
many domesticated beasts which employ microchips and user-
programming capabilities, for instance video recorders and washing
machines. Why should we worry about the computer and why do
many people find them powerful or threatening?

It is no accident that some of the most successful microcomputers
are those that seem to have their own personalities. They are being
designed around us and for us, and communication with them
occurs in ways that are easiest for us to handle. Such machines are
successful for a very simple reason: they are designed with human
capabilities in mind. They minimise our need to learn and remember
the procedures for communication. The so-called WIMP* interface
between user and processing unit of the computer can be operated
with minimum effort. It does not require the learning of anything
more complex than the number of clicks on the pointer (or mouse)

---

* WIMP is an acronym for **Windows**, **Icons**, **Menus** and **Pointers**. The idea is that the
user should think in terms of a desk top littered **with** things like folders, scraps of
paper, a calculator, a clock, and with a rubbish bin available. A Window can be
opened into one of these objects, to see what it contains, or to use it. A number of windows may be open at any time, just as a number of folders on a desk may be open
and ready for a document to be moved from one to another. Objects on the screen are
described to the user by an Icon, which is simply a picture (instead of a file name). For
example the icon for the rubbish bin, where unwanted files may be dumped, might be
exactly that – a rubbish bin. Menus are another way of reducing the load placed upon
the user's memory. Instead of having to remember the instructions for all of the operations that can be performed at any time, a menu of candidate operations can be pulled
down from a command strip on the screen, and the required operation then selected
with the pointer. The Pointer (often called the mouse), is used to indicate an object displayed on the screen or to perform some operation upon it. To select a file, the pointer
is moved until an indicator on the screen overlaps with the file, and then a button on
the pointer is pressed. The whole force of the WIMP interface is that the user does not
need to learn an obscure syntax of operation – instructions are executed by selecting
files with the pointer and by pressing a button. There is little to learn and there is
rapid transfer between different applications. Once the interface is learnt then any type
of program within it can be accessed very easily.

button. The desk top metaphor, which the interface uses, is easily assimilated and overcomes the basic human limitation of restricted memory. We will eventually use natural language instructions when communicating with computers, and instructions will be given by the spoken word rather than by the keyboard. As machines acquire features which make them more able to understand our instructions, they become more like other people that we know. It is this attribution of personal powers to the computer that intimidates many people. The fantasy world depicting the computer HAL in Arthur C. Clarke's *2001: A Space Odyssey* may not be too far into the future, but with it will come worries about the role of the computer in our lives. Can we maintain our autonomy when a more powerful being appears to have control of our environment? We have accepted factory assembly lines occupied by powerful computer-driven robots, but how easily can they be accepted in our homes and offices where we will be in more direct personal contact with them? Questions about the role of the computer need to be answered now, of course, because until we decide what we want them to do for us, we cannot make decisions about the design of the next model. More importantly for our discussion of the role of educational computing, we cannot make decisions about the kinds of software we should be encouraging until we decide what we want from them.

How should we view our relationship with the computer? What we will achieve with the computer will be determined by the uses for it that we can imagine. If we view it in the way that we view a pencil, as a tool with which to achieve some writing task, then we will obtain different results than if we view it in the way that we do a wristwatch. This is the distinction between machines that work for us (engines, watches and drill-and-practice programs) and those that work with us (pencils, garden tools and word processors), and it has been described most elegantly by Gavriel Salomon (1988).

Human–machine relationships can also be thought of in terms of their degree of transparency or opacity, defined by the extent to which the machine becomes an extension of the human user or remains as another-self, a significant other. Whereas a pencil or a spade is an extension of one's body, added to give a specific characteristic, other tools are not extensions so much as separate objects with their own identities. Ihde (1975) has argued that there are three levels or types of interaction between the human user and the machine according to their degree of transparency or degree to which they are extensions.

The first level in Ihde's analysis occurs when the human is using an implement such as a pencil or a car, in which the machine becomes transparent. At this level the machine or implement becomes an extension of the user's own body and the user can feel the environment, the roughness of the paper or of the road surface, directly through the machine. When using a telephone or watching the television, this direct tactile experience is lost, and we move to the second level in the analysis. A level of translucency is reached here as the machine still extends the individual's hearing or perceptions although the experience of the caller on the other end of the line, or the tropical island on the screen, is in a reduced form. In both of these types of interaction the machine can disappear into the background.

In the third type of relationship this extension of bodily experience is lost, the machine becomes opaque and separate from the user. In this case the machine may acquire an identity: 'In some cases relationships may actually be with machines. Here is a conversation with the machine and the "user" and the machine emerges as a quasi-other' (Ihde, 1975). The suggestion here is that the computer functions at this third level of opacity and is, therefore, fundamentally different from most other machines in our lives. Machines which operate at this level of opacity are in the foreground of our awareness. The mechanical aspects become subsidiary and the focal relationship is between the user and the quasi-other person. It is this personalisation that encourages us to discuss the 'user-friendliness' of the machine whereas we would not usually describe a pen or a telephone as being user-friendly or otherwise – the category label does not exist for this range of objects.

The essential difference between computers and other machines has been described more dramatically by Sherry Turkle (1984) in terms of their marginal status. She argues that they are objects on the borderline between the living and the not-living when she describes computers as 'a new kind of object – psychological, yet a thing'. Her anecdotal evidence confirms this feeling that computers are different. For example, she discusses the holding-power of the computer and the degree of parental concern, even fear, that is aroused by their children's obsession with video games. She also recounts instances of adults who are equally vulnerable to the fascination of this machine. This marginal status is not discouraged by programmers and systems managers who use a language which refers to 'killing' processes, to 'dead' systems, and to 'generations' of machines. It is not clear, however, whether Ihde and Turkle are talking about anything more than perceived complexity. Any system which is sufficiently complex not to be understood by the user will be capable of behaving in ways unpredictable to that user, and when it does then the user may attribute this wayward activity to inherent personality – as they may with other humans.

It must be noted that humans do not only communicate, but that they are also transformed by their communications. Messages of good fortune and of tragedy, for example, are those which will quite literally change our lives. Some messages can be described as being neutral in the sense that they convey information which may be acted upon, and then forgotten. These communications may have no long-lasting effects. We can think of educational computers as the carriers of messages, but their effects will be more profound than their predecessors such as the book or the television. Their effects will come through their ability to communicate in both directions, and through their ability to make use of knowledge, as other people make use of knowledge when deciding upon appropriate replies to our comments. What is important for us to understand as educators is that the computer is not neutral, but that it will exert an active influence on the learner. Once we have chosen to use it as an integral part of the classroom, as a tool with which to think, then its influence will be profound. There may also be secondary effects of this technological innovation, for 'what must be foreseen is not just the automobile, but smog and the parking problem; ... not just the television, but the rise of the advertising industry and the creation of the football widow and the TV dinner' (Lepper, 1985, p. 1).

Will we eventually say the same of computer-based learning? Classroom computers have a primary effect which is transparent, or at least translucent, but it remains for us to see what the secondary effects will be. Lepper was concerned mainly with the motivational and social effects of educational computing, and with the effects upon educational philosophy, but one of the most potent uses of computers is in the development of our powers of thinking. These are all influences which we should monitor and evaluate.

A contrary view is offered by Amarel (1984), who has suggested that the addition of computers to an established classroom does not necessarily bring about changes. Classrooms are intrinsically stable settings with well-established cultures, social dynamics and work-related agendas, all rooted in the established curriculum. Arguing from Roger Barker's tenet (1968) that 'settings have plans for their inhabitants', she suggests that this stable setting has resisted the influence of numerous innovations, and is unlikely to be reorganised by even such a powerful tool as the computer. The demand characteristics of the classroom will continue to be paramount in the determination of people's behaviour.

What can be achieved by our partnership with the computer will depend upon the distinctions that we see, and upon our views of the role of the computer in our partnership. The changes brought about by the use of educational computing will be extensive, if we allow them. There is a challenge to be met, once we have seen the potential for change.

Issues in the educational use of computers

There is evidence to suggest that many teachers are enthusiastic about the potential promised by classroom computers. In a survey of teachers' and trainee teachers' attitudes to computers in schools, positive responses were received four times as often as negative responses (Underwood and Underwood, 1989). Four clusters of teachers were identified along a continuum of those with highly positive to weakly negative attitudes, and with variations in attitude being directly related to computer knowledge and awareness. These results suggest that positive attitudes towards the computer can be generated by first-hand experience of its use. Indeed, practising teachers are often more enthusiastic than teachers-in-training because they have seen how the computer can motivate children in the classroom. There is also evidence to suggest that the machines that are available are spending most of their time switched off (Gardner, 1984; Opacic and Roberts, 1985)! There is a paradox here – on the one hand it can be argued that there are too few machines in the classroom and on the other hand research points to an under-utilisation of the resource.

Part of the explanation of this contradiction lies in understanding that while teachers may value the computer *per se*, when faced with it in the classroom they simply do not know what to do with it. In our own study, all the teachers were aware of the increasing impact of the technology on our lives and the need for children to be both computer-aware and computer-literate, even those teachers who were least accepting of computers and who did not want to be personally involved. The major difference in attitudes between the members of this sample was in where and how they might use computers. The least accepting group relegated computers to the mathematics and science curriculum, where mechanistic approaches to teaching were seen as applicable! The most knowledgeable and keen members of the sample saw possibilities for the machine across a range of curricula areas. In these attitudes we already have the seeds of non-use in schools.

Innovation is an exhausting process, especially in a system racked by change as we are seeing in education in the UK today. The process of change places demands on teachers' time and energies, and it questions the value of established skills while demanding the acquisition of new skills. Barriers to innovation can lie with the teachers, with the infrastructure of education, and with the technology itself. Heywood and Norman (1988) have attempted to model the teachers' perceived reasons for the level of computer use in schools. Overwork, often cited as a reason for not being involved in other innovations, was not significant here. There was no increase in workload because the computer was largely used for small-scale drill-and-practice programs managed by the children themselves. Nor were the teachers unduly concerned about the reliability of the technology. Although some felt the software was poor and that the computer added little to the classroom, it was used because the children liked it.

The significant difference in perceptions of computer users versus under- or non-users was expressed in terms of their confidence and competence with the technology. Not only did the under- and non-users express doubts about their own abilities to use the technology, but they were also unsure as to what to do with it in the classroom. Hence many took the path of least resistance either by using the machine for drill-and-practice or not using it at all.

It is increasingly apparent that new in-service training goals need to be set. Teachers need to develop not only competence but they also need guidance on how to integrate the computer into the curriculum. If children are to use the computer in ways other than as a drill-and-practice machine, then they need ready access to the machine for a block of time, and in a classroom with one or two machines this will necessarily result in some children having to forgo their personal computer time. If a principle of 'fair-shares-for-all' governs the way in which the computer is used, or if teachers are avoiding personal involvement, then more time-demanding packages cannot be used, and the computer is reduced to a practice machine or a simple reward system. Quite rightly, teachers are unimpressed by such applications, which are often seen as a trivialisation of education. Teachers may well feel little incentive to use their computer which, like all nine-day wonders, is gradually relegated to the corridor or to the back of the cupboard. If the machine cannot be used equitably for sound educational purposes, then it may as well stay in the cupboard – or so teachers seem to be saying.

Our educational system today is still a product of the Gutenburg-inspired print ethic, and the goals and values of our schools have been devised to instruct pupils to function in the print environment.

This may be considered as one of the reasons for the non-fulfilment of Patrick Suppes's prophecy, but there are others. In particular, workers in education, blinded by the technology, often have high expectations which they find are unfulfilled when they belatedly evaluate the quality of the learning experience. Richard Clark (1984) points out that we are continually searching for new technologies that will result in increased learning outcomes in comparison to 'older' media, and that the computer is seen as a particularly powerful technology in this sense. For example, consider the claims made by Mersich (1982), who argues that within the North American setting advances in computer-based learning (CBL) will soon make it possible for private enterprise to compete with the public education system, as long as the laws on school attendance are relaxed. He further predicts that this privatised educational system will flourish in comparison to the state system which it will 'whip in quality, and make a profit at the same time'. A similar belief in the value of the technology was expressed by the BBC, in its 1983–4 advertising literature, which posed the question, 'Will your children go to school?' The suggestion here is that the computer could take over the traditional role of the school in transmitting knowledge and fostering intellectual growth, leaving the schools to fulfil the role of socialising children and developing their physical skills.

This is not to say that the computer will replace the book or the written memo. They will survive, just as handwriting and the oral story tradition survived print. It should be noted that there are people who doubt this; for example Goff (1985), who made an impassioned plea for the retention of the book into the year 2000 at a United Kingdom Reading Association conference entitled 'Reading and the New Technologies'. The very title of Colin Harrison's (1981) paper on 'The textbook as an endangered species: the implications of economic decline and technological advance on the place of reading in learning' indicates a current concern. However, Harrison does sound a cautious note of optimism at the end of his paper by expressing the belief that the continued existence of the book is not ultimately in doubt. In any case, text displayed on a computer screen still requires the operator to be a competent reader. Reading skills would not vanish with the extinction of the book as a species, even if this did seem likely.

There are similarities between books and some computer applications, of course – they are both capable of storing information until needed – and the medium of storage and retrieval of knowledge is largely irrelevant. What is important is that we continue to have the means of storing this knowledge. It is important to be aware of the different limitations of these different media, and to educate users according to these limitations, but the argument about the relative merits of retrieval from the printed page and retrieval from the computer screen is largely a distraction.

A real concern is voiced by Clark, who questions the teaching role of the computer in education by arguing that it is very easy to mistake sophisticated technology for sophisticated learning. It would be a mistake to assume that productive outcomes will necessarily emerge when students communicate with computers. There are indeed many examples of complex technology being used to achieve low-level educational goals, and the use of drill-and-practice programs as electronic worksheets is a case in point here. The US National Science Foundation's project on Time-shared Interactive Computer Controlled Information Television (TICCIT), and the current development of distance learning, are two further examples. In these projects the machine is used for the largely didactic transmission of knowledge from 'teacher' to 'learner', and subsequent testing of the learner's acquired knowledge base. Although such programs often contain sophisticated models of concepts and operations within a subject domain, they have no knowledge of the students. At the present time, the machine delivers the information to the students and they must then attempt to interpret and assimilate that information into their existing knowledge structure.

One problem with these applications is that the role of the human educator can become minimised, whereas CBL has as much need for an educator with an underlying set of pedagogic principles as does any form of learning. Effective educators know about the background knowledge and ability of their charges, and describe new material and new concepts according to this knowledge and ability. Consider teachers faced with new students: how should they discuss a new concept on the first encounter? The answer will depend upon what the teacher knows about the new student, but suppose all that we have to go on is age. A teacher will talk in very different terms to a 5-year-old than to an 11-year-old, or to an 18-year-old. In part this is because the teacher has a good impression of the abilities of the average 5-, 11- or 18-year old student – and we can describe this impression more formally as a mental model. When the same teacher presents a talk at a public meeting, or to a group of undergraduate students, or at a scientific meeting, the talk varies. The material being discussed may be similar, but the teacher will vary the detail and style of presentation according to what is known about the audience. The teacher will have a mental model of the background of a typical member of the audience, and will present the material in such a way as to be understandable to that person. A book does not have a mental model of the reader, of course, although the author may have an idea of who might read it. We would not dream of putting a child into a library upon starting formal schooling, with the instruction to 'find out', because the educator needs to provide the mental model. The same holds for the selection of CBL packages. Material should be selected which is attainable by the abilities of the learner, and this is where current attempts at automated learning programs are having difficulty. Unlike the responsive teacher, who is aware of the capabilities of the children being taught and of their acceptance of, and difficulties with, the ideas being introduced, computer programs are often more like television programmes in that they run on regardless of the immediate audience reaction.

Programs being developed under the umbrella of 'intelligent computer-aided instruction' (ICAI) aim to teach at least as effectively as human teachers. Before they can do this they will need to know their students as well as the human teacher, and at the present time they cannot build the mental model. Accordingly, they cannot present material at a level of detail or difficulty to match the needs of the learner. The way around this problem, for the time being, is for the teacher to select the programs, and to select the uses to which the better software applications can be put. This raises the issues of how we should evaluate software, and what educational gains might be achieved by different uses. We shall be discussing the issue of evaluation in some detail, and considering some of the claims made for the effects of educational software on children's minds.

The computer is a very versatile machine which can be used to promote more sophisticated learning strategies in which the machine or the student, or both, take a more active part in the learning experience. It is this very versatility which raises fundamental issues about the future direction of education both in the UK and elsewhere. The computer can be used to great effect as a calculator, a 'teaching' machine, a processor of complex information and a creator of microworlds. In essence this means that the computer can support the full spectrum of educational philosophies: for example, acting as a tutor for those who believe we should return to a basic skills curriculum or as a key factor in stimulating the dynamic process of writing.

Dede (1986) suggested that instructional control strategies for the use of educational computers form a continuum based on the balance between the varying levels of passivity of the computer and the child. At one end lies the directed learning strategy in which the student is a passive recipient of wisdom unable to explore the material. At the other end lie the open-ended problem-solving computer-based tools such as LOGO, data bases and word processing packages. These programs give control to the learner but no longer provide guidance when the student has difficulty, although they may inform the child that an error has been made or an inappropriate action taken. One end of this continuum will appeal to those teachers who believe that there is a critical public corpus of existing preknowledge which all students need to be taught and to know, while at the other end are the teachers who believe in the need for the child to discover his or her own truths with varying degrees of support from the teacher.

In the centre of this continuum is the new breed of programs in which control can shift from student to machine as necessary, such as O'Shea's quadratic tutor (1982), and which can be considered as exemplars of approaches to teaching and learning such as the principle of scaffolding outlined by Wood, Bruner and Ross (1976). These ICAI programs are sometimes seen as the key to the new education where knowledge will be transmitted by machine. They are also the foundation for the belief that the computer will de-humanise education. Although Dede (1986) argues a very cogent case for the development of such software, two points should be raised. On a pragmatic note we have yet to see an ICAI program which can fulfil the role of 'coach' as Dede describes it. The programs to date are still very much content-driven rather than process-driven. Secondly, in denigrating the open-ended tool usage of the computer on the grounds that it does not support the child with individualised feedback, Dede has failed to understand that a different type of learning is taking place from that of the acquisition of facts or even concepts. In such programs children are not capturing past perceived wisdoms, but rather, they are honing their own thinking skills.

The questions to be resolved then, are how do we select the path to take when the computer offers such a range of instructional and learning strategies, and, once we have selected the pathway, what do we need to do to ensure that our educational goals are reached? These are crucial questions for education as a whole, both across the curriculum and across the age-ranges. One of these crucial questions concerns our use of computers as automated teachers as against their use as educational tools, for by using them as tools it remains for the teacher to make the important decisions about educational policy.

Computers as teachers and as tools

The debate concerning the most profitable ways in which we can use this costly and, in some schools, scarce resource, can simplistically be reduced into that of the computer as 'teacher' (the sub-skills tutoring/practice approach) versus the computer as tool. The most easily identified uses of the computer as a tool are those seen in most extensive operation in the world outside the classroom, namely data processing and word processing. At the moment, it is apparent that the practice of basic skills dominates the educational use of the computer, a fact which lead Chandler (1984) to suggest that this machine has made it possible for educational practice to take a giant step backwards into the nineteenth century! The complaint that there is a concentration on the development of low-level skills necessary for reading and language has been echoed by Rubin (1983). He argued that this is due in part to the nature of the computer, which encourages a mechanistic, detail-oriented education which focuses on 'correct' or unambiguous answers. But it is also due in part to the ease with which workcards, which concentrate on sub-skills, can be converted into classroom software.

Indeed, the most disturbing aspect of Bleach's report (1986) concerns the findings on the nature of computer usage. Drill-and-practice and learning reinforcement programs, concentrating on low-level cognitive skills of spelling or word recognition, predominated in these classrooms, with far fewer schools using their machines to stimulate higher cognitive skills such as the appreciation of story logic. These findings concur with other surveys in the UK (Jackson, Fletcher and Messer, 1986) and in the United States (Becker, 1982).

The use of drill-and-practice software does have its advocates, however. Amarel (1984) considers that the superiority of practice programs is compelling in comparison with the workbooks or sheets that they replace. In well-designed programs children can receive quick and accurate feedback, progressing at flexible rates, without public approbation of their errors. All too often we find children whose main motivation for wanting to use the computer is the patient, kind and generally non-condemning attitude it presents to their follies.

The practice of such skills is not inherently wrong – indeed practice is vital if skills are to reach the level of automaticity necessary to allow the individual to focus attention on higher-level problems (Underwood and Underwood, 1986). If we must concentrate on the spellings of words and on the formation of letters with a pencil, then we will have less time available to think about the meanings of the sentences being composed. As we automatise the lower-order skills, then so our minds become free to plan, guide and review. The tedious activities then take care of themselves, but only when they have been practised and over-practised. Drill-and-practice serves the purpose of releasing our minds. The tournament tennis player does not worry about the angle of the racquet head or the extent of the backswing of the racquet so much as where the ball should go next, and how the opponent would handle this shot or that one. We can think of few things at a time, and if our minds are trapped in thinking about low-level sub-skills like spellings and racquet positions, then there will be no time for the control of more creative and adaptive behaviour like story structures and game tactics. There is value in the addition of sub-skills to the child's cognitive toolkit, and the mind of the effective problem-solver has a variety of skills and knowledge to call upon.

But if sub-skills practice is all there is to education then it is sadly impoverished. Basic practice is essential, however, and the use of computer cannot only make practice less tedious for all concerned (by building it into a games-format package, for example), but can also make practice less of a focus of the activity (by integrating practice with the development of other skills). One of the great benefits of the high capacity machines now available is the facility of integrating activities at different cognitive levels. The same program may require sub-skills arithmetic practice and three-dimensional navigational mapping, with overall success in a simulation game depending upon success at both levels. The sub-skill is then appreciated in its rightful place, and serves a higher-order goal, rather than being an activity to be mastered for its own sake. For example, relatively simple programs such as Richard Phillips's ERGO or Anita Straker's GUSINTER deal with an understanding of multiples, but they also require the child to use that knowledge in such a way as to solve a more general problem. The user is engaged in sub-skills development through goal-directed activity. Drill-and-practice is necessary for the development of automatised skills, but it does not have to deal with children as automatons.

Although not yet in a majority, there is a growing percentage of teachers who are using the tool-like capabilities of the computer to show things, to say things or to provoke thought. The survey reported by Jackson's team found that teachers who had received a two-day in-service training course were significantly less likely to use drill-and-practice software than their untrained peers (Jackson, Fletcher and Messer, 1986). It is not possible to say whether this was a result of training or a matter of self-selection, because teachers who were more interested in innovative approaches to computer use were also more likely to volunteer for such courses. They did show, however, that greater computer experience did not necessarily lead to more innovative usage, when experience was measured by the length of time the teachers had been working with the computer. There was no difference between experienced and inexperienced teachers in their frequency of use of drill-and-practice, open-ended and data-handling software. However, those teachers with more than six months' experience tended to use more problem-solving programs.

It is often the tool user who has most fun and who gains most value from the encounter with the machine and, unfortunately in many cases, that tool user is the teacher rather than the student. Developments in CBL should emphasise the tool-like uses of the computer, and the learner should take the active role of operator. In encouraging children to use the computer as a tool, we are building upon out-of-school uses of the computer, with children participating in activities relevant to such environments as the electronic office, and engaging in an exploration of knowledge.

Many workers would argue that the computer can and should be used in more creative and liberating ways rather than as a drill-and-practice machine. Papert (1981), in particular, has argued eloquently against its use as a 'teaching' machine, suggesting that such a powerful technology can open up new fields of knowledge and encourage the development of higher-level cognitive skills.

It is deeply worrying that Sheingold (1981) should find that drill-and-practice programs are offered to low-achieving or disadvantaged children in the belief that they will benefit most from these 'highly structured non-judgemental, infinitely patient environments', while their advantaged peers enter the expansive world of the computer as tool. This differential use is seen as encouraging a questioning autonomy in one group of learners, while their less favoured peers are caught in an environment which sets limits on independent thought, curtailing the exercise of options and the opportunity to reflect. It also provides one group with the skills and insights into the uses to which a computer may be put outside of the classroom, while the drill-and-practice class sees the computer as an electronic worksheet, a concept of little environmental value.

The question of what we should do with computers in the classroom will continue to be a focus of educational debate, and not all teachers will resolve the question in the same way. There is a bewildering array of opinions as to the role of educational computers, and much of the existing software can be regarded as emphasising a more mechanistic or 'computer-as-teacher' policy of education. Software must be selected carefully and with general educational aims in mind. More than any other educational aid, the classroom computer requires teachers to question their goals.

We need to set the goals of classroom computer use. The questions which are being asked about the educational benefits of chip technology have resulted in the computer becoming a focus and catalyst for change in education. This is because they mirror the diversity of views about the proper goals and functions of schooling in general. The concept of the computer as a tool opens up new directions in education, challenging the roles of both teacher and child and questioning our definition of 'worthwhile' knowledge and skills.

Aims and structure

There are a number of pressing issues to be resolved following the introduction of the computer into the classroom. Although hardware provision has been generous to the schools there are still important shortages particularly in the provision of peripheral hardware. In the UK this was initially due to a lack of government support for equipment such as printers for primary schools. A second reason, however, is the failure of teachers to perceive a need for such equipment either because they are still using 'small' programs which do not require additional hardware, or because they feel that a second processing unit is more important to allow all their children to have that vital hands-on experience. The cry heard at many meetings at which educational computing is discussed is in praise of the next generation of machines. Whatever we have now, these technological soothsayers tell us, it will be much better when we have an improved model to work with. There may be some truth in this, but the message in the following chapters is that we can make outstanding progress towards our educational goals with what we have. Our emphasis is therefore upon children's minds rather than technological innovation. When we start to consider intellectual development to be of more interest than the next generation of machines, and place children in the spotlight of education, then we can see impressive achievements through the use of currently available data bases, spreadsheets and word processors.

A second issue arises out of the goals that should be set for computer use: the 'teachers versus tools' debate. Should we think of them as we think of pencils, books and TV programmes, or as tools with which to develop thinking? This debate is intricately bound to teacher expectations and underlying philosophies of education. Changes in computer usage can be achieved, however, following in-service training, although a rather more direct stimulus to change will be the Information Technology attainment targets which have been devised in the UK as part of the DES National Curriculum.

Training is itself the solution to the third issue, the lack of good software. It can no longer be said that all software is of dubious quality. The main problem now is making teachers aware of good material and how it can be used, and then persuading head-teachers to allocate resources to purchase a core of good material. Given that software that can be used for effective educational purposes is available, how should teachers select it? What are the characteristics of educationally effective software, and what are the educational effects which are attainable?

The central aim of this book is to demonstrate the usefulness of classroom computers. They are powerful tools, and they can have powerful effects upon children's minds. One of our principal goals is to suggest how computers can be used to aid teachers' purposes in fostering cognitive development.

Some of the specific claims made for educational computing are examined in chapter 2. Activities such as programming and data base interrogation have been claimed to provide benefits for the cognitive development of children engaging in them. What kind of benefits should we be looking for, and how should we go about evaluating the evidence? What, indeed, would constitute 'good' evidence of an educational improvement? Central to the theme of this chapter is the notion of a cognitive toolkit of sub-skills (categorising, questioning, debugging etc.) which are necessary for generalised problem-solving. The computer does not necessarily teach 'problem-solving' as such, but it can be used to give an appreciation of the sub-skills which are essential for effective problem-solving.

Information-handling skills are invaluable in modern society, and chapter 3 examines the potential of using applications such as data bases and spreadsheets in the classroom. The common feature of these programs is that they are tools. They do not have correct answers associated with them, any more than does a pencil or a telephone directory. They are process-driven tools which encourage cognitive development, and avoid the so-called tyranny of the product at the expense of knowledge of process. These applications can be used to demonstrate *how* things happen and how they can be made to happen, and minimise the correctness of final products such as are gained, for example, in multi-choice answer sheets.

Because this case for using the computer as a tool will not be readily acceptable to all teachers, the following chapters provide some demonstrations of computer-based tools in the classroom. Chapters 4 and 5 consider the information-handling skills necessary for the construction and interrogation of data bases respectively. Chapter 6 considers examples of how the word processor can develop not only writing skills but also reading and, perhaps more surprisingly, information-handling skills. These three chapters illustrate the cognitive benefits, and potential pitfalls, which can arise when using tools such as formalised data structure systems or word processing packages, by looking at examples of current practice in the classroom.

One reason that computers are left in the cupboard more often than not is that a single computer in a classroom gives either inequitable use for individual children, or requires massive reorganisation of class activities. This social impact of the microcomputer upon the classroom is discussed in chapter 7. This is a consideration of the changes in interaction between children, and changes in the role of the teacher, which have come about with the introduction of this new authoritative automaton. The examination of the effects upon paired-learning, and upon co-learning, also considers the question of why computers are sometimes thought to be only for boys.

The final chapter of the book moves away from current classroom experiences, and focuses upon two general issues concerning evaluation. All educationalists need to know how to evaluate the tools which are offered to them, and they also need to evaluate the educational outcomes derived from the use of those tools – otherwise how can they know that the current classroom practice is effective? In the present context these are the issues of the evaluation of the available software and of the classroom outcomes following use of that software.

We aim to demonstrate that educational computing is valuable not for reasons of the values of IT in society or the value of computer programming as the new Latin, however valid these claims may be. Classroom computers can change children's minds, but to do so they need to be used by teachers who do not view computers as surrogate teachers so much as tools with which their own educational goals can be reached.

2 Extending children's minds with computer-based learning

Can computer-based learning (CBL) activities be used to foster the development of children's minds? This chapter will consider some of the possibilities offered by currently available software tools, and will also consider the vexed question of how will we be able to know that our educational method has been effective. These are questions of educational benefits and their evaluation.

Just as the blackboard can be considered to be a valuable tool for educators (like the overhead projector, or worksheets, or even felt-tip pens), classroom computers can also be seen to have their uses and abuses. For a teacher to stand in front of a blackboard all day long would not be a recommended educational practice. But we would not want to reject all declarative teaching because of the *possibility* of abuse – there are times when exposition is essential. The blackboard is a useful tool for the effective teacher, when used appropriately. So the question becomes one of how we can discover the circumstances under which the blackboard would be a useful tool. There is a general question being begged here: how do we come to know that any educational tool is being used appropriately or inappropriately? To answer this question we need to consider our methods of evaluation. How should we determine whether the innovation has been effective? Part of our concern here is to emphasise the importance of evaluation in classroom practice.

In the present discussion we shall describe some of the uses of classroom computers as educational tools which can help cognitive development. We shall be considering these uses and their effectiveness in the context of their evaluation – how do we *know* that a practice will be effective, rather than feeling intuitively that it is a good idea. Instead of relying either upon 'common sense' or upon a philosophical stance which declares *a priori* that the innovation must be effective, we consider it preferable to observe the effects of an innovation upon the development of children's minds. For effects to be observed we shall need to know what aspect of intellectual development is being measured – what it is that is being developed – and we shall need to know that this development is a specific product of a classroom computer. To accept such effects we shall rely upon formal methods of observation using both experimental manipulations and case studies. These methods are preferred to guesswork and to declarations of a result before the jury returns. In place of spiritual inspiration we shall suggest objective evaluation.

In the development of children's minds there are two broad classes of activity to be considered, activities which serve to equip children with a toolkit of basic mental skills, and activities which require the application of those skills in generalised problem-solving. Whereas the toolkit of the educated mind will include specific arithmetic and language skills and more general cognitive skills such as questioning and categorisation, the more widely based activity of problem-solving requires the manipulation of information through the use of combinations of skills. The overall aim of this educational approach is to provide children with the ability to think. This is achieved by providing them with the basic skills – the cognitive toolkit – and with experiences of the use of different combinations of the components of their toolkit in problem-solving exercises. Computer-based activities which can be used to aid the development of the toolkit include the compilation and interrogation of data bases, the use of word processing packages, and LOGO programming. The feature common to these programs is that they are open-ended tools. In the sense that felt-tip pens and typewriters are open-ended, we suggest that the most useful pieces of educational software are those that also do not provide right or wrong answers so much as provide opportunities for the development and exploration of ideas. The aim of these activities is not an end in itself in most cases, but is to provide general skills which can be used in the solution of other problems.

The cognitive toolkit: acquiring basic mental skills

Drill-and-practice programs abound. Some are set in a games format and are motivating, and others confirm our worst fears of programmed learning. These programs can certainly be used to practise multiplication tables, or spelling, or the names of capital cities, but they make poor use of the potential of the microcomputer, and they are not the programs to be discussed here. The basic skills of numeracy and literacy can be fostered by software developed specifically for this purpose, but it often delivers little more than computeried worksheets. Skills can equally be acquired as part of more general programs – simulations of survival for example, or general problem-solving programs such as adventure games. The notion of a toolkit of well-learned skills is an important one for our description, as well as being potentially controversial. It is worth standing back from the issue of CBL for a moment to consider the desirability of cognitive skill, and the processes involved in its acquisition.

Practice is as important to the developing arithmetician as it is for anyone aiming to become a proficient pianist or a championship golfer, for unless the low-level skills become automatic, they will interfere with the performance of the general problem-solving activities which they are intended to serve. If a step in a long multiplication calculation is a stumbling block then the whole calculation is at risk. The stumbling block in this case may be a general operation which is not performed with certainty, or a specific component of the multiplication which requires thought and consideration. When we must dwell upon the performance of component skills, not only is the overall activity completed in a halting performance which is vulnerable to disruption, but it is more likely to be erroneous. When an activity is over-practised we no longer need to attend closely to each aspect of its performance. We can say that the stimulus itself seems to call for the response, whether it is a physical response such as turning a door key in a lock, or a cognitive response such as 'knowing' the answer to a question as soon as the question is asked. In each case attention is not required for the consideration of alternative forms of action because only one action is appropriate.

Miller, Galanter and Pribram (1960), in their seminal book *Plans and the Structure of Behavior*, described these actions as learned instincts. This label is appropriate because they are fixed action patterns produced to fixed stimulus configurations. They are invariant, and it is this lack of variation in the world and in our response to it that can be learned with practice. Once learned, the action does not require constant monitoring during performance. Elsewhere, this change from ponderous, attended performance to smooth, automatic performance has been described as the change from a 'closed-loop' to an 'open-loop' mode of control (Reason, 1979; Underwood, 1982). The 'loop' in question here is that which allows feedback of what we have done to be considered in time for it to affect the next action. With a closed loop this feedback can influence what we do next, but with an open loop feedback is kept out of the control mechanism, and we are then left with the original unmodified plan as the sole means of control. With closed-loop control we need to observe our performance in order to check that we are performing correctly, whereas with open-loop control we can rely upon the events around us to receive an appropriate response without our needing to think about the selection of the response. The major gain through the automatisation of an activity is that it can then be performed without close supervision – the mind is free to consider other activities.

Errors can arise when our decisions are ponderous, but when the component activities are practised and learned to the point of being automatic, then the performance is invariably appropriate. Consider the following question: what is the capital city of France? The average reader of this book will have about as much difficulty providing an answer as they would have with the simple multiplication problem of what is six times four, or as they have with turning a door key in a lock, or with switching on a light upon entering a room. These examples are chosen carefully, because what they have in common is that they are all component sub-skills which have the characteristics of automatic activities. We do not have to think about these activities in order to perform them correctly. When the question about the capital city of France is posed, the answer seems to offer itself, and when the key is entered into the lock the turning action also follows without deliberation. What has happened is that these activities, and hundreds like them, have become automatised. It is only when they are required in novel circumstances that our attention is drawn to them.

When errors do occur in the performance of these automatised sub-skills they usually take the form of a whole automatised activity being performed at an inappropriate time or being missed out of a more complex sequence of behaviour. For example, when making a pot of tea, people sometimes report occasions when they complete all of the component actions (filling the kettle with water, switching on the kettle, filling the teapot with boiling water, preparing the cups etc.), but have forgotten to put the tea into the teapot prior to adding the water. Reason (1979) has developed a model of automatised human behaviour which incorporates these examples of 'actions not as planned' in some detail. They are considered to emerge when attention is not available when decision points are reached in the sequence of activity, and then stronger actions take precedence and guide our behaviour without our conscious control. Reason suggests that at decision points we need to return to closed loop control, in which feedback is taken into account, and that when we make these everyday action errors we are tending to rely too much upon open loop control. Perhaps the best example of this is the case of the unposted letter: we set off on a familiar route with a letter to be posted at a point during the journey, and arrive at our destination only to find that the letter has been forgotten about. In this case attention was not dedicated to the posting task – feedback did not enter the control mechanism – and the familiarity of the route has called for certain well-practised travelling actions.

We have previously described the automatisation of printed word recognition as being an essential component sub-skill of reading, in that each word calls for a very specific cognitive response (Underwood and Underwood, 1986). The mental response to the printed word is, to use Miller, Galanter and Pribram's description (1960), a learned instinct. The meaning of the word becomes available as the skilled reader looks at it. There is no thinking about the shape of the word, or the sound that a particular combination of letters would have, and there is little pondering over the meaning of the word, unless it is set in the context of a cryptic crossword clue, for instance. We read without deliberating over the meanings of the individual words and only on special occasions do we become aware of their multiple meanings. The so-called 'garden path' sentences do call for inappropriate readings, and the recovery from misinterpretation makes us unusually aware of a cognitive action which normally progresses without conscious deliberation*. If we needed to spend time considering the orthographic structure or the meaning of each word as we are reading, then not only would our reading speed deteriorate, but our reading would also be less successful. We would impose a greater load on the memory system we use for sentence comprehension, and there would be more comprehension failures. When there is an invariant relationship between an event in the environment – for instance, a printed word, or the formulation of the question about the capital of France – and the action that is required

---

*   For an example of a garden path sentence, consider the following by reading it aloud. *When Cinderella was told that she couldn't go to the ball she felt very, very saddened and her sisters then saw the tears in her brown ball-gown.* The intended misreading of 'tears' (as those produced by crying) is not consistent with the final phrase of the sentence. The re-reading demanded by the misinterpretation makes us aware of part of the reading process which usually progresses automatically.

in response to that event, then the action can be automatic. The answer will appear in our minds without our having to attend to the problem. It will become effortless, and our minds will become freed for a more complex level of mental activity. This higher level of activity is, in the context of word recognition and reading, sentence and text comprehension, and more generally we can describe this higher level as problem-solving. In the case of reading, the problem is to understand what the writer has intended us to know, and to this problem the skilled reader brings a toolkit of relatively low-level cognitive skills. These skills are the processes by which we recognise individual words, and are normally performed without our attending to them.

Problem-solving, by definition, is not an activity that can be performed by this attention-free mode of cognitive control. If the activity does not require attention, and can be performed while we are thinking about something else, then it is not a problem in the first place. Problem-solving relies upon the low-level skills which we have acquired with practice and which together form our cognitive toolkit, and once we no longer have to think about their control then our minds can be dedicated to the higher-level problem. In addition to these low-level sub-skills acquired through practice, the toolkit also contains our data base – the knowledge about the world which can be described as semantic memory, or knowledge which is shared and agreed upon.

Without the toolkit we would have to allocate our limited span of attention to activities such as deciding what each word means, or whether the capital of France is Paris or Brussels, or whether six times four is twenty-eight or twenty-four. Attention, in this analysis of mental life, is required for decision-making, and if our minds are cluttered with low-level decisions such as these, then there will be less opportunity for using the available evidence when making decisions about general problem-solving strategies. This notion of attention and automatic cognitive performance, and their value in decision-making, is discussed more fully in Underwood (1978, 1982).

Component sub-skills of problem-solving activities are performed effortlessly and without attention because they are highly practised. These over-practised skills are valuable, and classroom computer programs which allow the development of a cognitive toolkit of sub-skills are to be welcomed, but they must be chosen with care. Practice does not necessitate drill-and-practice, and sub-skills can be acquired in the context of problem-solving activities such as simulation games and LOGO programming.

Acquiring the toolkit: why teach children to program computers?

The value of the cognitive toolkit is that it releases the mind of its user for more general problem-solving activities. Children have little difficulty in acquiring the sub-skills which form part of the toolkit, although the integration of relevant skills may be another matter. The educator has the choice of which sub-skills to emphasise, of course, and how to present them. Some of us still have memories of classes in which rooms of children could be heard to be reciting multiplication tables, or seen to be writing row after row of the same perfectly formed letter of the alphabet. These methods certainly present the child with a toolkit of sub-skills, but it is difficult to imagine a less motivating form of education. Of course, it is also questionable whether these are the sub-skills which should receive such emphasis. This educational philosophy has little to contribute to the development of flexible problem-solving. It is for the education of individuals who 'know what' rather than those who 'know how' – for the development of declarative rather than procedural knowledge. An exciting example of how procedural knowledge can be developed away from the computer is provided by Magdalane Lampert (1986). In her imaginative mathematics classes there is a use of story telling to make problems concrete – arithmetic problems concern the calculation of the number of people living on a set of similar planets, for instance. Martin Hughes (1986) has described how young children can grasp the concept of number using a similar technique – and this act of making problems concrete and accessible is what Papert (1981) suggests can be achieved so effectively with LOGO and microworlds.

The prominent alternative to rote learning is an educational philosophy based upon the work of Jean Piaget. The essence of this school of thought is that the mind of the child develops naturally through interaction with the environment, and that through this interaction the child discovers the properties of the world and the properties of the child's own relationship with the world. Interaction is of prime importance, because this is the only way that we can come to understand our personal world and learn how to operate within it and upon it. The reality that we come to understand is said to be a personal construction, and the process of construction is fostered through interactive experience. Cognitive development is seen not as the product of an accumulation of facts but as being driven by the child's own interactions with the physical and social world. Self-directed problem-solving, through actions in the world which teach us by the feedback which they generate, is the essence of this view of development. It is a view which transfers readily when we consider the possible uses of classroom computers, for here we can provide children with a rich microworld which can be explored with consummate ease and with little risk.

These ideas have had profound influences upon the organisation of our classrooms, and they also provide the basis for an equally dramatic reorganisation of thinking about the use of classroom computers. In place of drill-and-practice programs, Seymour Papert (1981) offers us a Piagetian vision of cognitive development driven by interaction not so much with the total world itself, but with a simulated microworld accessed through the LOGO programming language. In his widely influential book *Mindstorms: Children, Computers and Powerful Ideas* (1981), Papert points out that microcomputers can be used to simulate environments that provide children with the conditions necessary for the reorganisation of their understanding, and he argues that children can acquire powerful problem-solving tools very effectively by learning to program. By programming the computer to create graphic displays, abstract ideas can be made concrete, and the means of manipulating the world made personal and apparent.

LOGO is a list processing language which can be used to achieve a number of outcomes, including text processing, for instance with forms of the ELIZA interactive simulation, and music production. The language is best known for its graphics capabilities, however, and LOGO graphics have been used for many mathematical purposes including the acquisition of geometry and mental arithmetic skills, as well as the appreciation of general problem-solving heuristics such as the value of breaking down problems into smaller problems. Different versions of LOGO graphics are available, and have been extended beyond the production of graphical displays on the computer screen to a more concrete manifestation as turtle graphics. In this form a robot which can look remarkably like a turtle drags a pen around a piece of paper on the floor. Instructions to move the pen are given through the computer in the usual way, but the product is directly accessible in the form of a pen and paper drawing produced by the turtle.

The claim made for having children learn to program is that through interaction with a physical microworld, they will acquire a toolkit of general problem-solving sub-skills. Programming is a specific form of problem-solving – the problem might be one of how to get the microcomputer to display a spiral, or a row of houses, for example – and the act of programming itself requires the use of a family of sub-skills which are independent of any body of facts about the programming language itself. The specific sub-skills which can be developed by learning to program have been claimed to be as follows:

1 Programming requires rigorous thinking to be made explicit. There is no 'fudge button' when it comes to giving instructions about the movement of the cursor (the screen version of the turtle, or indeed the robot turtle itself) – it moves exactly as instructed and makes no assumptions of its own. Imprecise instructions are not recognised, and reformulations are demanded.

2 Programming provides an environment in which the general concepts of transformation, function and variable can be used and their consequences seen. These powerful, abstract concepts can be seen in operation through programs, and LOGO programs are particularly valuable on account of their graphical output. LOGO programs can be said to make thinking visible.

3 With problem-solving through programming, it is possible to appreciate the usefulness of heuristic approaches to a solution. These are the general problem-solving skills involved in planning the route to a solution, solving problems by breaking them into smaller parts, and solving problems by analogy. In particular, programming can foster the idea that problem-solving can be organised by parts. Small procedures can be seen as the building blocks from which large solutions are derived.

4 The interactive process of getting a program to run as intended gives an appreciation of debugging an imperfect solution. Errors can be helpful, in that the nature of errors can be informative as a diagnostic in locating the problem. This strategy of using errors as the starting point for improvement can be generalised to other problem-solving tasks.

5 The vocabulary of programming, and the necessity to openly discuss the process of problem-solving during programming, give an awareness of the process of problem-solving. This reflectivity of thought gives strength to the control processes which are necessary in the selection between alternative routes to a solution, and in the reviewing of resources necessary for problem-solving. This awareness of process has also been called metacognition – knowledge about our personal cognitive processes, their limitations and their application. Awareness of our ability to handle problems includes knowledge of the ways in which we know ourselves capable of solving and knowledge of the kinds of activities in which we must engage in order to find a solution. An important part of this awareness of problem-solving strategies is knowledge

that individual problems call for individual solutions. The selection of the most appropriate solution will depend upon a cost/benefit analysis of the alternatives.

These suggested educational effects of learning to program are the 'powerful ideas' of Papert's treatise. They are powerful because once they have been acquired they can be applied to a large number of situations with desirable effect. In the same way, being able to read is a powerful tool – it allows an individual to read a variety of materials for a variety of purposes, and with important consequences. (They are also powerful in another sense, because by making the suggested effects so explicit they have been made testable – we can evaluate them!) The essence of the claim here is that programming trains us to solve problems. The programmer must be able to formulate goals and routes to the goals precisely, to be able to apply a number of heuristics which apply to many types of problem, and to appreciate the usefulness of diagnostic errors. Once these 'powerful ideas' have been acquired through programming experience, they can then be applied to other kinds of problem. They are generalised tools which can be applied to a variety of situations.

Few of us need to be able to program anything more sophisticated than a washing machine or a video recorder, and there are very few advocates of programming as a discipline in its own right. The benefit of learning to program is that it provides experience of a range of concepts which are a useful addition to our cognitive toolkit. Papert goes further than this, however, and points to LOGO programming experience as a simulation of the kinds of interaction with the world which can foster the development of children's minds. The reorganisation of young minds occurs through the discovery of regularities in the world and through the testing of hypotheses about its structure. By exploring the computer-bound microworld with LOGO, children can discover the regularities in that environment, and will discover the effects of their own actions upon the world. These interactions will produce successive re-organisations of the child's understanding of how the world works, and LOGO programming can accelerate a child's normal course of cognitive development.

Here we have two kinds of claim to consider – a generalised claim about the conceptual development of children's minds, and a more specific claim about the stages of Piagetian growth. Piaget's claims about the course of intellectual development have received a very mixed press (see, for example, reviews by Donaldson, 1978, and Wood, 1988), and are beyond our remit. We shall restrict ourselves to the general question of whether learning to program, with specific interest in LOGO programming, has any demonstrable benefits for children's cognitive growth.

Evaluating the claims made about learning to program: techno-romanticism?

Experience with LOGO is claimed to benefit children's cognitive development, and the question to be asked here is how we should go about evaluating that claim. This leads us to consider the more general question of how we should judge *any* claim about the effects of an educational practice. We could, for instance, start from first principles and develop an educational treatment which should *a priori* have beneficial effects. Our method may seem sensible in that it is based upon worthwhile assumptions about the child's cognitive starting point, and about our overall goals as educators, and about the likely effects of our educational interventions in allowing children to move from their starting points to the desired goals. This is the route taken by Papert and his colleagues: we should follow their recommendations because their assumptions lead to the conclusion that extensive LOGO experience is good for the cognitive health of children. Regardless of the validity of the starting assumptions, the critical problem arises when a conflicting set of assumptions are proposed, assumptions which lead to recommendations about a different set of treatments. Suppose an educational theorist from a competing camp stood up and declared that not only was LOGO detrimental to children's development, but that some other activity was better able to provide the mental skills claimed for LOGO. How should we decide between these competing declarations?

Perhaps it is a matter of deciding upon one's personal educational philosophy and using a classroom practice which is felt to give some some voice to it. Kidd and Holmes (1984) recommend a slightly more cautious approach to the adoption of educational innovation. They would like us to rely upon informed opinion when deciding between alternative educational methods. When deciding between two methods of teaching, we should ask the people who have the greatest experience of teaching the topic, or who have the greatest experience of getting children to acquire a particular concept. This makes a lot of sense, but can we really ask those who have the greatest experience of teaching programming whether it is a good idea to get children to program with LOGO? At best we could ask these committed experts which language to teach, but even here it is difficult to get objective evaluations of programming languages from those who are committed to one language or another (try asking your local LOGO enthusiast why she is not advocating PROLOG, for example). What we can rely upon them for, however, is to say how and when we should teach programming. A second interpretation of Kidd and Holmes's recommendation is that we should get experienced teachers to make evaluations of the likely benefits of new teaching methods. The risk here is that insufficient time and resources will be allocated to the testing of the new methods for the potential to be achieved. How many classroom teachers have the time to compare the relative effectiveness of competing packages? And how many cases can be recounted of occasions where a teacher has had to be persuaded to try an innovation, only to become a convert?

If left to our own judgements, more often than not, we would like to continue doing things as we do at the moment. The better professional judgement, and the one that we do in fact rely upon, is to accept recommendations from colleagues who are, in some sense, better informed. They may have tried it themselves or may have heard it described elsewhere, or these colleagues may be professional evaluators. It is this objective evaluation that we shall come to recommend here. The third problem with Kidd and Holmes's recommendation of using informed opinion when deciding upon an educational innovation is that the best informants, the teachers, are not particularly consistent in their evaluations. Preece and Jones (1985) found teachers to be inconsistent judges of educational software, even after a short training course on evaluation. Their teachers tended to be uncritical and the final recommendations did not appear to be related to the conclusions about the separate features of the packages. The informed opinion which must be relied upon, therefore, is that offered by objective evaluation: the case study, and the educational experiment with its testing of performance before and after the treatment.

It must be said from the outset that the idea of having children learn to program has received very mixed reviews. We shall start with the more positive reports, on the basis that a single positive report, from a well-designed study, would be sufficient to establish the possibility of benefits from programming. The case in favour of LOGO is, it turns out, better than the negative reviews would have us believe, and there are a number of evaluative studies which show a variety of benefits from children's programming experiences.

One of the more popular debates to be heard when education researchers engage each other, is that between the proponents of the intensive case study and the proponents of the classic experimental method. We are fortunate in the present case to have examples of each of these methods which investigate the effects of programming upon cognitive development, and which show positive effects with each method.

An intensive case study is available in Robert Lawler's (1985) book *Computer Experience and Cognitive Development*, in which he describes in considerable detail the experiences of his 6-year-old daughter in a LOGO environment over a six-month period. Lawler himself acted as both personal tutor and evaluator, and concluded that the effect of the experience was to allow his daughter to demonstrate behaviour typical of a child in Piaget's stage of formal operations, far beyond the expected attainment of an average 6-year-old. The examples of her problem-solving, planning and debugging activities which he presents are certainly encouraging, and, as an example of the power of debugging skills, we shall consider just one example. First it is necessary to define 'debugging' in the context of skilled activities and in the context of writing LOGO programs.

When our achievements do not match our aims, then we could say that there is a problem or 'bug' in the plan. Debugging involves the identification and correction of the bug, so that achievements and aims can be matched. The plan can involve any sequence of actions and the goal can be anything from something as simple as tieing one's shoelaces or changing gear while driving a car, up to something as complex as winning a game of chess or pulling off a high-powered business deal. If the goal is not achieved, then there is a bug to be corrected. To take the example of changing gear manually, examples of bugs which are all too familiar to learner drivers are those involving the co-ordination of the foot pedal which controls the engine speed (the 'accelerator' pedal), with the clutch pedal and the movement of the gear lever. Ideally, as the clutch pedal is depressed the accelerator pedal is released slightly, to avoid excessive engine speed while the load on the engine is released. Once the clutch is depressed the gear lever can be moved, and the clutch pedal released in synchrony with depression of the accelerator pedal.

There are a number of things which could go wrong here – a number of potential bugs. If the accelerator pedal is not re-depressed after the operation of moving the gear lever and releasing the clutch pedal, then the engine speed may decrease dramatically and the engine may stall. We could call this an 'accelerator-inoperate bug' to identify it during tuition. Secondly, if the gear lever is moved before the clutch pedal has been depressed sufficiently, then there may be a grinding of gears – this could be called a 'clutch-operate bug'. And so on for each of the possible unco-ordinations that could occur during the operation. In each case the failure to obtain the desired goal could be described as resulting from a bug in the plan, and the successful learner will identify and correct these problems. Debugging of activities such as changing gear can have good similarity with the debugging of computer programs. The claim made by LOGO theorists is that experience of LOGO debugging is of benefit in the application of debugging procedures when it comes to other more general problem-solving activities.

We need to introduce some of the features of the LOGO programming language in order to demonstrate debugging in operation. In its most popular mode of operation, LOGO allows the creation of graphics effects with repeated sections, such as the petals on a flower, or trees in a wood. The programmer is asked to imagine a turtle which moves a pen around the screen in order to draw a picture. In some versions a mechanical turtle actually moves on a sheet of paper on the floor, holding a pen down to start drawing, and then moving itself to produce lines on the paper. In both versions the turtle follows commands to move forward by a stated distance, and to turn left or right a stated number of degrees. Combinations of commands can be given names, and then be used as procedures within other parts of the program by reference to these names. So, if we want to draw a flower with a number of petals, the instructions for a single petal would be given a single name, together with an instruction for moving to the starting point for the next petal, and then in order to draw all the petals with one instruction we would give a repetition instruction. Once the flower was complete, then all of the instructions necessary for the flower could be collected together with one name, and this single instruction would produce a complete flower. Similarly, a flowerbed could also be drawn with a single instruction which called upon the procedure for each flower, and so on. In the following example, Robert Lawler's daughter Miriam is writing a program for drawing such a flower, and has a bug with the length of the stem (Lawler, 1985, p. 83). It was appearing with a length of 35 units (created by a 'FD 35' instruction in the transcript), from an earlier attempt when a length of 85 units was required for good proportion. Miriam had therefore added 50 units during the previous programming session, but the flower was still appearing with the short stem. At the time, Miriam was a little over 6 years old.

1	RL:	Looks pretty good to me.
2	Miriam:	No.
3	RL:	Oh-oh. We got a bug, eh?
4	Miriam:	Yeah.
5	RL:	What do we do about it? What's our bug?

6	Miriam:	The stem is too short.
7	RL:	The stem is too short. How long is our stem? ... It's a 35 ... I know the trouble. We left out the 50. Remember?

:
:

8	RL:	Can you fix it?
9	Miriam:	How?
10	RL:	You remember what happened when you keyed the line 2 and the blank? And the old one went away and the new one got there?
11	Miriam:	Yeah?
12	RL:	Key a new line 5.
13	Miriam:	[*Keys*] 5, space. [*Keys the new line character, replacing the FD 35 command with a blank line*].
14	RL:	Would that fix it? That just made the FORWARD 35 go away. Now your stem will be no-long at all. It will be zero long ... I guess you'd better have a new line 5 that tells the turtle to go forward the right distance.
15	Miriam:	[*Keying*] 5?
16	RL:	Yeah. Space. And how far should he go? You ... had a 35 but you left out the 50. So it should be, –
17	Miriam:	[*Interrupting*] Hold it ... 85 ... CS, new line. PF.

The instruction CS in line 17 acted to clear the screen of the first, incorrect, drawing, and PF was the instruction to execute the corrected procedure (this is the name of the procedure, with the initials PF standing for Pretty Flower!).

Debugging has been a joint operation in this example, with Lawler himself analysing the bug (in line 7), and conceiving the correction (editing instructions which are suggested in lines 12 and 14). Miriam's contributions are considerable, however. Without prompting, in line 2 she has accepted the existence of a bug, in line 6 she has identified the nature of the bug, and in line 17 she has tested the correction. Shortly after Miriam has recognised the need to identify and correct bugs in programs, there is evidence of her using the concepts and language of debugging in her activities away from the computer. For example: 'One night at dinner Miriam struggled with a pork chop. Both lost – it skidded off her plate and onto the floor. "Miriam!"

her mother and I exclaimed. "You know what, Dad?" We waited. "My pork chip's got a jump on the floor bug" ... ' (1985, p. 86).

In another example, Lawler describes how he had Miriam teach him how to use a skipping rope. She diagnosed several problems with his technique, and suggested remedies. One problem was described as a 'too soon' bug, seen when he jumped before the rope had touched the ground. When he acted upon this bug the rope caught him around the ankles. Miriam saw this as a 'pull up' bug in which the hands holding the rope need to be raised at this moment. After a number of failed jumps the diagnosis is getting close (p. 104):

Miriam: You're jumping too low [the 'too low' bug] and too soon.
RL: I've got a too soon bug.
Miriam: And a low bug.
RL: And, ah ... which should I fix first?
Miriam: The too low bug.

There are a number of descriptions in Lawler's transcripts of the spontaneous use of debugging concepts out of the context of LOGO programming. There has been transfer in these examples, because microcomputer experiences have been useful in the identification and correction of more general problems. The examples provide a strong case for teaching of the principles of debugging skills, whether through LOGO or through some other medium.

Even if we take Lawler's daughter's cognitive development to be a 'best case' because of the intensity of the interaction between learner and teacher, and because of the qualities of both, the study serves to demonstrate what *can* be achieved under optimal conditions of intensity, stimulation and closely monitored teaching by a highly knowledgeable teacher. The study does not address the question of what might be achieved under more normal classroom conditions, with just a few hours available for the activity and with a less advantageous teacher–child ratio. Other studies are valuable in pointing to gains which can be made under just these circumstances.

After a manageable LOGO course of two hours a week for twenty-five weeks, 8- to 12-year-old children can be shown to show good transfer from LOGO debugging exercises to other tasks. This case of successful transfer was reported in a detailed study by Klahr and Carver (1988), and is notable for several distinctive features. The LOGO experiences were based around an explicit model of debugging skills. Children worked in pairs for lessons which each lasted an hour. After a few hours of programming experience they were given explicit instruction in debugging routines, and at the end of the course their debugging skills were assessed, to determine acquisition. Before the course, and again afterwards, the children completed another exercise to determine their ability in the application of these skills. These were the transfer exercises, and consisted of identifying the errors in a set of written instructions, given a desired state and an achieved state, and then correcting the instructions so that the desired state would then be achieved. One transfer task required corrections to a set of instructions for the arrangement of furniture in a house. Some two dozen items of furniture were to be arranged in three rooms, and two plans were available. One of these indicated the required positions, and the other one indicated the positions reached by following the instructions. Other transfer tasks involved checking for an error in instructions for the distribution of objects (e.g., paying wages), and in instructions to follow spatial directions (e.g., in playing golf). One instruction could be changed to correct the instructions in each of the tasks, and Klahr and Carver observed the search strategy used during correction.

Prior to the LOGO debugging sessions, the children tended to read the instructions line by line, sometimes failing to terminate the search for the bug upon detection. In the post-test they tended to be more selective, focusing upon the appropriate section of the list of instructions. In the transfer task involving furniture layouts, the discrepancy between the two diagrams was in the layout of one room, and so it is appropriate to inspect only the instructions concerning the items of furniture in this room. Further, when looking at the performances of individual children, the change to the use of a more selective search strategy in the post-test was found to be correlated with an improvement in LOGO debugging expertise during the programming course. Each child either improved on both tasks or failed to improve on both: there were no children who improved on just one task.

Identifying the errors in our solutions to problems is clearly an important skill – an essential component of our cognitive toolkit – and Klahr and Carver provide evidence that LOGO debugging experience can be seen to have positive transfer to non-programming environments. It is difficult to estimate the transfer of debugging to more general fault-finding activities. The transfer tests used in their experiments could all be described as being in 'near' domains, with transparent similarities between them and LOGO. They involved checking for errors in written instructions in all cases, with explicit instructions to determine the specific cause of the discrepancy between the intended outcome and the actual outcome. The transfer shown by Miriam is perhaps a more convincing example, when her fault-finding skills in LOGO were applied to the analysis of her father's attempts with a skipping rope (Lawler, 1985).

It is not only debugging skills which have been found to transfer from LOGO to non-programming tasks. An ideal example of transfer is demonstrated in a classic experimental investigation reported by Clements and Gullo (1984). In this study 6-year-old children were given pre-experience tests of cognitive ability, followed by LOGO activities spread over a period of three months, and then the tests of cognitive ability were repeated. The question was whether LOGO classes could influence the scores on the pencil and paper tests of thinking skills. This study provides a very simple answer to the question of whether cognitive ability changes as a function of LOGO programming. The answer is positive, and we know that the changes are not entirely a function of other activities during the three months of experience, because a non-LOGO group was pre-tested and post-tested in the same way. The non-LOGO control group used a variety of commercial software packages aimed towards the development of numeracy and literacy skills during the period when the experimental group were creating shapes with LOGO. The LOGO and non-LOGO groups therefore had similar computer time, and gains made by the LOGO group cannot be attributed to motivational differences due to them being in the only treatment condition. There were nine children in each group.

The battery of tests of cognitive ability used by Clements and Gullo included measures of reflective and divergent thinking, classification and seriation, and verbal memory. For the LOGO group, significant gains were made on the Torrance Test of Creative Thinking, and on a test of shape/object discrimination (the Matching Familiar Figures Test). These gains were not seen in the non-LOGO group. Further differences between the two groups were observed on a number of tasks which were presented once only, after the computer experience. Differences between the groups were found on three of these tests: two tests of metacognition (in which the children indicated when they had insufficient information to solve problems of two types), and a test requiring verbal descriptions of a route to be taken when presented with a map. There were no differences on the tests of classification, seriation, or the McCarthy Screening Test of cognitive development (which included sub-scales of orientation, verbal memory, drawing and numerical memory).

The three months of LOGO which the children experienced is arguably insufficient for us to see all of the benefits for their cognitive development, but even in Clements and Gullo's brief study there are improvements in a number of the components in the cognitive toolkit. The children were more successful with tasks requiring the generation of original ideas (Torrance Test), and the evaluation of their own knowledge (metacognition test). Less surprisingly, perhaps, they also performed well on a visual-spatial matching task (Matching Familiar Figures Test), and on a task requiring the extraction and description of directions from a map: these two tasks tap abilities which are central to LOGO programming.

In the Clements and Gullo (1984) study the general thinking skills of 6-year-old children were found to grow following experience of LOGO concepts. It is not surprising that a similar picture should emerge from Helen Finlayson's study (1984) of the benefits for specifically mathematical thinking. Using a classic experimental design with matched groups of subjects and post-testing with a different medium, one class of 11-year-olds had 28 weeks of LOGO exercises and projects while a second class had non-LOGO computer tasks during the equivalent periods. The two classes were matched on non-verbal ability and on mathematical ability, and at the end of the course they were assessed using pencil and paper tests of their mathematical skills.

The post-LOGO tests assessed the children's abilities to estimate angles between lines, and their understanding of the concept of a variable (using Chelsea College tests in both cases). These specific abilities are central to success when using LOGO graphics, and the study confirmed a successful transfer for the LOGO users in comparison with the non-LOGO class. A second test showed more general effects of programming, described by Finlayson as a test of the use of mathematical strategies, and required generalisation from patterns of numbers and the abstraction of underlying rules. For example, the children were given the following four 'number sentences' (as they were described), and asked to write two more sentences to show how the pattern continues:

$$2 + 3 = 5$$
$$4 + 6 = 10$$
$$6 + 9 = 15$$
$$8 + 12 = 20$$

The next item gave the following two number sentences taken from the same pattern and asked for them to be completed:

$$16 + \ldots = \ldots$$
$$\ldots + \ldots = 60$$

One question presented an incomplete number sentence, and asked whether it could be taken from the same pattern, and other questions asked for verbal descriptions of the rules which generate the pattern. These questions asked which numbers were allowed in the righthand column, and how could the remaining numbers be found from the first number in any sentence? The LOGO group outperformed the non-programmers in this test of generalisation and abstraction, but there was no difference between the groups on the questions asking for continuation of the pattern. The differences between the groups were in their ability to explain the rules which were used to generate the number sentences. This part of Finlayson's study shows transfer from the understanding of the rules embodied in programs, and which result in graphics patterns, to a more general understanding of how rules can generate numerical patterns. In combination with the Clements and Gullo study, this evaluation of LOGO demonstrates clear benefits for the development of mathematical thinking skills.

A number of other evaluations of LOGO exist – principally the Brookline LOGO project (Papert et al., 1979), and the Bank Street study (Pea and Kurland, 1983), which are available as technical reports and which offer mixed conclusions. The Brookline project report contains positive qualitative evaluations which are themselves difficult to assess, but the Bank Street study found no differences between a LOGO group and a control group on a non-programming planning task. The failure to find improvements in planning is important, because this is one of the few direct tests of the claims regularly made of learning to program.

More recent studies have confirmed the positive effects of LOGO programming for the early development of mathematical concepts. In both studies the children had recently entered formal schooling. In the first, Edinburgh children engaged in a six-month LOGO project with a floor-crawling turtle, and pre-test/post-test improvements were found on a number of components of the British Ability Scales (Hughes and Macleod, 1986). The sub-scales which enjoyed an improvement were all concerned with either number or shape, and even though there was no control group used in this study, these improvements are understandable in the context of the demands made in getting the LOGO turtle to draw shapes of pre-defined size and orientation. In a North American study of young children, 80 hours of LOGO tuition were based around the principle that progress follows from the use of problems that allow the discovery of solutions which are consistent with the child's current learning style (Robinson and Uhlig, 1988). In comparison with a matched control group, the LOGO programmers showed improved visual-motor integration, and improved performance on the Peabody Mathematical Readiness Test, a test which also assesses the Piagetian concepts of seriation, classification and conservation. Finally, the LOGO group had better school attendance than the non-programmers during the course of the experiment. Not only did they perform better, but they also turned up more often!

Not all evaluations of LOGO have found positive effects. Pea and Kurland's review (1984) comes to the conclusion that the idea that programming experience can transform children's minds is itself a form of 'naive techno-romanticism', and after reviewing a number of LOGO evaluations Tony Simon (1987) agrees. Whereas the evidence presented here does not support such a scathing dismissal (for benefits *can* be observed), we are compelled to acknowledge that there is a problem in accepting the claims of the LOGO proponents. Although certain benefits can be observed in children (e.g., assessing the state of their knowledge, in the generation of creative ideas, in spatial skills, and in numeracy), these are not exactly the profound developments which were claimed at the outset. The studies that have been performed do not map directly on to the five cognitive skills that have been claimed of learning to program: the development of rigorous thinking, abstract mathematical concepts, heuristics and planning, debugging, and metacognition. There are studies which show transfer from LOGO debugging to other debugging tasks (i.e., Lawler, 1985; Klahr and Carver, 1988), and also studies which show improvements in specific mathematical and spatial abilities after learning to program (i.e., Clements and Gullo, 1984; Finlayson, 1984; Hughes and Macleod, 1986; Robinson and Uhlig, 1988), but these are the principal achievements to date, and to be cautious we must conclude that the evidence is not overwhelming. There are also a number of reports indicating that there is little or no transfer from LOGO programming to other abilities. The benefits which can be observed are, in general, basic toolkit skills involving spatial ability and numeracy. LOGO users are highly committed, but their perseverance may be more an act of faith than the product of an objective evaluation. Evaluations suggest rather modest benefits relative to the extent of the user's enthusiasm, and relative to the extent of classroom programming experience which may be necessary for the general abilities to develop.

As with many applications of computer-based learning, one of the greatest attractions of LOGO is the motivation that it generates in the children using it. Hughes and Macleod (1986) commented upon children being able to sustain their work at the keyboard for 30–45 minutes even towards the end of the project, and the teachers who were involved in the project expressed surprise at the degree of concentration shown by their children. Robinson and Uhlig (1988) also found that their 6-year-olds were motivated by the LOGO classes. Motivation and concentration are infectious, and this may explain why there are so many LOGO enthusiasts in education, but claims for educational benefits must be based upon measures more profound than 'time-on-task' if we are to develop the quality of children's cognitive abilities rather than their powers of concentration.

One of the benefits noted by Hughes and Macleod was the willingness of the children to participate in co-operative working: we shall be returning to the effects of classroom computers upon social learning activities in chapter 7.

Acquiring the toolkit: classification, questioning and other basic skills

The idea of having young children learn to program with LOGO, so that they can discover the constraints existing within a simulated environment, is one which steps directly out of Piaget's claims about the necessity of cognitive reorganisation during development. There is little evidence to suggest that cognitive reorganisations do occur as a result of LOGO experiences, however, and this may be because they are difficult to observe objectively. We may not have seen evidence of cognitive development simply because our methods are inadequate to observe such comprehensive changes in the ways that children think about their worlds. Certain benefits are observable, as in the studies which we have described above, for instance, but these were improvements in performance on pencil and paper tests. It must be pointed out that when Clements and Gullo used more general tests of logical operations, such as classification and seriation, then no gains were observed. In agreement, Statz (1973) also found no effect of extensive experience of LOGO upon the classificatory abilities of 9- to 11-year-old children when tested with a twenty question game involving the identification of an item from a multi-dimensional set. If LOGO is to accelerate the development of operational competence then gains should be observable in classification tasks, and they are hard to find.

The ability to categorise the objects in our world has been identified as an essential aspect of intelligent behaviour by Bruner, Goodnow and Austin (1956), Rosch (1975), Homa (1984) and many others. We think with representations of the world we inhabit, and these representative symbols are abstractions taken from our experiences.

Thus, no one has actually seen an 'animal' as such, for this is a generalised category label rather than being an instance of an observable object; but we can have thoughts about the things that animals can do. We have experiences of individual objects which are classified as being animals, or birds, or as geese, or as grey lag geese, as the needs of description demand. What we actually see, of course, are specific instances. One of the purposes of categorisation is to reduce the number of instances that we have to deal with into a manageable set of concepts. By creating categories (for they have to be created as they do not exist outside of our common conceptual world), we reduce the complexity of our environments and thereby organise the components into familiar roles. Categorisation also eliminates the need for constant learning of properties by allowing a subordinate object (e.g., 'goose') to inherit the properties of its superordinate category (e.g., 'bird': can fly, lays eggs, etc.; and therefore 'goose': can fly, lays eggs, etc.). By categorising objects as we encounter them, our behaviour becomes more efficient because we can rely upon learned characteristics of objects to help us decide upon appropriate actions. If intelligence is demonstrated through our actions, then the ability to categorise is an essential characteristic of the development of intelligent behaviour. Categorisation skill is, in other words, an essential component of the cognitive toolkit and is a skill which education should foster. We have seen that LOGO experiences have little to offer this skill, but experiences with data bases are more productive.

One of our studies demonstrates the effectiveness of data base experience in the development of classification skills, and it will be described in some detail here (Underwood, 1986; see also chapter 4 where the study is discussed in the context of the use of data bases in classrooms). A version of Mosher and Hornsby's (1966) 'twenty questions' game was used in the assessment of categorisation ability, and children were tested before and after an extensive classroom project which required the description of a collection of cheeses with data base programs. The children were 9 to 11 years old, and there were ten children in each of four groups, two computer groups and two classes who performed the same exercise without using the computer.

The classification task required each child in the study to identify one of twenty-four objects by asking questions which would gain yes or no answers. The objects varied along three dimensions, and the measure of interest was the number of questions that was required for correct identification of the 'target' object. Ten trials with this game established the categorisation score for each child. The children were allocated to one of four groups on the basis of this pre-test categorisation score, and also on the basis of their reading age and their mental age as assessed by standardised pencil and paper tests. The four groups therefore contained children with similar abilities at the start of the project. All four groups took part in the cheese project, and all had categorisation experiences as part of the project, but whereas two of the groups used computer data bases the other two groups used a simulation of these data bases using filecards. The two data bases used different organisation principles – SEEK uses a binary tree, and FACTFILE uses a matrix classification – but as no differences were found between them, either when operated with the computer or when simulated with filecards, they will not be discussed further.

The cheeses project lasted for three weeks, and required the children to describe the characteristics of a set of common cheeses, to classify them using the data bases, and to interrogate the data file for associations between items and to identify items with specified characteristics. So that all children would consider themselves to be treated similarly, with the two computer groups seen as no more special than the filecards groups, the children not using the computer data bases engaged in a series of computer-based mathematical investigations: all children therefore had computer experiences during the course of the project. This eliminates the possibilities of Haw thorne effects in the treatments of the computer and filecards groups. At the end of the project the forty children were again each given ten trials with the 'twenty questions' categorisation task. The results were clear cut: whereas the filecards groups showed no change in performance over the course of the study, the computer data base groups required fewer questions in comparison with their pre-test performance and in comparison with the filecards groups. The computer groups achieved this improvement by changing the type of questions they asked. In the post-test they were asking more constraining questions and fewer specific questions: the ratio of constraining to specific questions was greatest in the computer groups after the cheeses project. Constraining questions are more efficient because they eliminate more alternatives than do specific questions, even though they contain fewer delineators. For example, a constraining question would be 'is it large?' while a specific question would be 'is it a large green triangle?'

Although the categorisation improvements seen in this experiment are encouraging, there remains the question of why it is that experience with a computer data base aids cognitive development whereas the filecards data base does not. There are a number of possible explanations. For example, the difference may have been due to the mechanical inefficiency of handling information written on filecards. The mechanical versions of the data organisation and interrogation tasks were certainly more tedious. Alternatively, the difference may have been due to the uncompromising rigour of interaction which is difficult to achieve in adult–child interaction in comparison with computer–child interaction. With the computer data bases, questions had to be formulated precisely. There was no room here for interpersonal negotiation over the meaning and form of a proposed data entry or of an interrogation, and it may be that one of the main benefits in using computer data bases is in the development of formal thinking.

It is not the case that all computer-based classes will show the same improvements as in the SEEK/FACTFILE experiment. Two further experiments with essentially the same design failed to show the same huge pre-test/post-test differences in the 'twenty questions' test of categorisation ability (Underwood, 1989, experiments 1 and 2).

In the first of these experiments the classroom activities were based around the LOGIBLOCKS 2 package of programs. As these programs are designed specifically to encourage the development of classificatory abilities, a large improvement was expected in post-test performance. The programs are based upon the development of thinking through tutorial guidance and practice in the categorisation of two- and three-dimensional shapes. The programs are carefully graded and offer practice in a games format, and the more difficult games have a time element which can be pre-set by the child or the teacher. The games are designed to be played individually but can be used by two or three children together, and are presented in programs which draw on familiar primary school activities. The software documentation includes a booklet of support exercises to be used by the children when not working with the computer. These exercises are generally board game simulations of the computer games and in the experiment they formed the basis of the work completed by the children in the control group, and were not available to the computer group.

The results of the LOGIBLOCKS 2 experiment suggested that the computer users had a marginal advantage over the non-computer users. The ratios of constraining to non-constraining questions were similar in the two groups of children both before and after the exercises, suggesting that the classification games in the LOGIBLOCKS package did not encourage patterns of thought which could be transferred to other tasks.

In the second experiment of the study a different class activity was introduced between the two tests of classification ability (Underwood, 1989). The program used was THINKLINKS, based on the notion of lateral thinking. It is a program to stimulate children's design skills. The open-endedness of design extends the child's thinking beyond the specific goal orientation of problem-solving, and encourages re-classifications of familiar objects. In THINKLINKS the children's ability to design is developed through a series of increasingly complex activities. Initially children are asked to classify, on a range of criteria, five randomly selected objects presented by the computer. For example, they may be requested to grade the following objects on the criterion of softness: matches, a shoe, water, a spade and a table. This encourages children to view objects in new ways. The second phase of the game is to use five randomly presented objects to solve a computer-selected problem such as crossing a stream, catching a fish, or getting into a house for which you have lost the key. Finally the children are asked to invent or design a device to solve a problem such as how to sort potatoes or how to catch a mouse.

At first sight this type of lateral thinking exercise appears to be an activity which can gain little from being computerised, as all that is necessary is a mechanism for providing the random list of words and design problems. Output to the screen is confined to text and the children's only input to the program occurs when they request another list of words or problems. The computer program proved very easy to replicate as a card game with appropriately marked cards and the adult experimenter randomly dealing out the pack. Again, there were marginal advantages for the computer users in the total number of questions required to identify a target card in the 'twenty questions' game, but no changes in the ratios of constraining to non-constraining questions for either group.

Although the didactic tutorial programme embodied in the LOGI-BLOCKS 2 suite, and the 'self-discovery' programme embodied in the THINKLINKS program, did lead to improvements in the classificatory abilities of the children using these programs, the greatest advances in rigorous thinking were seen with the data base programs. In these activities, in which the children first learned about cheeses and then classified them according to their multi-dimensional attributes, the children were compelled to think about the nature of questioning as much as the nature of classification. We shall be returning to the distinction between building and questioning a data base in due course. The development of rigorous thinking was seen in a number of the cases studies which are described in some detail in chapters 4 and 5.

The use of data bases in the development of analytic questioning has also been commented upon by Ennals (1984), who observed the enquiries made by 12-year-old children using a historical data file. The file concerned the population of their own town (Sunbury) between 1826 and 1876. Enquiries about population statistics, locations of specific families, and employment (e.g., 'what work did women do?') were answered through the data base itself, but the ease of collecting these data resulted in the children asking more analytic questions which could not be answered with the data base and which developed into further classroom and library research projects. Typical of these post-data base questions asked by the children were:

How did life in Sunbury change with the coming of the railway?
Where had the gentry got their money?
Why was insurance suddenly such a significant form of emplyment in Sunbury?

The mechanical ease of asking questions of a computer data base means that the answers to purely descriptive questions (such as 'Which people were publicans, and which pubs did they run?') are provided without effort. This frees the children to ask more reconstructive questions about the environment sampled, in this case life in nineteenth-century Sunbury. An important feature of this exercise is that the use of the computer data base has prompted the children to ask analytic questions which in turn could be answered only by more conventional library searches. The role of the computer here was to demonstrate the nature of enquiry.

The ability to categorise the objects and events in our environment is clearly associated with the ability to question the available data. Our study of the effects of using a computer data base found that more constraining questions were asked after children had taken part in a project requiring them to think about the ways that cheeses vary (Underwood, 1986). If there is no means of extracting information from a data file, then the data file itself is useless, however well organised it may be. It is a pointless exercise to form effective classifications of the objects and events in the natural world unless the acquired concepts can be retrieved as required. The ability to generate hypotheses about the structure of the world and to ask questions designed to understand more about the world is of clear importance to the professional scientist, but this is no more exacting than the task facing the developing child attempting to understand the regularities in the world which the adult takes for granted.

A striking demonstration of the way in which data base building and interrogation can sharpen children's thinking is contained in the following transcript. It was recorded during a group project in which three 8-year-old children need to develop the data base by adding a discriminative question. The transcript is taken from Underwood and Underwood (1987a), and the children were using the SEEK binary classification program. The task was to identify trees by the features possessed by their leaves, and when the children first use the data base they find that it is incomplete. Part of their task is to add to it with new information and new questions. C1, C2 and C3 are the three children working together on the project. C1 acts as computer operator throughout, reading aloud screen instructions, and entering responses via the keyboard.

SEEK + C1:	Is the leaf just one simple leaf on a stalk?
C2:	What does 'simple leaf' mean?
C1:	It means all in one piece and not in bits like a chestnut.
C2:	Oh, well it is then – press Y.
SEEK + C1:	Has the leaf got an edge like the teeth of a saw?
C3:	My turn. Well, it's got a curved edge but not like a saw.
C2:	Let's see – mmm, I agree.
C1:	OK, I'll put no.
SEEK + C1:	Has the leaf an oval shape and the veins going right to the edge?
C2:	Neither.
SEEK + C1:	Has the leaf got prickles?
C3:	No.
SEEK + C1:	Oak.
C2:	Let's tell Teacher.
C3:	It doesn't look like an oak to me!

The questioning attitude of C3 is the most remarkable feature of this interaction, although the progress made through co-operation is something that we shall come back to at a later point. When the events with SEEK were described to the teacher, further library research was suggested. The children confirmed that their mystery leaf was not an oak, by virtue of oaks having deep rounded lobes and two smaller lobes at the base – features which were not present in their leaf. They also learned that in oak leaves the top is wider than the base (theirs was the other way around), and finally that the veins of their leaf have a milky fluid which is characteristic of maples. They returned to the microcomputer data base with a new entry and with a number of discriminating features, and started by retracing their earlier steps.

SEEK + C1:   Oak.
C1:   No! Oh, what's happening?
       [The screen display is changing at this point.]
       It's disappearing. Wait, part of it's still on. It says 'What is it'?
Teacher: It's asking what the leaf is if it isn't an oak.
C1:   Oh, silly me. Right, let's put in maple. M-A-P-L-E.
SEEK: A question to give the difference?
Teacher: It wants you to tell it a question to show the difference between the two leaves.
C2:   Is the top wider than the bottom?
C3:   Does it have two small lobes at the base?
C1:   Does it have milky stuff?
Teacher: Which one do you want to use? Remember that it must be a YES/NO answer.
C3:   Use Jackie's (C2) – it's the clearest.
C1:   What do you mean?
C3:   Well, it's the easiest for anyone to see when they look at it.

The three children have three discriminating features to choose between, and are able to select objectively on the basis of a criterion of ease of use. There are a number of points to be made about these interactions between the children and SEEK – the non-acceptance a 'good question', the use of a classroom computer as the starting point for non-computer research, the appearance of group cohesion and group responsibility, and the problems for individual assessment which are associated with children working together in groups. These points will be raised in a number of places in this book where we shall refer to the foregoing as the Maple Leaf transcript.

Classroom computers can be used with the aim of aiding the development of hypothesis-testing and questioning skills, and this was demonstrated in a study reported by Simon, McShane and Radley (1987). The program investigated by this study was RAYBOX, a product of the Microelectronics Education Programme (MEP), in which the location of objects is to be determined. This is a problem-solving game in which hypotheses can be formed and tested by appropriate questions. The objects occupy locations which are the cells in an eight-by-eight grid (the 'raybox'), and the way of discovering them is by sending a probe (a 'ray') along one of the eight rows or one of the eight columns. If an object is hidden along a row, then the probe vanishes (the 'ray' is 'absorbed'), or if an object is hidden in an adjacent row, then the probe is deflected by 90 degrees, and if there is no object near the row, then the probe emerges at the other end of the row, and so on. Contestants can guess the location of an object at any time. The rules governing the behaviour of the probes are known to the contestants, and in Simon, McShane and Radley's study, the focus was upon the type of tuition which leads to improved questioning of the microworld of the raybox. There are a number of strategies used by skilled interrogators of the raybox, and Simon and co-workers reported that children taught the principles of the game with an 'informed training' regime performed better than those taught with 'blind training' or 'no training'. The informed training group were told about the appropriate problem-solving strategies and were told their underlying principles whereas the blind training group were only told to use the strategies*. The informed training group made fewer false predictions than the other two groups, and this improvement in questioning was still apparent in a re-test three weeks later. Computer-based activities such as this can be seen to improve the quality of questions asked by children, and this indicates an improvement in the quality of problem-solving. In the future it would be useful to have demonstrations of how these improvements transfer to other tasks which are not computer-based.

Hypothesis-driven questions were found to appear spontaneously in Chatterton's (1984) study of interactions in a science classroom in which conventional practice was supplemented by a computer-based lesson in a secondary school. A number of important changes were observed in the structure and style of the lessons, for instance, in an increase of pupil-to-pupil discussions and a change of role for the teacher who took a more supportive and less task-setting role. In addition, there were changes in the type of enquiry being made by the children. In the computer-based lesson there were fewer specific questions (e.g., 'What temperature do we use?' and 'How much do we add?') in favour of more predictive and analytic questions (e.g., 'What happens if we increase the temperature?' and 'Why has the yield gone down?'). Chatterton attributed the changes to the introduction of small group dialogue, in which hypotheses could be sug-

---

* For an example of a strategy, if a probe ray is absorbed (this is indicated by the disappearance of the probe), then the next interrogation should be of an adjacent row, since the point of deflection will identify the location of the object along the first row (except in cases of absorption being caused by a special case of two objects in proximity).

gested and discarded in an informal social structure without the embarrassment of presentations made to the whole class. There was also an inclination to question the data generated by the computer model of the chemical processes under investigation, rather than to accept it. The increase in the amount of pupil–pupil discussion in computer-based problem-solving is a feature commented upon in a number of studies.

Evaluation in education

In considering the uses of classroom computers as aids to the development of children's thinking, we have seen that learning to program with LOGO, using data bases, and using problem-solving games and simulations, can each be seen to produce changes in the ways that their users think about their worlds. There is no curriculum as such in the use of these programs – these applications are educational tools with open-ended uses – and the educational goal has little to do with the accumulation of declarative knowledge. The use of these programs can help develop thinking skills – the skills which young thinkers are assembling as a cognitive toolkit.

The specific skills which we have identified here as likely to be developed are, in the case of LOGO activities, spatial and numeracy skills, creative thinking, and metacognitive knowledge. In the case of data base and simulation activities, we are able to find developments of hypothesis testing, categorisation and questioning skills. Cognitive gains can be observed when children engage in computer-based learning activities, even though the gains we have discussed are those which are observed after only a short period of use. Education is necessarily a long-term activity, but educational research projects tend to look for changes after a few months of experience with the activity. As Snow and Yallow (1982) have shown, the impact of any one educational treatment may not manifest itself for several years, and equally may continue to show an effect when children have moved from one school to another. We cannot say whether any of the studies which we have reviewed would find any long-term changes in the cognitive development of the children who participated. The measures simply have not been taken. It is very sad that so few research projects look for changes over the course of years rather than weeks and months, and in an ideal world we would have the resources to evaluate our educational practices for their long-term effects. In the meantime we should use what evaluative measures we have available.

3 Why put information technology into schools?

This chapter is an introduction to the three that follow, which provide examples of the educational benefits that can be achieved using data bases and word processors. These are the tools of the 'informavores' – the consumers of information. Informavores are people who recognise that the world presents more information than can be processed by their own personal powers, and that artificial information processing tools are essential. Society has developed to its current state of civilisation by making use of the information gained by previous generations, and its future development is inevitably dependent upon our abilities to find new ways of making use of the information which technology presents to us.

These are the two benefits of using classroom computers with information processing packages – on the one hand society is increasingly dependent upon the information delivery technologies, and on the other hand there is evidence that thinking about information with these packages can act as a catalyst for children's intellectual development.

Education and information-handling skills

For some time now there has been a powerful lobby within the educational system arguing for a process- rather than a fact-oriented curriculum. In the fact-oriented curriculum the emphasis is upon knowing that Paris is the capital city of France or that a major export of Cuba is cigars, rather than upon the acquisition of atlas reading skills or library skills which would allow children to retrieve such data for themselves. Equally, it is about operating processes rather than understanding those processes. Lampert (1986) has shown a clear difference between these two curricula when discussing children using teacher-provided algorithms for completing multiplication problems, as opposed to children generating their own algorithms and multiplication stories. It was the children who produced their own explanations of the problems who understood the nature of multiplication. There is now a focus upon information manipulation, at the expense of the collection of facts, and this can be explained in a number of ways. Modern methods of communication have resulted in an exponential increase in the quantity of data impinging upon the individual. It therefore becomes imperative that each person develops information-handling skills in order to make sense of the world of information which is being created around them. We have more information being presented to us than we can possibly encode and remember. Our personal abilities are far exceeded by the amount of information created in the modern world, and so ours has become a problem of deciding which information sources to attend to, and which information retrieval systems to use when we know that we do not know something. In order to make use of an existing store of information we need to understand how the information within it is organised, and how to access it. These skills of information handling are underpinned by an explicit understanding of the organisational structure of categories. We need to be able to categorise the data which we collect from our personal experiences of the world in order to make sense of them. As we categorise events and objects we can be said to be forming the concepts which will be the symbols we manipulate during thinking. Indeed, the formation of these concepts appears to be important for many aspects of intellectual functioning.

The problem is not seen simply as one of individual survival, however. It can be argued that our future economic success depends on the degree to which children are taught to be sufficiently flexible and adaptable in their thinking and actions in order to handle the pace of change brought about by information technology. Gagné (1970) has argued that the most important things learned in schools are intellectual skills, not verbalised knowledge. This is the distinction between declarative knowledge (to 'know what') and procedural knowledge (to 'know how') which is central to the idea of a generalised cognitive toolkit. It is the acquisition of procedural knowledge which we should be looking for in classrooms that are dedicated to flexible problem-solvers. Longworth (1981) paints a very gloomy picture, however. He considers that what today's children learn at school, at best, has a useful life of half a generation, while at worst it is obsolete as it is taught! Competence with a variety of new technology machines and applications is a skill which will become more useful as we enter the 'Hole in the Wall' society, in which not only cash but also information will be dispensed to those who know how to gain access to it.

Building on the assertion that learning in schools is largely information processing, Labbett (1985) argues that teachers and pupils are already information-makers and information-handlers, and that all curricula are information-handling curricula. To a degree she is right, for we must all handle information to survive and it is not difficult to demonstrate that even very young children operate processes of discrimination. This is the thrust of George Miller's description of humans as informavores: we have a ferocious appetite for information, and much of our society is built upon our capacity to make use of the knowledge gathered by previous generations. Knowing is not enough, however: the relevance of a skill to any problem has also to be understood before it can be used to any effect.

There is also strong evidence that the emphasis in classrooms is upon factual knowledge combined with very limited structural organisation of information rather than upon information-processing skills. In the area of computer-based learning (CBL), drill-and-practice programs have so far predominated. This emphasis on knowing facts rather than applying cognitive skills was a worry highlighted in the Cockcroft Report (1982) on mathematical education. An evaluation of the use of mathematical software in schools also showed that, even with good support material, it is difficult to shift the classroom focus towards higher cognitive skills (Ridgway et al., 1984). These researchers observed teachers and pupils using non-drill-and-practice programs, which developed important skills of mathematics identified as neglected in most classrooms by the Cockcroft Report. They found that these programs led to an increase in discussions of hypotheses and improved problem-solving, but Cockcroft's missing 'investigational work' was not facilitated even though software aimed at stimulating such work was available to the teachers. Ridgway's team concluded that these packages were not used because teachers could find no way of fitting them into the existing curriculum.

We are being tyrannised by curricula which fossilise information into facts to be known, rather than into material to be manipulated and thought about. The fact-based curriculum may be nearer the truth for many classrooms than is described in Labbett's (1985) hopeful comments about what she sees as the underlying nature of the information-handling curriculum. Nevertheless, there is an awareness of the need to change the emphasis in education, although this may prove difficult as old ways have a habit of hanging on, and the new era of across-the-board educational testing may make it impossible. There is some concern in the UK that the National Curriculum objectives for much of the core curriculum will legitimise and support this emphasis. The focus on process and the need for procedural knowledge, highlighted by the Design and Technology Working Group, goes some way to ameliorate the problem. Information-handling skills are also emphasised by Her Majesty's Inspectorate, in discussing the need for children from the very youngest of school ages to be involved 'in the scientific processes of observing, measuring, investigating, predicting, experimenting and explaining' (DES, 1985).

The potential of information storage and retrieval systems

We have suggested that the classroom computer can, and should, be used in more liberating and creative ways to stimulate children's intellectual capacities, rather than as a drill-and-practice machine. While recognising the necessity of practice in the development of automated sub-skills, it is possible to give children this practice in the context of problem-solving activities. In the terms of Bloom's (1965) taxonomy we are discussing uses of classroom computers which place a high cognitive demand on children. Such uses go beyond the acquisition and comprehension of knowledge, and they encourage children to apply skills and knowledge, to evaluate and make judgements, and finally to draw together disparate information into a whole, in order to solve problems. To achieve these goals children should be encouraged to use the computer as a tool, particularly a tool to amplify their own thinking. One such tool use is that involved in processing data, but we are using the term 'information-handling system' here and elsewhere to include not only explicit data-handling software such data bases and spreadsheets, but also word processors, which can be used very profitably as flexible information-handling tools for the investigation of the structure and purpose of language, as we shall see later.

The view of Gagné (1970) and Labbett (1985), that teachers and students are already steeped in the ways of the information processor, questions the importance laid on the introduction of computer-based storage and retrieval systems into classrooms. These are the data base applications that we shall discuss in chapters 4 and 5. What can they offer in educational terms that the book-based data bases cannot? The computer is unquestionably the most appropriate means of storing, retrieving and classifying information, as it has the capabilities for processing large quantities of data at vastly superior speeds to anything we have previously had available. The printed page is a competitor only in its portability and familiarity.

The usefulness of the encyclopedic data base has been challenged by Chandler (1984), pointing out that in merely 100 pages the London magazine *Time Out* provides all the entertainments currently available in the city. To match this, PRESTEL's electronic viewdata system would need to set aside 200,000 frames, a highly uneconomic proposition. He argues, as many others before, that it is not the collected data which is of great importance, for he believes facts are the least important factor in thinking and learning. Rather it is the way in which data are used – knowing how to find, select, interpret and reorganise the material. The Schools Council (1981) put this succinctly when they pointed to not only the growth in the amount of information, but the ready availability of that information to individuals. They argued that children needed to be able to search out relevant information, critically assess the ideas and facts offered, and then make use of those findings. It was not only this goal-directed purpose to learning that they felt was missing in many of our secondary schools. The Council also maintained that in institutions whose main concern was learning it was surprising that teaching the skills of learning itself proved to be a very difficult task for the teachers.

In Piagetian terms, of course, the skills of learning are inherent in the child and cannot be taught directly, and the teacher's role in such a classroom is to provide an environment in sympathy with the child's level of development in order that appropriate intellectual leaps can be made as efficiently as possible. The teacher has a far more active role in classrooms operating according to the principles advocated by Vygotsky (1978) and Bruner (1983). For example, the teacher's role might be considered as being to provide a scaffold for children's problem-solving (Wood, Bruner and Ross, 1976). Here the teacher is a key interventionist, providing help when the child is in difficulty but standing aside when he succeeds, and generally supporting the abilities to select, remember and plan which are necessarily under-developed in the child. It is in this role of support facility that information handling packages such as the word processor and the data base are seen as most useful: 'Computerised information storage and retrieval is capable of offering liberation from "cluttered brains" and thus giving freedom to concentrate on the development of flexible thinking skills' (Chandler, 1984, p. 56). This view has sympathy with Rushby's (1979) classification of information-handling packages as being emancipatory, in that they free the user from non-essential work.

Moreover, the pragmatic argument that computer-based information systems are widespread in the world outside the classroom and, therefore, that there is a need to develop 'information literacy', is quite powerful. In our survey of eighteen classrooms using data base packages, the teachers at all age-ranges (5–19-year-olds) expressed the importance of children knowing *about* computers (Underwood, 1988). 'Knowing about computers is a necessity for all children' was one teacher's comment when discussing work with 6-year-olds. The feeling is echoed by parents. Rarely has it been so easy to gain additional funds for school equipment than when funds are to be raised for a new classroom computer!

Active learning

Papert's third guiding principle of appropriate mathematics is that of 'cultural resonance' (but arguably this is also a principle of appropriate education in general). He argues that knowledge must make sense in terms of the larger social context, and that it must be valued by adults and not simply seen as a 'kid's thing', which the adult population sees no reason to take or use themselves (Papert, 1981).

Chandler (1984) is particularly concerned that children should not only be aware of, and have access to, national and even international data bases, but that they also need to be contributors to the store. He argues that 'guided tours of someone else's frame of reference are not enough.' One of the most effective ways of understanding any body of knowledge is to reconstruct it. In some cases this corresponds to the building of a physical model, or of a computer model with LOGO graphics perhaps, and in other cases this may be the re-description of the body of knowledge with a personal data base. Children need to create their own systems for communicating information with one another, otherwise they will become alienated consumers of others' knowledge. Papert defined this as the 'power principle'. The learner must be empowered to perform personally meaningful projects.

Direct experience develops skills about the activity involved in gaining information, whereas mediated experience (for example using a pre-packaged information store) develops skills in using the medium. This is the view of Olsen and Bruner (1974), and it is a view which holds a warning for those educators who are at risk of losing sight of their educational goals in a maze of beguiling technology.

Both experiences are useful and provide information about the world, but for the majority of teachers the key educational goal is in stimulating cognitive development and not in training technical skills. This may not, of course, be true for those teachers who have committed themselves to the new technologies. There is no doubt that otherwise rational teachers can become fascinated with the technology itself. Wishart's (1988) primary reason for introducing TTNS electronic mail into a junior school classroom (10- and 11-year-olds) was to place technology firmly in the curriculum!

The premise that the child's cognitive performance will improve over a wide range of measures, if the educational experience builds upon the child's own experiences, is one which finds ready acceptance among practising teachers and theorists alike. Papert (1981) described this as the 'continuity principle', the first of his guiding principles for an appropriate mathematics, and it is the cornerstone of most theories of learning and child development. Publicly available viewdata systems such as PRESTEL, and the non-interactive CEEFAX and ORACLE which are available in the UK through television channels, make only minor concessions to children. Many teachers have felt it more worthwhile and, it must be said, cheaper, to use simulations of the original packages which are available on floppy discs, especially as children can generate their own PRESTEL-like pages. TTNS (The Times Network System), however, is a full information storage and retrieval system with the potential for national and international communication, and in which children can play an active part in building the data store. The use of such a package not only encourages children to collect their own data and prepare it for consumption by the computer, but it also encourages children to pose a range of questions of their own devising. The machine can respond to these questions, and through an analysis of the children's own data it can help produce a representation of the data in a restructured form.

The Wishart (1988) case study describes the use of TTNS to fulfil goals expressed in the Bullock Report (1975) and the Kingman Report (1988) which concerned providing students with a genuine audience for their writings. Here the children developed links from a school in the centre of England to another in the Shetland Islands. Much valuable work was completed as children passed daily weather data back and forth. This resulted in useful graph work involving comparative meteorology. The work floundered in the second and third terms, however, when the children were asked to contribute to a national data base for all schools. The loss of personal contact, the immediate relevance of knowing what weather their 'e-mail' friends were experiencing, resulted in a lowering of motivation, although they had by this time learned the importance of systematic data collection. Wishart argued that one of the most motivating features of the TTNS link between the schools was the immediacy of feedback. Immediate feedback from 600 miles or 6000 miles can distort children's perceptions of the world, of course: we wonder where children in the technology classroom actually think Australia is.

The value of enquiry

The introduction of TTNS into schools highlights one of the pitfalls of working with a powerful technology. That is, the ease with which the individual is subverted by the glamour of the machine into trivialising education. One of the early schools projects which appeared on the TTNS network was a national survey of secondary schools. The topic chosen for this costly operation was 'Pop Music'. The topic has of course immediate relevance to teenagers and it is quite possible that some useful mathematics came out of the project, but it is difficult to see what reasoned or evaluative statements could be made from questions of the type: 'Who is your favourite male/ female singer/group?'. This is an example of Chandler's concern that educational institutions in Britain have responded to the ever increasing threat to the place of facts in education by adding to the curriculum something called 'information skills', defined as the ability to 'handle' facts. He considers that the phrase itself has disturbing overtones because of the reference to 'skills' rather than 'strategies', and the implied focus on 'information' rather than learning (Chandler, 1984). Thinking about the computer in primary education, or indeed at any level of education, should not mean thinking about computers but thinking about education.

Sigel and Saunders (1979) have queried the assumption that a question-asking instructional strategy necessarily promotes thought. They argue that all the studies which accept the proposition that asking questions is 'good' are based on two implicit assumptions: first it enhances problem-solving skills; and, secondly question-asking by children reflects their own thinking, while question-asking by the teacher promotes the child's thinking. They suggest that previous studies have not provided a systematic conceptual base for advocating the use of question-asking strategies as an instructional model, nor have they explained why questioning should enhance problem-solving skills. Dillon (1982) and Wood and Wood (1983) are of the opinion that classroom questions delimit rather than stimulate enquiry, but this, of course, is when the teacher asks the questions.

[One reason for using information-handling packages in the class-room is to encourage the children rather than the teacher to ask the questions.] Sigel and Saunders argued that it is because enquiry can create discrepancy or a mismatch between sets of events that it provides a framework for cognitive development. This view of problem-solving as the resolution of uncertainty, in which ambiguity and paradox drives thinking, becoming a vital engine for the development of the individual, is at the heart of many theories of learning and child development (cf. Piaget, 1952; Bruner, 1966; Vygotsky, 1978; Papert, 1981).

However, it is not enough for children to ask questions, whether they are motivated by explicit or implicit hypotheses. It is also important that they come to appreciate that those hypotheses which build on a foundation of constraint, rather than hypotheses strung non-cumulatively together, are a far more effective problem-solving strategy. For example, one of the strategies in the Mosher and Hornsby (1966) twenty questions game, one which requires the identification of an object in a multi-dimensional array, is the 'hypothesis scanning' strategy. The optimal strategy for solving the problem is to ask questions which eliminate half of the remaining objects, and this focuses upon the target object by a process of elimination or constraint. Some children fail to maintain the strategy, however, asking questions which logically imply inclusion of eliminated objects. This failure to use questions in a focused, constraining strategy is characteristic of hypothesis scanners. Children operating an hypothesis scanning strategy can become confused and discouraged by the mass of disorganised information impinging on them and fail to see essential patterns in the data. It can be argued that practice in enquiry, in trying to figure things out for oneself, encourages the rearrangement and transformation of data in such a way that one is enabled to go beyond the evidence and assemble new insights. [Emphasis upon active learning encourages children to become autonomous and self-motivated thinkers, leading them to be constructionists – organising their data, discovering regularity and relatedness, and avoiding the kind of information drift that is symptomatic of non-goal-directed thinking, and which fails to recognise the potential usefulness of much of the data to hand.]

The argument for the flexible thinker leads us back to societal needs. We are often told that there is mismatch between employer needs and the educational responses. While the latter focus on disci-

plines and vocational skill the former see transferable skills and attitudes as more important. Although it is difficult to define such skills,
it is said that what employers are looking for are the skills of communication, co-operation and teamwork. One major company item-
ises its priorities as a need for workers who can set and achieve
objectives; communicate and influence others; solve problems and set
priorities; show leadership and work with others; and generate new
ideas and better ways of doing things. Essentially this provides us
with an argument for a problem-solving approach to education,
which is not content-oriented, and which allows the learner to make
decisions and to take on a variety of roles including project manager
and team member. These are the central goals of educational programmes involving computer-based information-handling packages
in the classroom, and which, incidentally, are ideally suited to the
type of group work which is encouraged by current child/computer
ratios.

In brief, therefore, information-handling packages are seen by
many as one of the most effective ways of using computers in school.
This is firstly because the software exploits the full potential of the
machine itself – as in the adult world, information processing by
computer allows rapid and increasingly complex manipulations of
data. Secondly, it offers the opportunity for children to collate and
interrogate their own material from the environment and form their
own mental reconstructions of the world as they understand it.
Finally, Goodyear (1985) argued that, prior to the advent of classroom computers, in any exploratory approach to data the amount of
'inauthentic' labour was high. Inauthentic labour here means work
which is not intrinsically valued as part of the learning experience.
Children spent far more time on tasks such as completing simple
computations or conducting frequency counts, rather than thinking
about the relationships within the data. This placed severe limits on
the amount of data that could be manipulated, and downgraded the
activity from being an example of real-world research problem-
solving to yet another classroom exercise.

These last two points each go some way to answer the concern that
the computer encourages the divorce of humans from the real world.
Students not only have ownership of the data, because they have collected it, but they are also able to use large bodies of data because of
the emancipation provided by the processing power of the computer.

There are, it would seem, compelling arguments for using information-handling packages in schools, but are they really such effective
tools in the classroom? In the following three chapters we present
descriptions of some classroom experiences of the use of information-

handling packages, considering the use of word processors as both text preparation devices and as aids to thinking, together with more conventional information-handling systems in the form of classroom data bases and spreadsheets. The aim of these chapters is to highlight through the extensive use of examples the educational benefits which can accrue when children make use of these packages.

Why should we expect children to fine-tune their information-handling skills unless they are presented with opportunities which exploit those skills? As the advent of information technology has, in part, forced us to revalue the direction of education, it seems most appropriate that we should use the new technologies to encourage those cognitive skills needed to process the growing flow of information.

4 Building a world of information

Information technology is an enabling technology. It uses computing and telecommunications resources to help the user to collect, organise, store, retrieve or deliver information. The benefits of computer use come from its speed and capacity: the speed at which many of these tasks can be done, for example sorting information; and the size of the information store that can be manipulated by the user. This provides the user with a tool of unparalleled power. There is a family of information-handling programs which fit under the IT label and which are currently being used within education. These include binary-tree and matrix data bases, spreadsheets and expert systems. This 'family' can be seen as a continuum of increasing complexity of operations from data bases to expert systems. In each case there is a body of organised data collectively called a file, most frequently with a hierarchical or tabular structure or a combination of the two. Network structures are found infrequently, and are currently absent in standard educational packages. The data in the file can be searched and sorted in a variety of ways in order to reveal patterns and relationships and to answer queries. In this chapter we shall be looking at some of the ways that information storage systems can be used in the classroom to help develop thinking skills. In particular we shall concentrate on the processes involved when children build their own files of data.

Data bases are most familiar and are in use with all age-ranges throughout the educational system. Although all information stores, including books, directories and computer data bases, are displays of organised data, the structure of that organisation is more overt in computer data bases. The importance of this transparency of the organisational structure for the efficient retrieval of information by school children is highlighted in our own studies (Underwood and Underwood, 1987b). The very method of constructing and interrogating computer data bases requires a clear understanding of that structure. This is not always so for a directory and certainly not so for retrieval of information from a book. This need for a mental map of the data structure, and the significance of this knowledge in the development of children's thinking is a theme we will explore further in this chapter and in the next.

Spreadsheets differ from data bases, not only in their mode of query but also by having an additional data type – the formula. Formulae are constructed: they are sets of rules for generating a new data point from other data inputs. Thus a spreadsheet can be used to generate automatically the sum and mean of a set of examination marks, to revamp costs after a change in VAT rates, or to allow children to explore mathematical number patterns. An expert system again consists of an organised data file structure, but in this case the questioning role lies with the system. Specific information is extracted from the user, matched to that in the computer's data bank, and through the use of probabilistic rules, the user is presented with a possible answer to the query. Perhaps the best known example of an expert system is MYCIN (Shortliffe, 1976), which diagnoses bacterial infections in human patients. Its purpose is to assist a physician who is not an expert with antibiotics in the diagnosis and treatment of blood infections – MYCIN provides the diagnostic expertise and the physician provides clinical observations in answer to MYCIN's questions. The following is an example of a probabilistic rule, a production rule, used by MYCIN:

IF: (1) The stain of the organism is grampos, and
      (2) The morphology of the organism is coccus, and
      (3) The growth conformation of the organism is chains
THEN: There is suggestive evidence (probability of 0.7) that the
      identity of the organism is streptococcus.

MYCIN requests information and suggests treatments, and in this case an expert system provides a valuable service. It was designed for use before the micro-organism has been identified (because laboratory identification can take two days, while a culture grows), but when treatment is necessary. Other expert systems have received a less positive press, being used for decisions about the buying and selling of shares and foreign currency, and for military decisions in simulated war scenarios. In each case information is given to the system which makes decisions and recommends actions on the basis of probabilistic rules. The building of expert systems is a useful educational exercise, however, in that it requires the formalisation of knowledge. These exercises are not generally available as packages for schools at the present time, although such a system can be built using the list-processing facility of programming languages such as LOGO.

Spreadsheets have moved from the electronic office and business studies course first into secondary and now into upper primary schools, where they are proving to be interesting adjuncts to the curriculum particularly within investigative mathematics. The use of expert systems is largely confined to higher education at present but many of the activities we have observed which involved data base use in the secondary school would have been better served using expert systems.

The premise on which much of the following research is built is that thinking skills are actively encouraged by the ready availability of data storage and retrieval systems, of which there are now a number specifically designed for educational microcomputer systems. Kemmis, Atkin and Wright (1977), in their classification of educational software, described data base programs as 'conjectural', in that they encourage thought rather than mere assimilation, and in that they emphasise the manipulation and analysis of data, the use of abstractions and the testing of ideas and hypotheses. This definition suggests that information retrieval packages will have an impact on classificatory skills, and many teachers are using such programs with this educational goal specifically in mind. Additionally, it is suggested that in quizzing a data base even young children can begin to ask 'good' questions and be introduced to a hypothesis-testing-strategy approach to learning. The issue of what constitutes a 'good' question will be discussed more fully in this chapter and in the next, which concerns questioning and retrieval.

The descriptions here are largely based on two long-running research programmes working with data bases in junior school classrooms, one undertaken by the authors and a second by a colleague, Janet Spavold, in association with the Derbyshire Educational Software Centre (DESC). We need to start by describing some of the types of systems which are available for classroom use.

The structure of data bases

Data bases are organisational structures into which information is placed and from which that same information can be retrieved. The nature of the organisational structure and the method of data retrieval are two key ways in which data bases differ one from another. These differing characteristics can have profound impacts on the ease of use of the program and on the cognitive experiences presented to the child using them. The organisational structure underpinning most educational data bases is either hierarchical, a binary-tree (SEEK and ANIMAL), or tabular/matrix (INFORM, GRASS, SUPERSTORE or QUEST). Network structures with their pathways and common links and nodes are not used in educational systems as yet.

It might be useful at this point to make clear key terminology of the tabular structured information-handling packages. The data base, spreadsheet or expert system is the program, the set of instructions which tells the computer what to do next. The user builds with that program a file, or files in the case of a relational data base, of data. If we think of a telephone directory, which is a non-computerised data base, then the person looking up a telephone number is the equivalent of both the computer and the program combined, and the collective data or information about people and their addresses and telephone numbers are equivalent to the file. If we look inside the file then there are records, each of which contains information specific to one telephone subscriber, and there are fields, the headings or categories of data that will occur for each subscriber (names, addresses, numbers).

A relational data base is one in which each data file can be linked to another by defining relationships between them based on data held in common. Each two-dimensional file can now have a third dimension defined by the common relationship between it and other files. For example, if we wished to organise information about animals in order to identify the characteristics of, say, a vertebrate animal, or of a mammal or of a badger, then we could use three interconnecting files. Initially a master (super-ordinate category) file would be devised, called Animals, with two records. One record would define the characteristics of the vertebrates and a second the invertebrate animals. At a level below this file we would need a second file containing the records defining the main classes of vertebrates: mammals, birds, reptiles, amphibians and fish. The purpose of this file would be to distinguish mammal from bird, but would assume that data relating to the characteristics of 'vertebrateness' were already captured in the master file. Again below this would be a file, or set of files, depending on the designer's choice, containing the data on individual mammals, birds, and so on. An individual record from such a file might contain our data on the badger.

The collective sets of files of data – the Animals file, the Vertebrates file, the Mammals file – come together in a relational data base when we link the record for badgers to that for mammals and vertebrates, so that records can be accessed one from another. The advantage of this organisation of data, in this case both hierarchical and tabular, is that information does not have to be duplicated; the badger record card does not have to carry information about vertebrate animals.

In relational data bases such as DATAEASE any number of relationships can be defined and all tables (or forms) can be linked together if necessary. Currently we are investigating what use undergraduates can make of a relational structure concerned with sixteenth-century wills and inventories (Spavold, Underwood and Newman, 1989; Underwood, Spavold and Underwood, 1989). The master file contains the personal data of the deceased and is related to sub-files concerning his property, legatees and trustees. This interlinking of tables in a relational data base makes the development of a cognitive map of the data base more complex and subsequent navigation around the data base that more difficult. But by increasing the dimensions across which data can be classified, larger and more complex bodies of information can be stored.

By defining the relationship between two or more files, the relational data base gains an economy of storage. In the example of the Wills and Inventories data files, if John Smith has bequeathed his candlesticks to Robert Jones, we would have a master file giving details of John Smith; a file, or files, of his possessions, including the candlesticks; and a file for the legatees, including Robert Jones. We can then define the relationship between John Smith, his possessions and Robert Jones. The important feature here is that the candlesticks would be stored in the data base only once. It is not necessary to duplicate their description in each of the files. With large numbers of people and items, this not only provides a considerable saving in the necessary storage space, but also encourages efficient identification of patterns in the data. The saving in storage here was captured in another artificial knowledge base by Collins and Quillian (1969), and was known as the principle of cognitive economy. In their simulation of human memory known as a semantic network, the properties of objects (e.g., *birds: can fly*) were stored only once, at the highest level in the hierarchy rather than with each example (*canary: can fly; sparrow: can fly;* etc.). In order to determine whether an example has a specific property, the network would consult properties stored with the instance and those above it in the hierarchy. Any property stored at or above the instance would be assumed to be possessed by the instance. Properties were therefore stored once only, but determining whether an instance such as *canary* has a property such as *can move* would take longer than checking on a property such as *lays eggs*, because *can move* requires comparison of instances stored further away from each other.

The exciting feature of the Collins and Quillian simulation is that it successfully predicted some aspects of human behaviour in answering simple questions about the properties of objects which might be expected to be stored in human memory in a hierarchical way. So, the question 'can a canary lay eggs?' would take longer to answer than the question 'can a bird lay eggs?' in both the computer simulation and in the test involving humans. In this example, the principle of cognitive economy requires that the property *lays eggs* be stored with *birds* rather than with *canary*. Such economy of storage is vital to efficient processing given the speed and capacity of currently available systems. Relational data bases are not as yet widely used in education, however, but their need is apparent. Even at primary level we have found examples where children could be better served by a relational data base.

Searching a data file involves transposing standard English questions into the command syntax of the machine using a variety of parameters to define the field values delimiting the search. One major difference between the least well developed of the educational data bases and other data bases is the absence of keyword search and partial word search from their toolkit. A keyword search is exactly as the name implies, the computer will search through the data file for *candlestick*. This is not a difficult task, many basic word processors have this facility, but, as we will show, the lack of such a facility severely restricts non-numeric searches and places additional strains on the field definition and coding skills of the data file builder.

Access to a data file is either through a menu or through the use of direct commands to the machine. Command selection requires users to instruct the program what they want to do next. That communication needs to be in a precise form and syntax – the command language. Command-driven data bases are ideal for the experienced user in that they allow rapid and precise formulation of queries but the user must have a high degree of competence with the command language and a clear mental map of the data structure. The alternative is menu selection, but this provides users with limited options at any given choice point; pathways through the data are in part already prescribed by the designer of the program. This limitation of choice and sign-posting of the possible next moves by the program to the user acts as a useful prop, an *aide-mémoire*, for the naive user. Such systems are cumbersome, however, and users may have to 'walk' some distance through the program to meet a specified goal and this can be frustrating as user-expertise develops. In our own use of DATAEASE, students who realised that the command structure of the data base is a language like French with a simple syntax which they must learn, rarely bothered to use the menu system again. For those who did not make the language connection, the menu system remained the route to data retrieval.

Natural-language query techniques are an attempt to build a bridge between the ease and supportive nature of menu-driven programs and the flexibility of command-driven programs. They are an extension of the command system with the advantage that they will accept instructions phrased in standard English rather than the highly specified command language of most systems currently in use. As with the relational data base, natural-language techniques have had little or no impact on education to date.

Building a data file: collecting, classifying and problem-solving

Our recommendations can be summarised with the twin statements that problem-solving is at the heart of process-oriented education, and that using the computer as an information-handling tool is particularly useful in stimulating problem solving. If children are to be successful problem-solvers, however, they must be able clearly to define the problem to hand. This may be through the more passive role of disentangling someone else's problem, or, as is increasingly found in our schools, by actively posing their own problems. In essence we are saying that children should be encouraged to ask good questions. In their report *Science from 5–16: A Statement of Policy* (DES, 1985), Her Majesty's Inspectorate suggest that encouraging children to collect things and to ask questions about them is one way of stimulating this problem-posing skill. Collecting maps, pebbles, fabric or census material can lead to a range of activities, one of which is the ordering of data to discover patterns and relationships. Data bases are particularly useful in supporting this task. They provide a formal but flexible framework into which children can place their data, and additionally provide search, sort and general statistical techniques by which patterns can be teased out. And because they allow children to handle considerably more data than would be feasible by pen and paper methods (the emancipatory role) they encourage children to explore situations in full rather than come to simplistic conclusions based on limited information.

Setting goals and organising data

We have spent some time arguing the case for classificatory activities in the classroom. At a recent meeting of the ITTE group (Information Technology in Teacher Training) held in Exeter, Jon Coupland (1987) asserted that classification is about putting things into little boxes and putting lids on them. In the light of our own arguments this assertion may be seen as heretical. He is arguing that working with data bases can be a sterile exercise, and in one sense he is right, that is when the work is 'box-filling' for its own sake. What children need is a purpose for classifying before they go on to the arduous, but potentially rewarding, task of creating a data file. The act of building a data file should require children to set goals or pose a problem, collect and select data, and organise those data in such a way that the initial question can be resolved. Each of these activities presents opportunities for exciting learning outcomes but this is a case of the whole being very definitely more than the sum of its parts. Good research questions are an aid to the definition of relevant data and suggest best-fit solutions for data organisation. A clear example of this can be provided with a description of a research investigation on road safety conducted by a group of 8-year-olds.

In this project to investigate pedestrian safety around their village school, the children clearly showed how the formulation of a good research question could make the selection and organisation of data relatively easy. The children conducted a field survey of those environmental features which they felt aided or hindered pedestrian road safety. This work included marking on a large-scale map the location of features such as zebra crossings the blind corners. Visibility was noted at key break points along each road in local area. The children also conducted a survey of traffic density and traffic type.

The children initially focused on these important road safety features and built their data file with a record for each of them. They quickly realised that an organisational structure such as this, which used such features as records and then used the criterion of place to designate fields, was not going to be effective. The spatial component, 'where' a hazard occurred, was critical for the solution of their problem. They needed a place name to be returned as the meaningful answer. This led the children to restructure their data file and to enter data into place-name records with road safety features defining the fields. Transposition of data in this way is a highly skilled activity. Should we be surprised that the children succeeded? The key to this achievement lay in the nature of the problem. Crossing the road had meaning for these children, they knew what the goal was and it was within their power to manipulate the material into an appropriate form.

This study illustrates Papert's (1981) 'continuity principle' in action, but such positive reconstruction does not always happen. Indeed the activity of constructing a data file does not necessarily develop good skills in selecting and organising data. In a second case study with children of the same age in the same locality these beneficial outcomes failed to materialise. The teacher set the children the task of building a data file to support their topic work on transport. A very standard file structure emerged with field headings such as speed, cost and number of passengers. On a technical level the file was highly successful, but it had little real world meaning and trivialised the activity of data collection. Both the teacher and the children appeared unable to operate a consistent criterion for choice of exemplar vehicles. They designated Concorde as their example of a plane, a highly atypical category member, but specified an 'average family car' (typical category member) as the car exemplar, when consistency demanded a Ferrari at least! It would appear that the teacher, or perhaps the children, was subverted by the glamour of Concorde into producing a file which would only confirm existing prejudices, such as 'flying is very fast but very expensive' perhaps. Why did this happen? The lack of clear, articulated goals for collecting the data on transport must have some bearing on the matter. A second associated factor might have been that the teacher appeared to be defining her goals in terms of information technology skills rather than in terms of the cognitive demand made on the children. This then became an exercise in understanding the technology rather than an appreciation of a body of information. Another case of techno-romanticism?

Similarities and differences

Classification is both about differences and similarities but it is the former and not the latter that we tend to emphasise. In a discussion on this point one group of teachers argued that this was sensible, indeed ecologically valid, because we need to identify 'them' rather than 'us' on security grounds. But nature seems not to work this way. Birds flock and fish swim in shoals for their individual security. Adolescent street gangs and Sloane Rangers operate by the group knowing what it is that makes each one of them a member, not by defining the multitude of characteristics which might exclude would-be members or predators.

That there are defining features which delimit a category (and the fact that those features both say this person is a 'Goth' and this person is 'non-Goth') may encourage us to think that identifying similarities and differences is one and the same thing, but this is not so. If we focus upon one rather than the other then a very different classification takes place. Essentially, similarities act to group objects or people and lead to super-ordinate categorisation, while focusing on differences leads to a miriad of individual cases. We will now explore why this is important in building data files using a very simple program called NOTICEBOARD.

NOTICEBOARD is a relatively new data base widely available in the UK. Although it is a small package, it is none the less a very usable piece of software. It is based on a simple word processing package WRITER, to which has been added an appropriate menu and simple search routines. Children can build a simple filecard-like data structure using standard language inputs. The children have one filecard for each entry and can define up to four keywords to allow searches through the data. These keywords perform the same function as fields in a standard data base. This program is often used with quite young children because there is no need to talk of fields and records, each filecard is a record, and because there is no requirement to code the data.

The program arrives with exemplar files and it is the file relating to British Birds that we will discuss here. In this file, which has great relevance to the primary school curriculum, are descriptions of approximately fifty birds. The data for each bird occupy a full screen (see figure 4.1) and consist of the bird's name and a short written description, under which are placed the chosen keywords. The program is based on the idea that a word processor with a FIND/SEARCH facility can also act as a data base.

From the command menu we can choose to page through the file, see the keywords listed, search on one or more of the keywords (the search allows a Boolean 'AND' but not an 'OR'), or search on 'anyword' chosen by the user. This latter choice 'anyword' has the equivalent of keyword in a standard data base. On using this particular data file with both students and teachers, it became rapidly apparent that the best way to retrieve data was to page through or use the anyword search. The keyword search which should have provided young users with a ready-made entry into the data was of little use. Why should a potentially useful investigative tool fail here? The answer lies in the selection of keywords. For this exemplar file selection is perhaps too strong a term. The keywords are idiosyncratic, showing little inherent logic other than that they focus upon the characteristics which make each bird different from its neighbour.

—————————————————————————— 11 ———

SWALLOWS
have long pointed wings and forked
tails. They fly fast, catching
insects. They commonly perch on
wires, rarely on the ground. Often
found in mixed flocks. 4–7 eggs

Key: FLOCKS, FORKED, INSECTS, PERCH.

Press RETURN

—————————————————————————— 12 ———

CROWS
are large, gregarious, black and grey
birds, with heavy bills. They nest in
trees. Their call is raucous. They
are often chased by other birds. 3–7
blue-green speckled eggs

KEY: BLACK, GREGARIOUS, RAUCOUS, TREE

Press RETURN

Figure 4.1   Screens 11 and 12 from the British Birds file
NOTICEBOARD. Note the lack of overlap in selected data and
keywords between the two records.

For approximately fifty birds, each with four associated keywords, we have collectively 100 different keywords in use. These keywords are meant to represent the core characteristics of the birds in the file. They perform the same function as fields in a standard data base, but they actually emphasise features which have caught the designer's eye. This lack of consistency provides the user with a serious difficulty when searching through the file.

Few birds share the same keywords. There are eleven 'black' birds but most keywords apply to one or two birds only. Why is this a problem? One reason is that it makes nonsense of the power of computer searches. There is little point in asking a restrictive 'AND' search. For example, if only one bird is 'brown' and only one bird has an associated keyword 'nocturnal', then asking the question *Find all the birds which are "brown" AND "nocturnal"* ' will at best return one bird but more likely will result in a null result, if the brown bird is not nocturnal in habit. There are times when null results are illuminating and add significantly to our understanding, but when a file produces this answer to the majority of searches, as is quite possible here, then it is neither illuminating nor motivating. As one teacher said, surely its better to flip through and retrieve the data as from a book rather than having all these disappointments.

The problems with this particular file are not unique, as we have shown with the transport file, but it is unfortunate that so much good work should prove so unproductive. How can this body of data be made useful? The answers are simple. Know what your goal is and remember the keywords are the classificatory mechanism of this data base. They should therefore emphasise similarities within the data rather than differences.

If we look again at the file and take as our goal the production of a file for use by young ornithologists composing a birdspotting diary, then our first questions should be what do these users need to know? The following are some suggestions:

1   What birds might we expect to see at different times of the year?

   Keywords: All Year, Spring, Summer etc.

2   Where might we expect to see different birds?

   Keywords: All UK, Scotland, N. England etc.

3   What types of bird will I see in habitat X?

   Keywords: Garden, City Centre, Hedgerow, Seaside, Wetlands etc.

4   What kind of bird (eater) is it?

Keywords:Herbivore, Insectivore etc./or Seed eater ...

(NB: Some changes to the data will be needed to accommodate these keywords, as keywords must also occur in the text.)

These keywords will rapidly return the answer to questions such as 'which birds can I expect to see at the seaside in summer?', and could provide useful lists and descriptions for children to take on holiday with them. Questions about colour and size are best dealt with in the descriptive passage and can be searched for using the anyword search function.

What we are saying here is that the classification should be put back into the data base. Indeed, one should debate with the children what keywords should be used and come to a collective view about the purpose of the data file. This same file of birds could be set up with different keywords depending on the age of the users and the research questions they wish to answer. One cognitive value of building a data base is in helping children to see patterns in data, but without a task which relates the data to the children's worlds the whole activity is likely to prove disappointing. Like the pen or the bicycle the computer data base should be seen as a tool with which to achieve a goal – it will not achieve the goal without the purpose of the activity being clearly specified and clearly related to concrete, understandable experiences. Hughes (1986) and Lampert (1986) also had their successes, in their case in early mathematics teaching, for the reason that their methods made thinking visible.

Category boundaries

While the ideal usage of data bases encourages children to be an equal, or dominant, partner with the teacher in setting up the research problem and creating the data file, valuable experiences do occur in less child-directed situations. The next case study shows that classificatory decisions can be important even for files where the structure was pre-defined. This example shows the potential for testing category boundaries that entry of data into such a structure can offer. Six children were working together to describe and identify a number of small animals that they had collected from an afternoon's field work. The teacher described the children's problem thus: Joanne 'immediately homed-in on the field which was giving her some difficulty. Stinging and biting was one feature of the creature about which she had not been able to make direct observations.' There then followed a discussion as to what constituted 'stinging and biting'. Philip argued that all creatures which could eat could also sting or bite, and went on to note that the creature in question had a rear structure which looked very similar to a scorpion, and that it would therefore attack people.

Despite Philip's contribution the children had still not resolved the specific point of whether their creature was one which would sting or bite, nor had they resolved the global issue of what was meant by the field heading 'stinging or biting'. Joanne argued that meat-eating and biting, in the attacking sense, were synonymous. This idea was taken up by the other pupils who now assumed that any insect with visible mouthparts would attack by biting. The property of stinging was now ignored by the children. It was some minutes later that John commented that biting to eat plants was not an attack. This insight was ignored by the group and the teacher concluded that if the program had offered an option of passing over a field, the children would have taken it. This example shows that even pre-formed categories can act as a stimulus to discussions on the structure of knowledge. The children were drawn into active decision-making and operated a number of strategies to resolve the problem; these included solution by analogy (the scorpion) and by possession of physical structures (the occurrence of mouth parts).

These examples have highlighted intimate links between research goals and the collection and organisation of data. Other seemingly mundane activities can provide valuable learning experiences but also barriers to those experiences.

Transparency versus machine efficiency: the costs and benefits of coding the data

We have commented upon the use of menu selections versus command language access to data bases, and upon the trade-off between ease of use (good for novices) and efficiency and flexibility of use (good for experts). Either mode of use will produce difficulties for one group of users, and a similar problem is encountered when we come to decide upon the nature of the entries to be made into a new data file. Collaborative work with teachers in a number of primary schools highlights some of the difficulties faced in coding data entries. In producing a FACTFILE data file related to their project 'Sound in the Environment' 10- and 11-year-old children designed a number of fields and field entries which did not exploit the full potential of the program. Such field entries suffered from an inability to maintain congruency of command (see Carroll, 1982; Underwood, 1983). In their file the production of a sound was attributed to the object making the noise if it were a car, but to the human operating the object, in the case of a drill or a piano. The ability to maintain consistency over the criteria of classification is essential but it is not always easy. We are all drawn to the most obvious rather than the most significant feature of an object. This is why we tend to define birds by flight, rather than by the unique characteristic of having feathers (although bats and aeroplanes fly too). There was also a strong resistance, in the 'sounds' project, to numerical coding even for those entries such as noise level which are inherently numerical. Numerical coding, despite its advantages for sorting activities, presents material in a more abstract form, and it does not seem surprising that these children were unwilling to let go of the immediacy of a descriptive field entry.

Janet Spavold (1989) has conducted a trial of data base use for local history with two groups of top junior school children (9 to 11 years old) and this highlights some of the difficulties of organising the entries to a data file. Here the children were working with census material, and decisions about what data to capture and about how to capture them were already made. The children joined the project at the level of coding of given data. Initial problems came in understanding the census enumerator's handwriting and in coming to terms with coded field names and field entries, but both problems appeared to disappear over a period of six weeks. The problem of data coding is a perennial debate for data base usage. Coding is machine-efficient: it reduces memory usage and aids search speeds. For these reasons it is widely used when constructing large commercial files such as payrolls. Naive users, whether children or adults, tend to code to reduce keying-in. The keyboard can be a real barrier to computer usage by non-typists. Coding, however, can lead to a reduction in transparency of the information to hand and as such can reduce children's understanding of the material under discussion. This problem is further compounded if the data file is to be used by groups other than the constructors.

Although the children showed great facility with the codings in this project by the seventh week of continuous activity, it must be said that their depth of immersion in the project was exceptional. The length of time could be justified because identical files were being created throughout the children's county area (Derbyshire) which would allow these children to share information with schools in contrasting environments, and for which these specific codings would continue to be relevant. In the situation where children are designing in-house files it is perhaps best to avoid coded entries where possible except for those cases were they are universally understood, such as 'F' for female. One way to alleviate this problem when working with a data base such as GRASS, which produces standard ASCII files, is to allow the children to enter coded abbreviations. Through the use of a standard word processor's FIND and REPLACE facility, the teacher can put in full word entries before the children interrogate the data file.

In seeking cognitive ends, children may be forced into new ways of representing data. Coding can become more than simple reduction in keying-in time, rather a useful skill in its own right. The children conducting the road safety project had identified a clear research goal – to identify accident black spots and safe places to cross the road. Their first attempt at retrieving this information from the file was not successful. The nature of the data format inhibited access to the information the children knew to be in the file. They had used lengthy string, rather than numeric descriptors for most field values, but the children came to appreciate the need for numeric coding after several fruitless attempts to access the data base. For example, in categorising certain road junctions close to their school as heavily used or not, they employed a five point scale; 1 represented a junction with low flow and no commercial traffic and 5 a junction with plenty of heavy commercial vehicles. The children made an important breakthrough here in their understanding of the way in which data bases and computers can be used efficiently. They came to appreciate that the computer could be used with other tools, in this case it was worksheets displaying a full explanation of each field's structure. Secondly, they learned that it is often necessary to represent data to pick out essential patterns, and that this might involve putting the data into a different form, collapsing the data and even discarding material. Of course what these children really needed was a relational data base and in effect that is what they built but with the third dimension as paper files off the machine.

In Janet Spavold's study (1989) the children constructed their understanding of the data file through a model based on playground games. In INFORM it is possible to move both forward and backward through adjacent fields and records during data entry and correction, a characteristic shared with GRASS but not FACTFILE and OURFACTS. The children referred to the completion of a field or record as a 'turn' or a 'go' and the instruction 'miss a go' was frequently heard to indicate that a field had no entry and was to be passed over.

Cognitive skills in data organisation

Does constructing a data file have any impact on the development of children's minds? Our own study addresses the question of the influence of data base use on children's classificatory abilities (Underwood, 1986). This was introduced in chapter 2 as the 'cheeses' project and we will spend some time here trying to understand the benefits gained by the children who used the computer data bases.

The experiment was concerned with the development of classificatory abilities in top juniors (9- to 11-year-old-children). These are abilities identified by Bruner, Goodnow and Austin (1956) as being necessary for perceptual discrimination, for ordering the relationships between objects and events, and for efficient encoding and retrieval, among other cognitive activities. An efficient categoriser might be considered to be a perceptual alert and efficient learner – someone who is able to see similarities between objects and between events, and who is able to take decisive actions on the basis of the ability to categorise.

Groups of children were matched on chronological age, on reading ability, a strong correlate of classificatory ability (Turner, Scullion and Whyte, 1984), on non-verbal IQ and also on a pre-test categorisation task. This pre-test required children to ask questions in order to identify which of twenty-four pictures the experimenter was 'thinking of' – the 'twenty questions' game. All the children then engaged in a three-week class project in which the main task was to classify a range of cheeses. The experimenter was not involved in this part of the project. Half of the children (the computer users) used commercially available data bases (the tabular structured FACTFILE and hierarchically structured SEEK) on a BBC microcomputer, and the rest (the non-computer users) simulated the structure of the data bases using index-cards. So that each group of children had similar computer experience, the control group completed a series of computer-based mathematical investigations. The children worked at the design and structuring of their data files over a three-week period and completed the task by interrogating their files. At the end of this time the categorisation task with twenty-four picture cards was repeated. The children also completed a general knowledge task to assess their factual learning of the material they had been working with.

Three results are of importance here. First, the computer users showed an improvement in the number of questions they needed to ask to identify the target picture in the categorisation task. An improvement meant that they required fewer questions to identify the target. Secondly, they asked more constraining questions and fewer specific questions. A specific question in this context would be 'Is it soft and warm and cuddly?', a reference to the teddy bear, and a constraining question would be 'Is there more than one object on the card?'. The computer users were showing a great awareness of the classificatory structures of the objects represented on the cards – recognising those features that were in common, rather than individual differences. The type of file structure, whether tabular or hierarchical, had no effect on performance. The non-computer users did not show these improvements in classificatory ability. The third finding was that factual recall was linked to reading ability across all the groups and there was no difference in performance between the computer and non-computer users.

There were certainly overall gains in performance between the pre- and post-categorisation task but the strength of those gains was governed by the teaching strategy employed, computer users outperforming the non-computer users.

Why should this disparity in skills acquisition occur between the computer-users and non-computer users? As the categorisation task did not involve the use of a computer it might appear surprising that any effects should be discernible. Nevertheless there are a number of possible explanations of this result. Two arguments are suggestive of a disparity in the treatment received by the experimental and control groups: first, it might be argued that the data-handling packages on the computer exhibited a superior organisation to the hand-operated system generated in the study; and second, it might be argued that the interrogative mode, in both SEEK and FACTFILE, was superior to that operated by the adult worker with non-computer groups. Other explanations stem from the intrinsic nature of the computer. Were the children simply more motivated because they were using this new technology, or was there something more specific than an overall stimulus to work, in the nature of the interaction between the computer and the child?

In conducting the experiment great care was taken to match the operations off the computer to those presented by the machine and the appropriate software. This would have minimised, if not removed, any effects of the differences in organisation. Possible support for the rejection of this organisational hypothesis comes from the lack of disparity in performance between the children using the two different types of organisation; linear SEEK versus matrix FACTFILE. This same argument – the careful matching of the interrogative style of the computer by the adult worker – can also be put forward to reject the superior interrogative performance of the computer.

Are we left then with the motivational aspects of the computer as the sole cause of the improved performance in this study? Certainly the comments of the children using the computer were encouraging. The children appreciated the colour, the layout and the animated aspects of the programs, which were either absent, or had to be provided by the children themselves, in the control situation. Those children in the control groups, using the computer for other activities but not for their cheeses project, were also willing to complete the most mundane of tasks over and over again if the computer was involved.

There are perhaps other factors to be considered, however:

> It is clear that the attempts to train abilities must go well beyond simply manipulating practice and feedback, or coaching and teaching expectations, they must provide substantive training on the component processes and skills involved in task performance. (Snow and Yallow, 1982, p. 548)

This is precisely what building a data file is about, each classificatory decision is set within a larger problem-solving task and has implications for that task. In this study, although care was taken to mimic the computer in all relevant operations, in human operations it is difficult to operate the same rigidity of control. The demands placed on the learner for precision in data presentation may be significant here. Each user must have thought very deeply about the material to hand not only to enter it into the machine but also to allow worthwhile questions to be asked of that data. This is no easy task, and both adults and children may initially have great difficulty in preparing material for entry into programs such as FACTFILE, although newer programs are less inhibiting.

In this study the children operated five-point taste and group-preference scales alongside their descriptive fields, such as cheese colour. Children may not come to these decisions easily, however. In devising the road safety data file, the children numerically coded both traffic density and road visibility. They came to accept the need for such coding after several fruitless attempts to access information from the data base in which the field entries were highly descriptive.

In the road safety project children had to reorganise their data and discard some of it before they could retrieve the answers to their queries. It is this process of stripping data down to the essentials that could be responsible for the differential improvement in performance of the computer and non-computer users in the cheese project. This is a persuasive argument as careful observation and naming of objects should lead to improved classificatory skills. In both the construction and interrogation of either a SEEK or FACTFILE data base the program exercises considerable control over possible operations, and so the children may also have felt a sense of control when working with these programs which was not achievable when the adult took the role of the computer. Such a sense of control might lead to greater self-esteem and be motivating in itself, a point not lost in Papert's monograph (1981).

Anecdotal evidence confirms that children appear to produce differential responses to the authority of the machine compared to that of humans, as Turkle (1984) has shown, and pilot work to our project adds weight to her evidence. Observations of less-able 11-year-olds working with a drill-and-practice mathematics program show that far from being castigated by the response to an incorrect answer, the children were highly delighted to see the computer displaying a seemingly harsh message of

WRONG   WRONG   WRONG

in bright red letters across the screen. These young boys produced a string of palpably incorrect responses in order to enjoy what appeared a savage reprimand. It appeared that the ability to disregard an authority figure was almost a cathartic activity which they enjoyed to the full, and regardless of the mathematical task in hand, they had taken control for themselves. The machine was doing what they wanted it to do. This is very similar to Turkle's children pulling out the batteries in the 'SPEAK AND SPELL' machine. The inability of the computer to punish might be one of its greatest advantages in the classroom.

One final explanatory factor for the classificatory advantages of the computer users in the cheese project might lie, yet again, in the nature of the interaction between the child and the computer. Alongside the 'control hypothesis' it could be argued that the swift response of the computer to the children's queries, particularly on more complex questions, might have led to a stronger association between question and answer. Although the adult in the control condition would have provided rapid answers to simple searches, there may have been delays on the more complex material. For the less-able subjects in this experiment, the immediacy of feedback may have proved particularly important as answers could be provided before attention strayed and memories of the question under review faded.

A comparison of the effects of the computer condition on the learning of facts about cheeses and on classificatory skills is illuminating. While the computer groups produced significantly better performances than the non-computer groups for classification performance, there appeared to be no such benefit of the computer on information recall. There are several possible reasons for this result. It has already been argued that the computer emphasises the organisation of data rather than the data themselves. If this is the case it could be argued that there is no legitimate reason for supposing that factual information should be preferentially available to the computer user groups. One flaw in this argument lies in the fact that the conjectured superior skeletal model of that data, provided by the computer programs, might have been expected to aid the organisation of the data in the child's memory and thus have aided recall, but this was not the case.

It was also apparent that children certainly had difficulty in providing an appropriate answer as the questions became increasingly complex when the question specified more than one defining feature of the cheese. This would be predicted by the work of Shepard (1967), who cites considerable evidence for the failure of adults to use all the information available to them in making decisions. His interpretation is based on limitations in information processing in that, when pressed to make decisions about multi-dimensional stimuli, we generally have a tendency to simplify the problem. We economise by collapsing all information on to one single dimension, with the attendant loss of detail. Decisions are then made on this reduced information base. On the test of knowledge about cheeses, the decline in performance as questions increased in complexity might well have been a result of this simplifying of the problem to a single dimension by a number of the subjects, particularly the less able children.

Snow and Yallow (1982) suggested that one of the key questions in education concerns the relationship between intelligence differences and instructional treatments. They reviewed a number of studies which have shown that didactic teaching with paced individualised learning tends to eliminate intellectual differences, but that discovery learning tends to emphasise initial ability differences to the advantage of the more gifted child. The findings in our study do not fully support these suggestions. Activities in the classroom, and which involve the use of data bases as a support tool to the exploration of a particular data set, are generally viewed as good examples of discovery learning. Yet the less able children in the computer groups made strong performance gains on the post-categorisation task and appeared to be reaching a level of mastery commensurate with the more able children. Such gains were not evident for the less able non-computer users, nor for the less able children in either condition on the recall task.

Another explanation of these results might lie with the formality of thought necessary both for data encoding and query specification. Although the classroom activities were explorative and, therefore, should have benefited the more able, the rigidity of acceptable input to the computer provided the low-ability children with a step-like sequence of moves which one would normally find in an individual-ised learning package. These children were, therefore, exposed to dis-covery learning with clear structure which proved very beneficial to them. Because the work on the computer did not specifically direct attention towards the acquisition of the specific knowledge of cheeses, the low-ability children failed to make similar gains on the learning task, performing in a similar manner to the non-computer users, considerably below the more able children.

The lack of impact of the two data organisations on children's clas-sificatory abilities or, indeed, on their ability to recall factual informa-tion, is consistent with the findings of a study of the effects of data structure upon data recall reported by Underwood and Underwood (1987b). Children of 9–11 years of age did appear to treat hierarchical and tabular structures in the some way in that study.

The use of data bases provided specific advantages for the com-puter users in the cheeses project, and failed to provide advantages in other performance tests. The arguments offered as a partial expla-nation of these results, imply that there are specific attributes of the medium, in this case the computer and accompanying software, which influence the way that information is processed in learning. In his criticisms of the effectiveness of new media in education, Clark (1983) was only marginally less sceptical about 'media attribute research' than he was about 'media comparison studies'. He argued that although certain attributes of any given medium can model cognitive processes, they can only serve as a sufficient but never necessary condition for learning. The rigidity of response acceptance, the explicit nature of organisational structures and the rapidity of response to a child's question, are all attributes of information-handling packages. They are what Clark calls operational vehicles for methods that reflect the cognitive processes necessary in order suc-cessfully to perform a given learning task.

Clark's concerns rise out of a perceived need to produce a general theory of learning, and, if the use of the computer is only a sufficient and not necessary condition for learning, the achievement of this goal is not furthered. Citing the work of Dixon and Judd (1977), which compared teacher and computer use of 'branching rules of instruction', he concluded that most of the methods carried by the new media can be performed equally well by teachers, and that no learning differences can be unambiguously attributed to any medium of instruction. In the face of such criticisms, based on extensive research evidence, it is perhaps important to reiterate that the cheeses study did find strong evidence of disparate skills, but not of factual learning, between the computer and non-computer groups. These results were obtained even though the children had identical learning experiences for the first part of the study and experiences were matched on and off the computer in the second half. Also the 'teacher' was the same adult throughout. The learning experiences of the children, and the abilities of the children, were closely matched, and yet here is a case of a computer-based activity producing cognitive advantages.

The disparity between Clark's views and these findings might be simply accounted for in terms of the poor experimentation in the studies he considered. It is clear from the research cited that crucial variables, such as the impact of individual teachers and the matching of groups, have been widely ignored. On a more pragmatic note, however, we should perhaps argue that any successful method should be welcomed into the classroom, particularly when the attributes of that method are structural and, therefore, available for use by all teachers.

Data bases can be useful in helping children to learn to think and significant gains can be made in classificatory skills when children use information-handling packages. There are caveats, however. Children need to be involved in purposeful classification, acting as research workers resolving problems they find both interesting and valid. The data which they organise and interrogate must be related to worlds which they are coming to understand. Classification for the sake of classification is indeed a sterile exercise. If the children are fully involved with the project then the data will be at least partially transparent to them, and many of the problems of structure design and coding, and indeed of interrogation, will be minimised. The remaining problems will be resolved by discussions within the peer group or with teacher support. Computer software designed to help children to organise data can act as a stimulus to cognitive development by providing a learning tool which is highly flexible and content-free, but with a well-developed and proven structure.

5 Questioning the file

In the previous chapter we discussed how children's cognitive development can be enhanced when they build data files. In many aspects of life, however, file users are presented with ready-made files, and their need is to extract information from existing files. Outside the classroom we are usually putting information into a pre-set file structure with pre-set codes, which is a simple keying-in exercise, or we will want to extract information to resolve a particular query. This chapter draws on eighteen case studies of classroom data base use, which have been summarised in Underwood (1988), to illustrate how cognitive development can also be enhanced by the questioning of data files. This investigation found that primary school data bases were used largely for the building of the data file but that in secondary schools and FE (further education, post 16 years) the emphasis was on information retrieval and hypothesis testing.

Our survey revealed that in the primary schools the ordering and organisation of information was as important as the information itself. This is very typical of primary education where a theme or topic will be used as the vehicle to teach, for example, linguistic, mathematical and artistic skills. In secondary and FE classrooms the pupils had need of the information itself, perhaps to join together their plastic and wood, or to form a picture of dental health across a school year, or to test their hypotheses about the development of island populations. In these cases the children's cognitive development was largely dependent upon designing the research questions to be asked and from specifying the query. This is not to say that hypothesis testing or the formulation of good questions was not important in the primary classrooms which we investigated, but that the focus of the studies tended to shift from data capture and organisation towards data retrieval with the move from primary to secondary and tertiary education.

How then do we question a data file, and what learning opportunities does this present us with?

Developing skills of questioning

In the survey of data base use in the classroom, the questioning of the data base was seen as an important cognitive goal by each of the teachers in the sample, but not all questions act as a stimulus to the higher cognitive skills of hypothesising, seeking relationships and reasoning about our world. The issues of the approach taken to questioning, who designs the questions, and whether they are seeking facts or testing ideas, are each of considerable importance in the assessment of the potential cognitive development of the children.

It is in the nature of data bases that all the questions asked have closure, for such packages are driven by algorithms and they lack the heuristic structure for probabilistic reasoning necessary to begin to cope with open-ended queries. A question with closure would be 'Who has more dental fillings – boys or girls?' while an open-ended question asked of the same file might be what causes dental decay? The preponderance of closed questions in our case studies does not mean that the questioning was at a low level. In a study of mammals, for example, quite simple factual questions were combined to answer complex theoretical questions. The appearance of a large number of simple questions did not necessarily imply a low level of thought was taking place. Indeed the use of simpler data bases such as FACTFILE made it very difficult to ask complex, or highly specified questions and the children often found it necessary to split relationship or hypothesis testing questions into component parts, and then to piece these answers together in order to resolve their initial query.

The following classification was devised to aid in the analysis of the questions asked of the data bases. These questions were grouped on the basis of the structure of the sorting procedure which was required to answer the query, and on the purpose of that query. This produced a simple three-fold division with two of the groups further subdivided:

1   *Page the data retrieval*   In this mode the child simply asked the computer to reproduce on the screen, or printer, specified blocks of the file with no manipulations. This is analogous to looking for a word in a dictionary by opening each page in turn, and often consisted of a complete record across all fields.

2 *Fact seeking retrieval* Here the machine was used to manipulate the data, but the type of questions were sub-divided into: (i)
Fact1 – list all the known examples of ..., these are simple sorting
procedures on one dimension and were used, for example, to list
all the housewives or marsupials; and (ii) *Fact2* – identification
questions, for example, find the mammal, person, type of transport, which possesses the property of ... Children could, of course,
answer both of these fact seeking type of questions in the paging
mode, with the children manipulating the data themselves, and
this did happen in a few cases.

3 *Relational retrieval* In these questions children looked for
relationships and patterns within the data through the testing of
hypotheses which could be either: (i) implicit – implied by the
type of question asked; or (ii) explicit – clearly articulated hypotheses. For example, the children might generate the hypothesis that
large dinosaurs will be meat eaters: a falacious but none the less
a legitimate explicit question. At other times children might ask
questions concerning the two variables of size and eating habits
but with no specific question in mind other than a feeling that this
could be interesting, implicitly indicating a belief in a relationship.
General research questions were often a feature of work which
involved such questions.

It was not surprising to find that the youngest children were concerned with factual information retrieval and not with the testing of
ideas. Our two youngest groups paged the data and never asked a
specific question. One teacher commented that her 6-year-olds were
unable to formulate questions, but that they did derive great pleasure from seeing their names and personal data appear on the screens.
By age 7 the children were asking simple but logical questions, such
as 'who has an elder brother?', or identifying leaves using a pupil-
constructed data file on trees. A more questioning approach was evident in later primary years. Although there was still some paging of
the data, this now had a clear purpose, and the use of *Fact2* questions
occurred in all studies.

It is worrying that the teachers of the youngest children should
assume that questioning was beyond the children's capabilities. One
response to this assessment might be to argue that the task had not
been presented in a way that the children could understand. The
acceptance of structuralist models of cognitive development, such as
those of Jean Piaget, can lead to teachers' assuming limits to children's behaviour at any one time, and thus, with the best of motives,
to an unwillingness to stretch children's minds. Commentators such

as Donaldson (1978) and Wood (1988) would argue that under-developed language or memory skills might be the underlying cause of what *appears* to be a failure in conceptual understanding, and that the simplification of instructions, particularly with relevance to the child's own experiences, might produce conceptually high-powered thought from children as young as those discussed here.

In the secondary/FE case studies there was a strong emphasis on factual questions and only two studies showed evidence of rule test-ing and of questions which explored relationships. In part, this fail-ure to achieve one of the key aims for using data bases, identified by both the educational software designers and the teachers themselves, was due to the limited purpose to which the programs were put. In three of the six secondary studies the programs were used as refer-ence texts to identify specific materials, careers or books, given a set of constraints. This, of course, is the most frequent use of information packages outside of the classroom. While it gives little opportunity for the direct development of cognition, it does require skilled information retrieval and such questions can present the user with conceptual problems which require a solution before data can be accessed.

It is quite possible that the better the retrieval facilities of the soft-ware the less likely the user is to be faced with challenging cognitive experiences. For example, the overall goal of allowing adolescents to match their interests, aspirations and qualifications to a potential career, would be better served by an expert system rather than a data base. An expert system includes not only a data bank but also a set of production rules which guide the user from question to question. As information is provided by the user, it serves as the conditions under which the next production rule fires, and this next rule will generate another question or provide a solution to the initial enquiry. In addition an interpreter determines how the data base should be interrogated. This allows the system to make ostensibly intelligent decisions in selecting between two or more production rules whose conditions of firing have been satisfied. The user will find that the difference between an expert system and a data base is that the for-mer asks the questions, as a doctor questions his patient, in order to resolve the query. In a data base, as we have seen, the user has to pose the questions, but it is here that much of the more fruitful cog-nitive activity occurs, and while the adolescents would have resolved their career queries far more quickly using an expert system, theirs would have been a cognitively passive role. The selection between a data base and an expert system comes down to the selection between a system that requires the user to develop good questions as against a system that (if designed appropriately) may provide good answers.

The three investigative studies carried out in secondary schools – a historical study, an ecological investigation and a data file to support the human biology curriculum – each provide contrasting approaches to the use of data bases. In the first the children did not question the data file, but simply paged through the material and extracted the data by 'eye'. In the second, the teacher developed a spiral curriculum from first (11-year-olds) to sixth form (18-year-olds), each with its own research problems on speciation in mammals. He offered global research questions to each of his third and sixth forms, rather than more specific queries. For example, his sixth form were asked to identify and account for species variation in any one genus. A number of subordinate questions needed to be posed to address this problem, but the teacher felt that it was critical that the pupils constructed those questions themselves. Over-specification of questions, he suggested, would produce clones who thought only as the teacher thought, and who would learn nothing about the process of generating hypotheses. It was important, he felt, that children came to recognise the multiple routes to the solution of any problem and to value their own approach, where it was effective. Many educational thinkers would agree that self-constructed knowledge is more memorable and easier to make generalisations from, than is given knowledge (cf. Piaget, 1952; Bruner, 1966; Papert, 1981). The replacement of data bases with solution-providing expert systems might have a detrimental effect upon cognitive development by eliminating the need for knowledge organisation and interrogation.

The idea of self-constructed knowledge has some notable advocates. Einstein raised the problems which result from the use of pre-digested ideas and concepts in scientific enquiry, and offered a pragmatic justification for encouraging novel thought patterns:

> In the attempt to achieve a conceptual formulation of the confusingly immense body of observational data, the scientist makes use of a whole arsenal of concepts which he imbibed practically with his mother's milk ... He uses ... these conceptual tools of thought, as something obviously immutably given; something having an objective value of truth which is hardly ever ... to be doubted ... And yet in the interests of science it is necessary over and over again to engage in the critique of these fundamental concepts, in order that we may not unconsciously be ruled by them. This becomes evident especially in those situ-

ations involving development of ideas in which consistent use of the traditional fundamental concepts leads us to paradoxes difficult to resolve. (Einstein, 1957, pp. xi–xii)

In the third study in a secondary school, children produced a data base to help identify the nature and causes of dental problems. Their questions were both factual and relational. One of the important points of this study was the way in which children re-formulated questions following output from the data base. For example, the children felt that brushing teeth twice a day would lead to an improvement in health, that is, fewer fillings, extractions and bleeding gums. They were surprised to find that the evidence did not support this hypothesis, but still felt that their initial assumption was valid. The hypothesis was therefore modified to explore the effects of not two, but one, cleaning per day and this indeed was correlated to dental health. The questionnaire used in this classroom study was as follows:

Dental Health Questions

1   Do girls have more fillings than boys?
2   What kind of teeth have most fillings?
3   What % of pupils take fluoride tablets?
4   How many people use fluoride toothpaste?
5   How many people still have primary teeth?
6   How many people suffer from bleeding gums?
7   What are the habits of people who have fillings and have not lost teeth?
8   Do people who clean their teeth twice a day have more or less fillings than people who clean less frequently?
9   Does the addition of fluoride to tap water help?
10   Do sweet foods and sweet drinks affect the number of fillings?

This investigation was successful partly because it stemmed from the pupils' own self-interests. We have acknowledged the importance of the principle of starting from the child's own experiences and interests in order to maximise learning: the 'continuity principle' found in many theories of developmental learning. There are times when self-interest can also be inhibiting. In one of our studies a girl involved in a social survey of her village was very eager to question the data base. With great enthusiasm she asked the computer to identify all the village people who wanted to start a tennis club. The answer 'none' was totally unacceptable, for she herself was a very keen player. She refused to have any more to do with the project since her own interests could not be met!

We must conclude that cognitive outcomes were most apparent in the late primary studies. The youngest children had not developed the conceptual base from which a systematic enquiry approach could be built, nor were they aided to construct one. In the secondary/FE sector skills of enquiry were often highly developed but the use of data bases with these older pupils was often restricted to reference seeking rather than an exploration of ideas. Of course the use of multi-field sorting procedures, as practised by many of our 8- to 11-year-olds, does not necessarily mean that thought-provoking questions were being asked. A group of 8-year-old children were able to cope with technical aspects of asking highly constrained questions. But it is doubtful that queries such as 'How many children have birthdays in June, brown hair, blue eyes, a height more than 130 cm, and take a size 2 shoe?' have any real value. The children here were simply playing a game with the computer by testing its ability to hold all the variables in 'its mind', a task they themselves would find extremely difficult. They could be said to be operating a hypothesis scanning strategy, with no clearly defined cognitive goal or outcome. This is the trivialisation of information and is in stark contrast to the work on dental health, or indeed a further 'Ourselves' file constructed by children of the same age, which we will consider in detail shortly. They were, however, gaining considerable expertise in information retrieval, and without this skill many cognitive outcomes can be stifled.

Navigation

To retrieve information effectively from any data store the user must have some understanding of the structure of the store. We come to learn that the index of a cookery book will help us find all the recipes containing lamb or chocolate, that the first few letters of a word are necessary for retrieval of its spelling from a dictionary, and that the last few pages of a 'Who-done-it?' novel will reveal the guilty party. Our expertise with such data stores is built up over time and with increasing frequency of use, and this same ease of use is required to retrieve data efficiently from a computer file, but such files are more opaque than books. This lack of transparency is a result of the characteristics of the computer file. In one case the file cannot be handled all at once, as it comes up screen by screen. This is not a simple equivalent to the page by page of a book. In the other case a handy finger can keep a second page available for comparisons. In most educational data bases this is not true, although the increasing use of multiple window environments will make within-file comparisons increasingly convenient.

Opacity is also caused by the need to reduce data to a 'manageable' size and form, where 'manageability' is defined in terms of efficiency of use of the available memory and of the sorting procedures. Computers use reduced data, that is, coded data, and especially numerical data, whereas people like linguistic descriptions whether in well-formed sentences or readily accessible phrases. Optimising either user or computer demands will lead to a reduction in either the efficiency of the computer or accessibility for the user. In general, software designers have increasingly allowed machine efficiency to be compromised, so that the machine operates at a sub-optimal level, to the advantage of the human user – as with the development of the WIMP environment, for instance (see p. 12). Because of the overall power of the machines, the user does not recognise this operational compromise. Data base work in education is better described at being at the stage of optimising machine efficiency, however, and we still sacrifice legibility of the data file to achieve this efficiency. Feeding the computer what it wants, reduced data, instead of more descriptive data, can also have benefits when building the data file. The act of accommodation to the dumb machine, a real problem to be solved by children, can be a powerful learning experience, as we have shown. This accommodation by presenting data in machine-friendly form, leads to greater opacity of the file and can cause subsequent retrieval problems for the users, especially if they are not involved in the construction of the file.

A third possible cause of opacity is the organisational structure of computer data bases. Unlike the simple one-dimensionality of a book presentation with a beginning, middle and end, data files may have one of a number of two-dimensional structures based on hierarchical, tabular or network organisations. Users may not be equally familiar with all the types of organisational structure found in data bases, and this might in turn affect efficient data retrieval. This problem has been recognised by a number of investigations of how people organise and retrieve data (Durding, Becker and Gould, 1977; Brosey and Shneiderman, 1978; Underwood and Underwood, 1987b). The underlying aim of this research is to facilitate the use of computer information packages by matching software structures to the organisational structures most readily available to humans. If matches are not possible, then the software designer and the potential users at least need to be made aware of potential problems in the operation of any program.

A number of organisational structures appear to be readily available. Humans are not restricted to the use of one data organisation, because we have the flexibility to adapt our cognitive processes to changing information structures. Durding, Becker and Gould (1977) confirmed that adults, when faced with word sets exhibiting a range of pre-defined organisational structures, were capable of recognising and making explicit those structures. There was, however, a ranking of ease of use, in the order lists, hierarchies, networks and tables. Tables were the only organisational type with which subjects achieved less than a 50 per cent success rate. This order was not maintained when subjects were primed as to the appropriate organisation to use, by the inclusion of a skeletal diagram accompanying each word set. Lists and hierarchies were still the easiest to organise, but they were now followed closely by tables. The provision of an overt structure did little to facilitate the recognition of networks. Rather than asking their subjects to construct organisational structures, Brosey and Shneiderman (1978) asked them to access information from data bases, with either a tree (hierarchical) structure or a tabular structure. The tree structure proved to be an easier retrieval format, and it was also easier to commit to memory and reproduce, in comparison with the tabular structure.

The two sets of experiments together suggest that after lists, the most accessible form for data is in hierarchies or trees. Other organisational structures may be used with some measure of success, however if the subject is made aware of the relevance of that structure to the task in hand. Our own experiments with 9- to 11-year-olds showed that these young children were not very successful in discovering the inherent organisation of information, and showed a marked tendency to impose a standard structure (a list) on all data regardless of their inherent organisation (Underwood and Underwood, 1987b). This result held true whether the subjects were primed to the appropriate organisational structure or not, although skeletal priming did improve performance on the non-list organisations. Hierarchies and tables were perceived as equally difficult by these young subjects, while networks were somewhat easier to construct. On a more hopeful note for those working with young children, a third experiment showed that the children were able to extract data from existing hierarchies, networks and tables.

What do these findings mean for the use of information-handling packages in school? If information-handling packages are to be used in school, then teachers will need to ensure that children have had exposure to the relevant structures and have come to value the different methods of organising data, in order to achieve successful outcomes. Research by Bransford (1979) adds another caveat to the application of these results. In a discussion of concept formation, he points out that in the majority of concept-identification experiments, participants had to identify which member of a set of known concepts the experimenter had in mind. Once the the correct concept had been identified, or once the experimenter had made the rule explicit to the subject, problem-solving became relatively easy. Bransford argues that this is a very different situation from that normally existing in the classroom where children are generally provided with the definition of new concepts rather than being allowed to discover them, and thus they fail to understand adequately or to transfer knowledge. The Hughes (1986) and Lampert (1986) studies give practical demonstrations of the cognitive benefits for children in generating rather than receiving concepts. Essentially, this suggests that data structures must be made transparent to children if they are successfully to organise or extract information from a particular structure.

This problem of transparency of the data structure was addressed by Fitter (1979) when he suggested that in order for users to feel in control of the system they need to have an adequate knowledge of it, which in turn means that they must know where they have been, where they are, and where they can go from there. Essentially the user requires a mental map of the system but also a reason for navigating through the system. In constructing her census data file Janet Spavold showed that children used the playground language of 'turns' and 'goes', but in interrogating the file they adopted a TV gameshow analogy. The queries were seen as quiz questions, with output data as the 'prize'. Children's behaviour was often a parody of the gameshow contestant as the printer began to deliver the prize, with cheers from the participating audience, and exaggerated gestures of anxiety, relief and triumph from the contestants.

Children are aware of the need to develop this mental map of the data structure. A group of 8-year-olds who were in charge of their interrogations, once having constructed their file wanted to see it used by a parallel class. There followed an animated discussion on the best way to introduce the second class to the file the outcome of which was two question sheets. The first sheet required the children to page through the FACTFILE data base, while the second sheet contained more constraining questions, which were to be answered using the search routines. The 'teacher-children' argued that paging would give a feel of its structure to those children who had not constructed the data base, a necessary precursor before moving on to more complex interactions with the file.

Although the second set of questions was ostensibly geared to helping the children understand more about European countries, they were in fact constructed in such a way as to provide a stepped learning sequence through the information retrieval skills required to use the file. Questioning in this case had little to do with hypothesis testing, but rather it was a means of interacting with the file and it produced benefits more in IT rather than in cognitive skills. By formulating their knowledge for communication to other children, the cognitive skills of the 'teacher-children' may have been enhanced. The teaching of an idea to others is one of the more effective ways of coming to understand that idea oneself.

There is a danger here that the children, and possibly some teachers, will begin to think that the IT skills are more important than developing thinking skills or becoming attuned to the role of the research worker. This is again a case of trivialising the body of knowledge. Anne Sheward, working with us on a project with 11- and 12-year-olds, recognised that for the children the task of getting the machine to manipulate the historical data correctly in IT terms was far more important than making sense of the historical data and concepts. We must guard against the danger of teaching the machine at the expense of teaching how to think. One other point should be made here: the concentration on IT skills and on mental mapping of the data base seems sensible on many counts. New programs are breaking this link, however. Galloway (1989) showed that his most adept user of MacWrite and the Apple Macintosh had a completely falacious understanding of what was taking place when she called on the functions of the MacWrite word processor. She was a skilled operator with little or no conceptual understanding of the machine or program – an effective driver who never looked under the bonnet. As programs generally become more user-friendly we will have an increasing population who lack conceptual understanding of the processes they are involved in. Does this matter? To the purist of course it does, the IT goal is lost, but pragmatically perhaps it does not.

Statistical tools

One of the major changes in educational data bases during the past few years has been that the addition of simple statistical tools has become the norm rather than the exception, as with OURFACTS, which is the upgrade for FACTFILE, and GRASS. As we have observed, in infant and lower junior schools (5- to 8-year-olds) children often operate a paging technique rather than questioning the data file by using search facilities. Statistical tools have added a new dimension to the retrieval of data by young children in that they allow easily constructed pictures of the data to be produced in a number of graphical forms. In our work on house types, part of a local village project with 7- and 8-year-olds, once the children had paged through the data, to check that all 48 houses were there, we began to identify patterns by drawing simple bar graphs. The children were working with the data for the whole school and were given the responsibility of analysing and presenting their findings in both oral and written form to the rest of the school. Working in pairs, the children identified one aspect of the house that they wished to investigate, drew the appropriate graph, which when printed was personalised, analysed and mounted for display.

The choice of which graph to draw hinges on the fundamental question of what it is the child wants to know, and once this research question has been posed it may appear that little additional cognitive effort is required. Essentially the children's task here is to ask for a graph of roofing materials or types of windows using the simple menu display. Data bases are used to their best advantage, however, when handling large files, as in this case. Small files can often be perused as efficiently, if not more efficiently, using card records. Such large files do present children with choices. For example, some data had a large range (house dates 1700–1978) and the children had to decide whether to graph the data in six, nine or twelve groups. The children debated which graph was more easily interpreted and decided on nine groupings. It would have been pleasing to say that this decision was due to an intuitive statistical sophistication, but it was in fact due largely to the size of the symbol representing each house. Twelve groups produced very small images which the children rejected, but they also realised that the choice of six groups hid a lot of data, and nine groupings became the compromise choice. Even a compromise can lead to educational discussions and the children's reasoning was sound.

One problem of using restricted packages such as OURFACTS is the quantity of data that they can handle. Although all the data were accepted in our housing project, for fields with only a few defined values – such as 'Has it a dormer roof? Value: yes/no' – the computer was unable to graph the data as it has a maximum input value of twenty-five. This threw the children into a quandary which was resolved first by asking for a different graph, and secondly by returning to the original question and helping the computer out of its difficulty by producing their own sticky-paper graph for the computer! This is an important extension of the work, because not only could the children interpret ready-made graphs but they could reciprocate for the computer when necessary.

Another of our local teachers, Maree Coates, working with her 6- to 7-year-olds on the ubiquitous 'Ourselves' theme, found that the children were able to evaluate the merits of their own graphs versus the computer's output. Comparisons of the information recorded on both manual and computer graphs were easy to make, although the tendency of the children to record values along the horizontal axis while the computer placed values on the vertical axis, meant that the children had initial orientation problems. Maree observed that there was general agreement among her children that the computer graphs were neat and produced the work very quickly, but that their own graphs, which were larger and more colourful, were easier to understand. If the children's own graphs were of sufficient quality that data could be extracted from them, then it is not surprising that understanding was enhanced by doing it themselves. This is exactly the argument that we have put forward for the benefits of data file construction on classificatory skill.

The last few paragraphs have introduced a subsidiary question about the retrieval of information from data bases: are there benefits to be gained by the use of statistical toolkits? Should children be encouraged to manipulate the data themselves or should they use the 'quick fix' from the computer? As the examples we have discussed so far all involve very young children, perhaps there are different answers for young children as opposed to secondary or higher education students. Let us first remove the age-range question. Although different emphasis may be placed on the depth of question to be asked by older pupils and students the processes of asking questions and seeking patterns are fundamental to all age-ranges. It is obvious that our 6-year-olds were trying to classify and re-classify data about themselves in order to find some understanding of the patterns they had identified. When our undergraduates have been introduced to new data files they have been observed to follow a similar pattern of exploration to these infants. First they page the data to get a feel of what is there, thereby establishing the mental map of the data file, and then they produce a series of graphs to further their understanding of the data. Of course this pattern is not followed by students coming to a known file to seek a specific piece of information, as they do, for instance when collecting information about their teaching practice schools before going out on their placements. In such cases the students will use the search and sort facilities to gain access to the specific data they require. For these more experienced users the file has acquired transparency and retrieval can be more selective.

That the undergraduates make the same initial moves as young children is illuminating, but are these techniques legitimate at any age? One benefit of the statistical toolkit is that it allows users to get a feel of the pattern of data. Although graph production may be an end in itself, in that it provides a first level of data processing and pattern identification, it is often a stepping stone between the initial 'eye-balling' of the data on paper and the more analytic testing of hypotheses through the search facility. The use of computer graph facilities as opposed to hand-drawn diagrams has the added benefit, as our young children have noted, of being quick. Speed of processing in itself has several benefits. As in the 'Ourselves' project, for example, in which a large data file had been built and the production of certain graphs required the children to make choices between six, nine and twelve groupings. The children printed all three possible graphs and discussed with their teacher such issues as why all the graphs were valid, thus questioning at this very early age the assumption that there is only one right way of representing reality. This activity of re-scaling data could quite happily form an important part of a study of news media in secondary social studies, or for that matter at higher education level in discussions on how we are manipulated by advertisers. Similarly, in programs such as GRASS or on the DOMESDAY DISK, users are encouraged to select the most appropriate graphical presentation for data. Is the bar chart adequate or would a pie-chart or cumulative frequency graph reveal more?

We also find that this emancipatory statistical tool use is particularly valuable as a motivator. Social studies in one FE college takes an active approach to learning with sixteen-year-olds collecting data using questionnaire techniques. The course stumbles each year on the need to process the data once collected. The students, who are motivated by the research topic itself, are rapidly demotivated by the quality of their pencil and paper skills and by the amount of effort required to glean the most elementary conclusions from their data. An in-depth understanding occurs at best for a minority of persistent students, who are not usually boys. On being introduced to the GRASS data base the course tutor became converted to computer data handling, although feeling that the students should still produce one graph by hand to know how it is done.

The flexibility in data handling which even simple packages such as GRASS bring to research to the classroom can be one of the causes of Coupland's assertion that classification is a sterile exercise, if it

becomes much more interesting to see the range of alternative patterns that can be distinguished through the manipulative techniques
of the machine than to think about the data themselves. Sterility
comes from purposeless exercises: it is not necessary to put a lid on
the box.

If using the statistical packages is so good as a classroom activity,
then why are we showing any reservations about this approach to
data retrieval? There are sophisticated stand-alone statistical packages with a wider range of tools into which we could put our data.
At first sight this would eliminate the need for a data base, so should
these packages be preferred? The answer is in our need not only to
identify patterns but also to pin-point specific data points or combinations of data characteristics through the search facility. But there
are also costs in the use of statistical tools for the processing of our
data. One classic example comes from using the INFORM program
and a very useful file of data about child road traffic accidents. This
file compiles, for a full year, data taken from generally available
police sources. We have found this file useful with students training
to be teachers and we use the file to help us design a road safety
policy in a school management simulation. After an initial brainstorming session where the students usually reach such conclusions
as we should direct the policy in winter because of the dark nights,
and at the smallest or the oldest children because they are most
vulnerable, we then check our assumptions with the help of the
data file.

Students quickly abandon the specific question of how many accidents in each month, a tedious twelve queries, and ask for a graph of
accident frequency across months. It is important to note that the
months have been accorded an appropriate number, January = 1 and
so on, and not entered as a letter string. The computer obliges and at
first sight produces a very useful graph, but as INFORM in our current version only allows data to be divided into ten groups, there is a
spurious output. If we look again we realise that the first column
must consist of data from January and part of February. That is, the
interval breaks occur at 1.2, 2.4, 3.6 months and so on (figure 5.1).
One key question must be, how does the computer decide which bit
of the February (month 2) data should be grouped with the January
data? There is of course no sensible answer to this question. The
numbers as applied to months are nominal data and it is illegitimate
to apply such arithmetic operations to them, but the graph is a very
powerful image and such mathematical niceties are often ignored
because interpretation of the picture appears to be so simple!

It is at this point that the tutor must understand what the com-

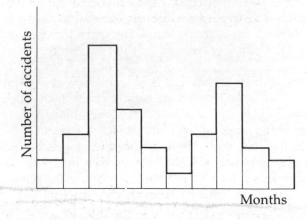

Figure 5.1   Ostensibly a frequency graph of the number of child accidents per month

puter is producing and help the students to achieve a level of sophistication, in order fully to evaluate automatic data output. In a study of data base use in undergraduate social studies, Welford (1989) recorded that all seventy of his first year students expressed a growing confidence in their own abilities to work with data bases in particular, and computers in general. However, only 18 per cent of the group expressed any increased confidence in using statistics. The automatic processing of data by the machine, a black-box approach, had not led to further understanding. This concern is not new, and Cockcroft (1982) and others have raised it, particularly with regard to the use of calculators and of simulation packages, both on and off the computer. There is a danger here of such learning experiences becoming mechanistic, capturing us once again in a product-rather than process oriented curriculum.

Welford suggested that the use of spreadsheets, in which the data manipulations are usually less hidden because statistical formulae are generally visible, should help in furthering the user's understanding of those techniques. The greater control over the operation of those statistical techniques, and the ability rapidly to update statistics makes spreadsheets a powerful mode of information-handling if the data are largely numerical and with text input confined to labelling. They can be a considerable aid to developing an understanding and excitement about the nature of numbers. We have had several jolly, even revelatory sessions with math-phobic teachers playing with spreadsheets. One simple task for the spreadsheet, and highly tedious task for the human operator, is to compare the outputs of the following series of arithmetic and geometric operations:

Number	Formula 1	Output	Formula 2	Output
10 (x)	10 (x) + 10 (x) =	20	10 * 10 =	100
20	20 + 20 =	40	20 * 20 =	400
30	30 + 30 =	60	30 * 30 =	900

This is a simple task, but to watch the numbers grow in the two different progressions, to feel the size of the geometric series, has proved to provide genuine insight for many teachers. Understanding comes from the user constructing the initial formulae to be applied to the number 10, which are then copied for 20, 30 etc. The heightened awareness and sense of wonder come from the speed of the spreadsheet producing the answers. This speed element is important: it is rather like watching time-lapse photography with all the inherent benefits that technique has brought to our understanding of the physical world. As machines become faster, of course, there is a danger of this unfolding of operations being lost. It is relatively slow machines that show us the succession of products of the operations. Speed also allows the user to concentrate on the question at hand, that is, what is the difference in the number patterns produced, rather than on the mechanics of number crunching: a slow process even with a calculator.

The use of data bases and spreadsheets in combination, an alternative now readily available for all but the very lowest age-range, gives the best of both worlds. One difficulty is that the increased sophistication and choice available with the use of such integrated packages can cause further navigation problems.

An inappropriate use of the graph facilities is not necessarily illegitimate, but it may simply be unhelpful and a general waste of time. In figure 5.2 children working on a file of data consisting of their own body measurements have just completed a search for the tallest members of the class. They have sampled all children taller than 170 cm. While it may be a truism that 'a picture tells a thousand words', it is hard to see what value this pie-chart has. Why, other than being a picture, should it be seen as superior to a simple list of three children's names? Further, what confusions are developed in the children's minds in trying to explain why Tom is worth 34 per cent and the other two children only 33 per cent each?

Is Tom wider as well as taller? Welford talks of his social science students having a lack of understanding of where the 'line of best fit'

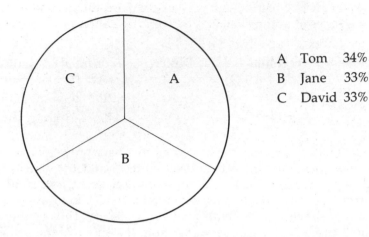

A   Tom   34%
B   Jane   33%
C   David 33%

Children greater than 170 cm

Figure 5.2   A pie chart of the height of children greater than 170 cm

came from in their statistical analyses, and in the same way young children regard the production of bar charts and pie charts as magic. This excitement of getting the machine to do clever things, things the children find difficult, can produce some misleading results, just as it can lead to the asking of highly complex but essentially meaningless questions. At this point the operation of the computer, to make it jump through mental hoops, can become the children's goal, but it is difficult to see the educational objective in that.

Formulating a search

Natural language versus query language

The quality of query formulation is the key to the effective questioning of a data base. There are two problems here. The first is to get the child to ask a worthwhile question, and as we have seen this is no small matter. The second problem lies in translating the question into the query syntax of the specific data base being used. Thus the child needs to be clear about the goal of the search – what information will provide an answer to the enquiry? – and also clear about how to ask the computer to provide that information in an intelligible form.

The vagaries of some computer data bases, for example FACTFILE, can cause problems for children. Lower primary school children querying their file on 'Ourselves', asked the simple question 'Who has an elder brother?' to which the computer responded by producing a list of names each with a number denoting quantity of brothers to the right of it. The equally simple question 'Who has a brother?' was complicated by the structure of the data base, for there were two fields relating to 'elder' and 'younger' brothers. The two questions were similar in syntactic and semantic terms, but the second question demanded a two-field sort. FACTFILE again returned a relevant list of names, but the numerical data appeared odd to the children; for example Child 1 was on the list but accorded no brothers. In fact the file had returned the last quantity requested only, the presence of one or more younger brothers, of which this child had none, but the child occurred on the list because she had an older brother. The children found this very difficult to grasp and decided to ask only one-field questions in future and to piece their answers together from these building blocks. Here it is not the query specification *per se* but the opacity of the computer's thinking that has nonplussed the children.

In the investigation conducted for Derbyshire Educational Software Centre by Janet Spavold (1989), the children were engaged in a local history project working with standard census material. Not only was the command-driven program, INFORM, likely to be opaque to these children, but the information itself is coded in a standard format with little initial meaning for these relatively young researchers. In this case it became necessary to provide help sheets, in the shape of a CENSUS ENQUIRY SHEET (figure 5.3).

The children were encouraged first to specify their query in standard English, then to highlight the essential elements of the query, 'What information do I need and where will I find it?' They were then to use the second half of the form to translate their query into command language. They experienced a high level of frustration when they tried to convert from personal language to machine language, finding it much easier to interpret queries and put them into English than to convert discursive enquiries into query syntax. The children also found it difficult to separate the query parameters from output and frequently asked for the redundant query data to be returned alongside the essential data required to answer the initial research question. Thus, if asking about the occupations of females in a specified age-range, the children asked for their output to include age and sex as well as occupation. This may well be a problem of translation from discursive enquiry to query language as Janet Spavold has suggested, but it may be that the children were checking up on the computer and generally making sure that it did not include

CENSUS ENQUIRY DATE

Name ....

Place .... Census date ....

Entered by .... Checked by ....

I want to know

....

....

These are my search conditions:

1. field ....   The tests are:
    test ....   E = Equal to
    value .... [R]   N = Not equal to
                    AND/OR   L = Less than
                                             G = Greater than
2. field ....   C = Contains
    test ....   D = Does not contain
    value .... [R]   S = Starts with
                    AND/OR   X = Does not start with
3. field ....
    test ....
    value .... [R]
                    [R]

I want to print out these fields to get the results of my
search:

....

....

My title is:

....

....

For use with the INFORM package   JS/DESC

Figure 5.3   The Census Enquiry Sheet designed to aid children
formulate machine-ready queries from natural language (After
Spavold, 1989)

any wrong information! This checking would be natural for children who are often surprised by the answers produced by the machine, particularly when asking constraining questions. Our undergraduates also seemed to show a lack of faith in the machine's ability; or was it that they were checking on themselves? It could be that they were testing whether they had asked the right question in the first place.

The census form only allows space for triple-condition enquiries. Here and in our own work we have found that upper primary school children (9–11 years) have great difficulty in formulating more than two-condition enquiries. This has not proved to be so difficult when the children are using menu-driven programs such as GRASS.

Cognitive benefits of query language

Cognitive benefits, which can accrue when children wrestle with the problems of query language, are often the result of the children having to think as formally as the machine and this, in many cases, is counter-intuitive. Novice users of all ages do have problems in coming to terms with query languages but such languages can provide important cognitive opportunities by presenting children with problems of understanding the computer's way of retrieving information. We will outline some examples from case studies.

In one case a child, confused by a zero matching on a multi-field query, re-ran the search to check the accuracy of the answer. The problem here, which was shared by the group as a whole, was in coping with the counter-intuitive nature of the search. They felt that the more fields they specified the more records should be matched. They were unable to come to grips with the logic of a constraining 'AND'. With considerable help from the teacher, the children learned to operate a two-field search successfully, but only when the problem became very concrete, as in the case of the pairing of parameters frequently found in their natural world. For example, they could understand that a query asking for all the females (parameter: sex) over 21 years of age (parameter: age) would produce a sub-set composed of older females, but they were confused when only a sub-set of the females was returned when posing questions such as 'Find me all the females who work (parameter: employed) and have children (parameter: parent)?' It may be that the children here expected most of the women to be returned, perhaps because they saw motherhood as the main reason for not working, or that they were again matching the concept of 'more' fields with the expectation that 'more' records would be produced.

At first sight it appears that these children had not fully come to grips with the concept of class inclusion/exclusion by their failure to reach an understanding of the more constraining questions, but it may well have been a problem of semantic associations: the children connecting AND with mathematical terms such as 'summation' and 'adding', each of which implies an increase in the final result. The linguistic and logical meanings of AND are different, however, and these children were struggling to understand complex issues. The problem here is with the logical values which can be attached to the AND operator. In everyday life AND indicates an association. It is summation leading to more items or features. For example, we might describe a person as being both male and over thirty years of age: in this case we have provided more information than if we had used either feature alone. When searching through the data base, however, it is not the additive value of AND which determines the response to a query so much as the restrictive value represented by the Boolean value of AND. Using the same example, if we select from the population all males who are older than thirty years, then the search is defined for people with the characteristics 'male' AND 'over thirty years'. There will therefore be *fewer* people in the sample as a consequence of introducing AND, in comparison with the number of people returned if we had used any one of the defining characteristics alone. This reversal of the usual meaning associated with AND poses some interesting problems for children engaged in searches. The pragmatics of everyday life do not help us come to terms with the logical AND and as a result this is a situation in which the 'continuity principle' cannot operate.

Children can be helped to come to terms with such linguistic conundrums, however, as is shown by another case study. The teacher successfully tackled the problem of class inclusion and exclusion by using a knitting needle for a hand-sort on a binary selection, with data stored on punched cards. The aim was to aid her children's understanding of the nature of a computer search before they used a machine-stored data file. Although the teacher did not articulate this intent, she was also to confront the children with the logical AND. The principle of such a searching procedure is that a knitting needle is placed through the hole marking the attribute that is to be retained, for example 'girls', and all the cards not pierced by the needle fall off, leaving cards representing 'girls' on the needle.

Her children had had some initial difficulty in answering the query 'Which boys had bikes' [boys AND bikes = true]. The child conducting the sort had great difficulty in understanding why when he put one needle through 'boys' and another through 'bikes', he retained not only all the cards of boys with bikes but those without bikes and the cards of girl cyclists too. This is the reverse of our previous search problem: here the children were expecting a reduced number of cards with increased specification of the question, but the nature of the search resulted in the inclusion of more records than expected. The problem was finally resolved when the children came to appreciate that they should search on one field at a time. This would remove either all the girls or all the non-bike owners. Through this the children came to realise the equivalence of 'boys with bikes' and 'bikes with boys', the reversibility of class inclusion. The teacher in this case reinforced the learning by enacting out the problem, grouping the appropriate children (boys with bikes, girls with bikes etc.) around the classroom. The children then transformed this knowledge into a living Venn diagram. The initial form of the enquiry was as follows:

The data from each child was:

Name   Sex   owns a pet   owns a watch   owns a bike
can swim   ?? metres

The questions were:

Find all the boys with bikes.
Find all the girls with pets and watches.
Are boys better swimmers than girls?

The children now wanted to identify all the girls with watches and pets using two passes through the data only. However hard they tried, their simple binary sort resulted in a loss of data, either some of the girls with pets or with watches were dropped out of the sort. A prompt by the teacher to look at the cards which had fallen off the needle and to remember the equivalence of 'boys and bikes' and 'bikes and boys', led the children to try a sort in the order pets, boys and then watches, but this too failed. After further inspection of the discarded cards, one boy had what can be described as an 'Aha!' experience. He carefully explained to the rest of the group the importance of the order of sorting. 'If you have watches and pets first then those that drop off we don't want at all, that just leaves the people with watches and pets. It's easy then to split those into boys and girls. Hey ... we can use either hole. We don't need a hole for boys and girls do we, because if you're not a girl you must be a boy.' He had come to terms with two problems simultaneously, the under-standing of the concept of the logical 'AND' plus a procedure for operationalisation of a search procedure to realise it.

These 8-year-olds were indulging in thinking similar to that required by the Wason and Johnson-Laird (1972) 'Four Card Prob-lem,' in the sense that it was important for the children to come to grips with the nature of the discarded information, the 'not-watches, not-pets, and not-girls.' The teacher noted, however, that despite dis-cussions of negative questions, no child posed such a question dur-ing the lengthy period of this work. Again the children were faced with a situation in which everyday pragmatic use of the language did not coincide with specialist use required for data sorting. The natural choice is to use negatives to falsify presuppositions and assertions but in such situations as here the function of the negative is to verify. The Four Card Problem demonstrates that individuals are reluctant to use the negative in this way.

These insights were crucial to the successful use of the computer data file. In posing the question 'Are the boys better swimmers than the girls?' the children ran into problems resulting from the structure of the FACTFILE data base. They initially wanted to identify all swimmers before operating a 'goodness' criterion to their sort, but this is no easy matter with FACTFILE (see Underwood, 1986). It required an application of knowledge from the previous needle and punched card work, for one girl to offer the solution of asking the computer to identify all the swimmers who could not swim zero metres, that is a negative question to ascertain all the swimmers regardless of distance.

Retrieval and understanding

Perhaps what these children are learning most in these classroom data base exercises is about the structure of knowledge and about the relationships between knowledge and the language we use to describe it. The specific variety of knowledge is largely unimportant – provided that it is material of some personal interest then the cog-nitive gains derived from its manipulation will be similar. Children are able to find ways of describing their knowledge in the form acceptable by the data base, and of interrogating the newly formed store of knowledge in order to answer hypothesis-driven questions, solving logical problems on the way. The building and questioning of data bases are activities which represent the essence of the pro-cess-oriented curriculum. Acquiring knowledge can be an unmotivating and difficult activity when the organisational structure of that knowledge is not transparent and when the knowledge store has only rudimentary means of selectively retrieving information from the store. Once knowledge-organisation and knowledge-questioning techniques have been acquired through the use of classroom data bases, then the knowledge gains personal meaning and becomes self-constructed.

Making retrieval as simple as possible is important in some situations. In these cases the knowledge itself is of greater importance than the skills of classification and questioning. If retrieving the factual material is the start of a process and not the end product, then simple retrieval is to be advocated as it might be if a teacher wishes to discover the grades of a particular child, or a student wants a specific answer to the question 'Which is the appropriate bonding agent for acrylic' for example. In these cases the use of a pre-defined route of investigation can be the solution. This is of course the essence of an expert system. It is clear that searching a data base requires much careful thought from the user. For many queries a simple alternative is to use the powerful sort facilities and then extract data by eye. Indeed obtaining the three tallest children from the group is faster by sorting than searching and removes the difficult problem of deciding on a threshold value. If answers to the student's questions can be obtained as easily by sorting as searching, as is the case for many factual questions, then the use of a spreadsheet, particular one in which blocks of data can be highlighted for manipulation, can prove to be both quicker and easier than the use of a data base. In addition, the greater transparency of operations can reduce the confusion in the student's mind. The data base may not always be the appropriate information-handling tool. As always it is necessary to know one's goals or end points before starting out on the route.

The case studies described above have been presented as demonstrations of the cognitive gains which can be made when children retrieve information from data files. We have seen instances of the development of hypothesis testing and of the formulation of precise questions when answers are required of the uncompromising data base. Statistical tools can be used to reconstruct data files, and formal thinking can be seen to emerge. The greatest gains were seen in the late primary school studies, but before we can accept this as the basis for a general recommendation on classroom practice we shall need confirmation of the trend. Early primary children tended to produce non-systematic searches, while secondary school and further education students tended to use data bases like reference manuals. In the late primary school, however, we can witness the exploration of ideas and the development of thought. For these developments to occur it is necessary to use data structures which are transparent, for what may be happening when children form efficient questions is that they may be using a mental model of the data structure to constrain their interrogation.

6 Reading, writing and the word processor

One of the most commonly available information-handling devices for the classroom is the word processor. The ensuing discussion of some of our classroom experiences, which includes recommendations based upon successful encounters, views the word processor as more than a device that can be used to produce smart printing. It can be considered to be an open-ended and flexible tool with which children can learn to think about the structure and purpose of language.

Many people equate word processing to typing with a rather swish electronic typewriter, but this is a poor metaphor. Both a word processor and a typewriter do use a keyboard to enter information into a machine, but after that there are only superficial similarities between the two. For example, it is possible to be a very poor typist and still achieve a professional finish to any document with a word processor. The unskilled yet professional finish is possible quite simply because the word processor allows easy correction of errors before ink is ever put to paper. It also allows the addition, deletion and movement of words, phrases and whole blocks of text if there is a change of mind after reading through what has been written. It is because it is so easy to re-structure text to make the maximum impact, that it is preferable to think of text processing rather than word processing. It could be suggested that a word processor is more analogous to a tape cassette than a typewriter because they share the facilities of fast forward and backward searches, easy editing, and cut and pasting. Essentially they are both tools to manipulate ideas, operating in two-dimensional space, but the typewriter is a linear mechanistic beast. The word processor is a tool of considerable power and there are a number of valuable learning activities which can be performed with even the least sophisticated packages.

The word processor as an educational tool

Writing to read

That the word processor is a tool for writing is obvious, but it can also be used as a tool for developing reading skills, and its use encourages better and more rewarding performances from learners of all ages and abilities. Indeed this word processing tool can be used effectively with the non-writer!

One of the views currently held widely by teachers of reading is that children should develop writing skills as a way of developing their reading skills: they should write to read. The statement appears contradictory but is based on that sound learning principle of using the child's own knowledge as a platform for development. An adult keying-in an oral story for a child, and then providing a printout, produces reading material for the child which is personally relevant. But because the poor reader is reading materials in context, and is therefore more likely to be successful, this personal relevance encourages the development of reading skills. When employing this approach to the teaching of reading, the role of the adult is critical. If adults take an active part in the writing process then the whole social balance will have changed and the learner will defer to authority, losing that all-important personal involvement and the motivation for story production may be lost. Adults are there as a medium by which the child achieves the story goal, not as censors or assessors. Collaborative writing between child and adult may come later, when the child has sufficient skills to feel confident of sharing the task with the adult.

It is possible to argue not only that children can create personally relevant stories using conventional language-based approaches to the teaching of reading, but that extended oral stories can be captured adequately on audio tape. Indeed one of the more pleasing pieces of work conducted by a recent post-graduate student was such a tape produced in conjunction with a 10-year-old child with language problems. The story was stimulated by a drawing which the student had asked Paul to describe. On hearing the tape, Paul felt that the story had not come out right and asked to do a second recording which he felt did justice to his ideas and this was eventually played to the whole class with acclaim. This was a valuable learning experience for Paul, so how might the word processor have improved on an already successful outcome? In the first place it could have provided Paul with a written final product which he could then have attempted to read. Paul could not revise his story, however, and so he had to re-tell it. In this case the written and oral recording of the story might well have proved a double benefit. Before the re-telling of the story Paul could have been encouraged to work on the written text and then used it as a script to aid his re-telling. Indeed the written form could have been a paraphrase of the fuller, richer oral story and it would have provided Paul with personally relevant reading material to be used at a later date.

Reading for meaning

The use of specific word processing features such 'find and change' and 'pick and put' offer further opportunities for language development. We have used the 'group sequencing' approaches to reading comprehension advocated by Lunzer and Gardner (1979) with some success. The purpose of this activity, which is one of a number investigated by this Schools Council project team, is to re-introduce a purpose to reading. Rather than having children engaging in one-directional, passive and monotonous activity, Lunzer and Gardner piloted a variety of activities related to reading and which required an interactive involvement with the text. In the group sequencing activity a passage was presented with a few sentences typed on each of a number of pieces of paper. Children were given the pieces of paper in a jumbled order, and so the natural sequence of the text was disrupted. The task required them to consider the meanings of the components of the story and to reconstruct the text. During the restructuring it is necessary to become aware of the story grammar, and children readily grasp the purposes of the introductory and concluding sections. In completing this task the reader must extract the meaning from the sentences, and be aware of the signals to text cohesion which give a clue to order. Such detail might include grammatical structures, dates or times and, of course, plausibility of the sequence of events. Lunzer and Gardner commented on the active class discussion which was generated by the task: reading was no longer a process by which language entered a passive mind, but was the starting point for an understanding of the structure and purpose of language. The advantage of the machine versus paper version of this exercise, other than the motivational aspects for some children, is two-fold. Again we have a high quality final copy of the text but equally importantly children who do not succeed first time in this re-construction process can easily revise their answers and reconsider their initial readings. Accuracy is achieved through approximation, and there is no punitive effect of an unsuccessful first draft.

We have used this approach with adults to teach the technique of 'pick and put' itself, with word processors. In this case a set of instructions, written in such a way as to make their relative order quite obvious, were themselves jumbled in a word processed file. The task was to use the material contained in the instructions to re-order the instructions themselves. The teachers responded well to the games format of the exercise and were pleased to have an accurate set of notes to take away with them. This is an excellent device for conveying factual information and ensuring that the text is read for meaning. We would offer one caveat, however. It is important that the students are aware that it is the text which is important and not the demonstration of machine competence. It is necessary when working with the machine in this way to leave time for discussion for the final texts of the children. In some cases only one text is plausible (and our use of 'pick and put' instructions is a case in point here), but this is often not the case and it can prove a valuable experience to discuss why some sentences have a specific place in the text and others have not. This can lead children to an appreciation of the planning of text. In history classes, for example, it may be useful to have key events highlighted and explanatory material inserted later. Such exercises, which start as a problem-solving task involving directed reading of a specific body of information, can be extended to a discussion of story or report structure and finally to the relevance and nature of planning text. Here reading and writing tasks are complementary skills, one leading to the discussion of the other.

Basic skills

Ease of editing is of course an important feature of the word processor. Short exercises on the machine, in which the student identifies and rectifies mistakes in punctuation or grammar, have the advantage over pencil and paper in that the child can be required to produce a perfect copy even if a number of attempts may be required. The demand for perfection from the teacher in a pencil and paper exercise can be daunting to those with poor skills in the mechanics of writing. For the majority of children, however, the low technology method may be perfectly suitable and have the advantage of not tieing up a scarce resource. On the other hand, the 'find and change' facility, particularly if associated with a dictionary as in PENDOWN, adds a new dimension to the development of spelling skills. There is something magical about the computer changing mistakes into a corrected form! At the same time this methodical replacement of an error with the correct word places that word at the focus of the writer's attention. Automatic spelling corrections, as found in many advanced systems, may be less useful, however, as there is a problem of the child not attending to changes when they are done automatically.

'Find and change' can also be used to analyse the structure of the text. This is the basis of the program GLOT but can equally be done on a standard word processor. The student investigates a given passage, already placed in the computer, such as the introductions to Lawrence's *Rocking Horse Winner* or Green's *Brighton Rock*, by searching for keywords, names or phrases in the passage. For example, a search for the word 'like' (as an indicator of metaphor) in the two passages shows that Green has a much richer descriptive style than Lawrence. The word 'money' dominates the Lawrence story. This obsession with a word is also shown in *Odour of Chrysanthemums*. Is this typical of his work, the student might ask. This type of work does involve much keying in by the teacher, or a helper, but definitive text passages could be built up over time. In other areas detailed analysis of patterns and distributions may well be better accommodated by the use of data bases and spreadsheets, but in literature and possibly in areas such as history, the reader requires the full text to regain meaning rather than the reduced data set available in a data file.

A comment often made about writers of all ages is that they do not read their own work, or if they do, they read what it is they intended to write rather than what is actually on the page. Equally when first using a word processor, students are obsessed with immediate corrections. They seem unable to enter that state of getting the ideas down and correcting minor flaws later. This was brought home to us when a group of 19-year-olds admitted they found it difficult to leave any inaccuracy up on the screen. Whenever they spotted a mistake they had to go back and correct it.

Developing information-handling skills

The role of the word processor in developing information-handling skills and as an introduction to information-handling packages, may not be immediately apparent, but it is none the less very exciting. At all levels of education, and indeed in many jobs, we are frequently asked to précis a text. One interesting reversal of this is to provide students with either a summary of a text or one containing only key content words and then ask them to reconstruct the passage in their own words. Their text and the original can then be compared. Such activities can encourage students to focus in on the structure of text and to consider what is, or is not, redundant. Such activities can be completed with pen and pencil but they are essentially messy, active language games requiring re-thinking and editing as the writer goes backwards and forwards through the text. The word processor not only facilitates completion, but also allows repeated revision without penalty. The non-linearity of such exercises really benefits from the use of the word processor. Indeed, Maxted (1987) has argued that word processing is more akin to discourse, rather than pencil and paper writing, because of this non-linearity and because of the facility to revise, correct and expand at any time between conception and delivery. This is a point Daiute (1985) endorses when she talks of putting 'the voice' back into text construction (writing as the presentation of externalised thought) with the aid of the word processor.

These are examples of relatively conventional uses of the word processor. More interesting is Robinson's (1988) suggestion that the word processor can also be used as a prototype data base. Although lacking the flexibility of query specification and statistical tools associated with data bases, word processors are less restricted in the amount of data they can hold and they do not suffer from limitations in field or record size. As we have already observed, these are very real problems for users of educational data bases. The keyword search (find and change) facility of the word processor, as used in GLOT, allows us to move easily through such a data file. This is particularly useful if the word processor is case-sensitive and can distinguish between ADDRESS, Address and address. Here three levels of data organisation have been identified. Robinson overcomes the problem of non-case sensitive systems by prefixing labels with a code mark, as in *address, @address and address. Children have no difficulty in using programs in novel ways, and the development of flags to distinguish one level from another is readily taken on board. Robinson has used one page of the word processor to represent the record, producing a series of identical forms using headings, tabulations and other formatting facilities, and data are placed within these pre-defined structures. A data base does offer more sophisticated search and data manipulation techniques, and in particular word processor data bases have limitations with the handling of numeric data. But as Robinson points out, we often only need a very simple keyword search.

A matter of choices: what should we do with the word processor?

The creative teacher can, therefore, use the word processor in many different ways: as an electronic worksheet for basic skills practice; for the development of advanced reading skills; for the decoding of text; to develop an understanding of story structure; and to encourage planning. The word processor is a highly versatile tool which is ill-named by commerce: thinking of it as a 'text manipulation tool' or as an 'ideas organiser' will give a better feel of its capabilities. It can support reading and writing of course, but it is also an organiser of thought and a scratchpad for the exploration of ideas. Many of these uses are machine-hungry, however, and with limited hardware a teacher may have to restrict the number and type of activity, or make decisions as to which children will most benefit from machine time.

Writing with the computer

Why write with the computer? From forgiving typewriter to ideas organiser

Writing with the computer is a valuable activity for students of all ages. Why should we assume this and where is the evidence of a benefit? Papert's description of an alienated writer who moved from total rejection of writing to intense involvement (accompanied by rapid improvement of quality) within a few weeks of beginning to write with a computer (Papert, 1981, p. 30) makes for convincing reading. Sharples goes further, offering an explanation of children's use of few of the high-level skills of editing and revision when writing with a pencil and paper:

> To be a writer is empowering yet every word that a child forms on paper is confirmation of inferiority. However carefully and neatly a child may write, the result is a poor substitute for adult typeface. If we want children to become adult writers, we should equip them with adult writing tools. (Sharples, 1985, p. 10)

This statement begs the question of how any child ever learned to write, but it does make a useful point. Children tend to be involved in the minutiae of text production which leaves limited cognitive capacity available for the higher-level organisational and other more demanding activities of the writer. If our minds are trapped by decisions about spellings, they cannot be used for the consideration of story grammar. But does writing with the computer actually achieve a shift in emphasis from spelling to story logic and plot production? This is the essential question to be answered here.

In essence these views are founded on the characteristics of the word processor itself. The ability of the word processor to edit text easily and, with a printer, to produce a clean, error-free copy every time, should help the development of written language which concentrates on the content of the text rather than upon the grammar. By releasing the writer from the constraint of concentrating on low-level aspects of text production, the mind is released for the development of the text as a piece of communication.

Using a word processor allows the writer to concentrate on the process of writing; that is, the acts of drafting, editing and revising the text. Colette Daiute (1985) describes writing on a word processor as more like talking than writing; an interactive exchange between the writer and the machine. Text is entered into the machine which then displays the writer's ideas for reconsideration. If, on reflection, things do not look right, modifications can be made. The machine responds and a new, clean version of these thoughts appears on the screen.

Those enthusing about the word processor, or more accurately, text processor often speak from positive personal experience. At first the benefits are those of a forgiving electronic typewriter facilitating easy error correction, extending to the production of an elegant edited text. In this mode, users often bring fairly detailed hand-written copy with them to the machine. They are not actually creating at the machine, this is copy-typing without the need to be as accurate or skilled as a trained keyboard operator. A significant change in the writer's strategy occurs with the move to direct input to the machine, without the initial paper phase. Here the adventurous begin to use the computer as a tool with which to compose and create text. The text processing package encourages the organisation of ideas, sometimes through the help of advanced organiser software. In the latter case the writer is encouraged to think out carefully the skeletal structure of a text after which the detail can be fleshed out. Organisers are extremely useful for writing structured documents but they can also be valuable in more creative writing where characters, scenes and plots can be designated. Such additions to the standard word processing packages are available across the age-ranges, for example PENDOWN, designed for the primary sector, incorporates an advanced organiser facility.

Often, however, the writer may only have a very rough plan of where to go, and ideas are 'scribbled down' quickly. This period of active brainstorming is followed by a period of reflection when the work is tidied up and reorganised. This is not simply an editing job.

It involves careful revision and redrafting of the material. Ideas are moved around and new relationships formed in the manner of putting together a giant jig-saw puzzle, but in this case there may be a number of 'optimal' solutions to the puzzle depending on the goal (purpose or audience) of the text.

These two approaches, the 'planned structured' approach and the 'quick free writing with much revision' approach have been noted by a number of workers. The planner operates a top-down strategy, a Mozartian composer compared to the bottom-up, basket of eggs approach of the Beethovian style (Daiute, 1985). The suggestion here is that although individuals have a tendency to one style or another, the writing task may also influence the chosen strategy at any one time, the top-down approach being more suited to scientific or report writing while creative writing benefits from the more informal style. Our work with undergraduates has shown, however, that students are very resistant to changing their styles of writing, and that whether writing with or without the machine, strategies of writing remain fairly well set. Again, good writers who have developed their skills with pen and paper are dominated by a linear model of writing.

Rosson's (1984) study of experienced word processor users (many hours with the machine) found a similar rigidity of practice. Writers tended not to use the full editing facilities; the initial way of solving a problem was often the one that continued to be preferred even when more elegant strategies were available. Only a small group of users were explorative and keen to find optimal solutions to problems, and these people tended to be interested in computers themselves and/or they had used more than one word processing package. This latter experience seemed to give the users a greater perspective of what a word processor might be expected to do. This is a cogent argument for giving learners as wide an experience with available packages as possible and allowing them, from top primary school age (11 years old) and upwards, to select word processing packages which meet the needs of the specific task to hand.

A large study reported by Dalton and Hannafin (1987) observed eighty seventh grade children (12–13 years of age) composing with and without the word processor over the course of a full academic year. The study found that some of the word processing group reported neglect of the planning process. Some children appeared to feel that editing was so easy that planning was not vital as in pen and pencil writing. Here the children had changed their writing styles. Dalton and Hannafin found that ability differences were of importance in predicting who would benefit from word processor use, and this comment is consistent with observations from other workers (Burns, 1984; Daiute, 1985; Woodruff, 1984).

One explanation of the disparity in our own and Rosson's (1984) observations, compared to those of Dalton and Hannafin, could be that lower ability children had not developed a writing strategy of their own and were therefore susceptible to the influences of the writing medium. The word processor is of great benefit to the compulsive reviser of text and it may well be that it is such writers who will most benefit from its use. It will be interesting to monitor the changes in writing style of children over the next few years and it may become necessary to re-emphasise the advanced organiser features of programs such as PENDOWN. We already have anecdotal evidence of a slippage in skills. A current British training film on office automation includes an interview with one unhappy secretary who is complaining about the extra work that the word processor has brought her. When she used a standard typewriter, before the word processor was introduced into the office, her boss planned his dictation but now, knowing changes can be made very easily, he had stopped this careful preparation. As a result of this he might ask for as many as five drafts of a letter. For this secretary the word processor has been anything but emancipatory and her boss was allowing his own skills to atrophy. Similarly, when word processors were first introduced, there was talk of the paperless office. Anyone working in a computer-rich environment will testify to the joke in this promise.

These individual differences in text production may in part explain the confusing data that has come out of experiments, largely with adults, to test the benefits of writing with a processor. Mixed, and generally inconclusive findings for the benefits of machine- or handwritten text are the norm. Linguistic ability may prove to be a more significant factor, however, and we will return to these issues of individual differences when we discuss some of our work in the classroom.

If the first stage of using the text processor is largely to do with editing text and the second stage with the act of creating text, then the third stage is more one of creatively editing not text but whole documents and a number of documents together. This occurs when desktop publishing (DTP) packages are tied to a standard word processor to produce professional standards of document presentation. There are now a number of these packages designed for the production of classroom newspapers, but there is some controversy over their use. For some they are simply a 'prettying-up' of important language work and, as such, are largely time-wasters. However DTP, as a group activity, has the potential to encourage many traditionally valued classroom skills: decision-making, research and enquiry, language production, aesthetics and presentation and communication or the appreciation of audience in writing. DTP is again non-linear because it is an act of synthesis; it involves the juxtapositioning of text with text, text with graphics, and each of these with data. These changes from linear to multi-dimensional thinking are important and are discussed more fully in chapter 8.

We and many other happy users of text processors have felt the release from the tyranny of low-level writing skills such as handwriting and spelling as suggested by Rubin (1983) and Sharples (1985) and the resulting freedom to focus on the act of writing itself. In the first case as editor, but editing becomes a polishing process rather than the nightmare of increasing errors described by John Holt (1969). He applied a rule of three mistakes only per page to a young girl with spelling and handwriting problems. To his consternation she did not produce, as he expected, more careful and neater compositions on the second and third drafts of her story. Instead the child became very upset; she was so worried about having to re-copy her paper that she could not concentrate on doing it, and hence did it worse and worse (Holt, 1969, p. 135). Our experience of children and students in this situation is that not only errors proliferate but also that writing becomes such a chore that many reduce the quantity of text to alleviate, in some little way, the pain of copying the material yet again. Of course the advent of correction aids such as 'liquid paper' has reduced the chore in no insignificant way.

We have also come to appreciate the computer as a machine with which to think actively, as an aid to the manipulation of words and ideas, and in effect as a tool that encourages revision rather than editing. On questioning experienced teachers about how they approached the word processor, the answers were not encouraging for this view. All of the teachers, who were in the second year of an advanced course in educational computing, felt that the benefits of text processing to produce good copy were important. They were able to make informed choices of word processing packages according to the job type, for example WRITER or PENDOWN were used for children's worksheets or for notices, and VIEW, INTERWORD or WORDWISE for their own course work or for school documents. But only one out of seventeen composed at the machine! There were two main reasons offered for this non-interactive style of writing. A number of teachers saw little advantage in this way of working as they had always produced detailed, carefully structured notes when writing by hand and they carried this tradition with them. A second group felt the power of creating at the machine but argued that a home computer was a necessity to enable this mode of writing to take place successfully. Interestingly, this survey showed that the writers in the first group restricted their use to simple editing and layout facilities of the text processing package. A number had never tried 'pick and put' facilities. Among the group of would-be creators at the machine, many more of the 'advanced' facilities of the package were used. The dichotomy highlighted here, and the issues it raises, is very relevant to a discussion of text processing in schools. Lack of time on machine, or the overall lack of hardware, is a reason many teachers offer for not using such packages. The evidence from this group also suggests that established writing styles may influence the way in which children will use word processors and therefore the effectiveness of that experience. Before going on to discuss these issues it will perhaps be beneficial to reflect on the nature and value of the writing process itself.

The writing process

Children generally agree with their teachers that writing is an important skill, and Whitmarsh (1988) found that children valued good handwriting, although this will not concern some teachers. But what is writing and why is it important, and if it is held in such esteem why do so many children have difficulty in learning to write with any level of proficiency?

Graves (1983) describes the writing process as a repetition of three functions, 'select, compose, read, select, compose, read'. Other views suggest that writing begins as a visible form of speech, but that over time the child incorporates words and phrases from other written language either read to, or by the child. Writing does not provide an exact transliteration of speech sounds, as the two modes each have their own patterns of organisation between which the child must learn to differentiate. This adds to the problem of learning to write for the normal child as speech codes are learned first.

Good writing depends on having something to write about; it requires from the writer such non-linguistic qualities as truthfulness, vigour and imagination (Perera, 1984), and should not be put at risk by attention being focused on low-level details as spelling and handwriting. A child's story writing should be spontaneous and may well be compared with an adults' undeveloped English usage, such as personal letters, diaries and memos, which often share the spontaneous property of spoken language. These items are characteristically hand-written, contain personal ideas, and are to a known audience, but they tend not to be extensively planned, do not undergo drafting, revision or re-writing, and are not usually kept for posterity. Children's story writing should share some of these properties, but at least when the writing requires original thought or is to be kept, pupils should make several drafts and this in turn will enable them to learn written structures. Because writing, unlike speech, produces a permanent creation, it can be re-worked, manipulated and altered. This permanency is important and tape can give the same longevity to the spoken word. We have already referred to one 10-year-old's taped story. On hearing it played back he felt it had lost a lot of its punch and was very happy to make a second tape so that the story in his head was properly laid down for others to hear. This re-working is important; while mistakes in speech may pass unnoticed, in writing they remain to confuse the reader and to remind writers of their own inadequacies (Martlew, 1983). In agreement with these ideas the Bullock Report (1975) clearly pointed out that there has been insufficient encouragement of children to produce first drafts of text followed by a second more refined product.

Thought and language are necessary prerequisites for the skilled writer, but whether child or adult, the writer needs specific techniques for forming ideas. These include the generation of constraints such as scene setting, specifying audience layout, vocabulary, plus the need to generate advanced organisers, and the development of proof-reading skills to verify the text, coupled with the revision of initial drafts. Few children in the primary school have these skills available to them, and those that they do have are not used because of the physical constraints in the pencil and paper approach to writing. This is particularly so in the case of re-drafting.

Writing is a multi-layered skill, with the writer's attention being directed to the lowest level of skill which poses performance difficulties. In chapter 2 we outlined a model of the relationship between attention and skill, and the model applies to writing as it does to other mental and physical skills. The notion of novices attending to different aspects of performance is well recognised:

> writing is a communicative action that results from multiple cognitive processes that operate simultaneously, producing text through their interaction. For example, there are processes that draw a letter on paper, those that select words and order them in sentences, and those that generate select and organise ideas. While an expert writer can operate competently on these many levels, a novice tends to become locked into more local levels, a

phenomenon called downsliding ... (Levin, Boruta and Vascon-cellos, 1983, p. 220)

It is at these local levels involving spelling and other detail that the computer allows children to rectify mistakes easily, and releasing them from the tyranny of errors and at the same time increasing their self-image.

In theory, the finished product may have gone through a number of drafting, editing and revision stages, but as John Holt found, the copying process may result in more errors and an emphasis of the child's weaknesses. In this case the child was left-handed, had diffi-culty holding a pen and frowned with concentration as she struggled with her work. Many children's handwriting is slow and laborious, and with poor letter production. As a result the train of thought may be lost and text can become muddled and incoherent. Children often read only the last word of their work when they come to add to it, and so can easily lose the thread of the story or argument. Martlew (1983) has claimed that slowness curtails the number of ideas held in short-term memory, and so slow writers may seem unimaginative and produce poor work as a direct consequence of their writing speed. Slow writers may be aware of the problem, and it may be slowness that inhibits them from producing text. In a similar way, slow reading can lead to increasingly poor comprehension. If the ideas presented in the beginning of a sentence have been forgotten by the time the slow reader gets to the end, then there will be no opportunity for the integration of the ideas contained in that sen-tence. Underwood and Briggs (1984) provide a fuller discussion of this problem of the consequences for reading comprehension of the slow decoding of written words. Poor writers may produce as little text as possible to keep their workload at an acceptable level; re-copying and correcting provides a heavy workload when a child has difficulties in letter production.

Children also tend to be poor at identifying their own mistakes, and their weaknesses in revision processes have often been attributed to an ability to see their texts from a reader's or an objective point of view (Scardamalia and Bereiter, 1983). From Ellen Nold's (1981) use-ful review of research on revising we have evidence that remedial adult writers have difficulty correcting their work, simply because they have difficulty in reading it accurately enough. When they read aloud what they have written they simply read what they had intended to write, rather than what they have actually written. Chil-dren appear to have similar problems. They may be capable of revi-sions and improvements but the executive burden may be too great and this may disrupt the composing process. It seems that children may avoid revisions beyond local deletions as the distractions of crossing-out or restructuring their ideas may cause them to forget what they were writing about. Why should the word processor help? One of the problems is that children and adults bring well-tried methodologies to the machine and continue to under-perform, hence the teachers' failure to use the full facilities of the word processor. Revision, as opposed to editing, is not an automatic consequence of using the machine, as the adult studies show. The machine gives the opportunity to make revision part of the writer's methodology.

More able pupils are more aware of the possibilities of text revision than their less able counterparts, who tend to be more concerned with producing neat, error-free texts. Less able pupils often persevere with written structures which are causing them great difficulties, rather than crossing them out and re-phrasing their work. This highlights the dangers of an over-emphasis on neatness and the avoidance of errors. Approaches to the writing task should be fostered that will be beneficial in the long term. Graves (1979) suggested that the status of a piece of writing is changed by crossings-out; it reverts to a working draft rather than a final copy. The shift from low-level skills such as spelling and pencil control to high-level skills of composition occurs when the child need not worry about getting everything right the first time (Martlew, 1983), and this should be an even more powerful stimulus with a machine which takes away the need for fair copying. Perera (1984) argued that learning by writing is only possible if there is an acceptance that the first draft is a tentative formulation and that revising is not correction of mistakes but rather a process of searching for the best expression of the child's developing meaning. In such instances the child is able to exploit fully the cognitive and expressive resources of the written language.

Writing, then, involves a complex basket of skills, from the mechanistic skills of making marks on paper, through careful editing to essential text revision. It appears that this latter skill is not well developed by many writers of all ages and it may well be that pragmatic considerations have taught us to reduce as far as possible major changes in our texts. The word processor can help us to develop this important skill.

Children writing with the computer

In this section we shall discuss some of the work we have conducted with the help of experienced teachers and undergraduates in education and psychology. These are a number of studies with top juniors (9–11 years), and in the first study the children worked individually. The focus of the second study was on shared writing experiences and the children worked in pairs. Much of this work was conducted by an experienced primary school teacher, Richard Eagles.

Although children value writing and see handwriting as a valuable skill, it is also apparent that not all children enjoy writing. We found that the reaction by 8-year-old children, to the question 'Do you enjoy personal writing', was divided along ability lines with good writers expressing positive views while the 'not so good' said they did not. This is not a surprising finding perhaps, but it is important to remember that although writing is valued it is not viewed with equal pleasure by all participants.

The perceived prominence of error reduction

Children have a clear view of what writing is about. We found general agreement as to the problems that writing brings: 'Trying to remember what to put in ... making sure the spellings are correct and that I haven't missed anything out'; and 'If it's for display, trying not to make a mistake.' When children were asked the question, 'What if you have missed something out?' the eventual reply was, 'You tag it on at the end or leave it out altogether.' These comments are illuminating. Children are aware of cognitive demand and those pressures are made worse by the need to produce error-free material. The children focus a large part of their attention on trying to minimise errors. Indeed error reduction is more important than completing a story into its best possible form. Editing is a necessary evil to be avoided, where possible by getting it right first time, and revision and re-drafting are not mentioned.

This focusing of attention on errors is apparent when children are first introduced to the word processor. The first reaction of Lindsey (10 years old) to the delete button or 'magic rubber' was 'Cor, that means you don't have to keep re-writing out all your mistakes!' Other children thought it might help because you could do 'inserts'. Graham, also 10 years old, reacted on first using the word processor that 'It was good how you could go back and rub it out' and 'It helps you with spellings this, it's all right'. Graham had a problem with spelling and it is perhaps the one thing that put him off story writing. When presenting his first piece of processed work, he was not bothered about the content but got in his bit about spellings straight away. 'I don't think some of these spellings are right,' he said.

The point to make here is that children are focused on error correction. They are at a very basic editing stage. It seems unrealistic to expect them naturally or automatically to develop those higher skills of revision just because they are using a word processor. After all, the anecdotal evidence we presented at the start of this chapter, plus a wealth of supporting experimental studies of students in the United States shows that many adult writers rarely if ever consider re-drafting (see Rosson, 1984).

The Bullock Report (1975) emphasised the importance of re-writing, and yet there is still perhaps too little attention paid to this aspect of writing. Even once re-drafting has been taught to children it may find restricted use because of time constraints and because of the purpose for the writing is being produced. Often this is to satisfy the teacher or an outside authority. We rarely have the opportunity of writing for ourselves. If we pass the exam, or convey the message in our memo, do we really need to look for the most elegant or parsi-monious design for our written thoughts? It is important, however, to achieve some level of competence in error reduction, and the chil-dren, commenting on their first experiences of machine-produced text, were quick to spot the benefits of the word processor here.

Approaching the keyboard

Teachers tend to have two main complaints about the keyboard. They argue that their children will not be able to cope with the 'qwerty' layout or, if under 8 years of age, with the upper case let-ters. For beginner writers keyboard entry can be reduced, or even eliminated, by the use of other input devices such as touch pads and screens. For example, the concept keyboard is widely used in schools in the United Kingdom and it is an easy matter to program this input device to simulate a lower case keyboard, with the alphabet in the standard sequence. Rubin (1983) produced an early computer version of an hierarchical story tree with the intention of focusing children's attention on story logic. Eyre (1989) presents a practical example of this type of program composed for the concept keyboard, while retaining the benefits of direct input from the computer keyboard.

If children do cope with the standard keyboard, as many do, then some teachers feel this may lead to deteriorating standards of pen-manship. The penmanship argument is a legitimate concern but, for the foreseeable future, there will be too few machines in our schools for it to suffer. And mastering the keyboard can be especially helpful to those with poor pen skills and can give a pride in work which may be carried forward to the production of handwritten material. Emphasis on layout, including underlining, and spaces between paragraphs are easy to achieve with computer, and if the child is taught to appreciate this then the quality of presentation and increased readability can be transferred to pen and paper.

Returning to putative difficulties with the keyboard, Daiute (1985) has argued that computer writing is fun, and that it turns what for many is an unpopular activity into a game. She points to children's appreciation of the physical ease of computer writing. It is possible to underestimate the ease with which children take to the keyboard, for it is not only the keyboard which can act as a barrier. Screen displays are not always helpful to early readers. One able 10-year-old, Clare, argued that writing is quicker by hand. She had tried the word processor at home and found it very difficult. She changed her mind on using the program WRITER saying, 'This one's much better because the print is much bigger. It's easier to see if you've made a mistake.'

The ease of using WRITER may well have been the reason for Clare's change of heart but it might also be a result of working successfully with other children with the program. We had a similar experience with PODD, a language extension program widely available for home as well as for school use. In this program the task is to discover the range of actions that can be performed by the cartoon character PODD by typing in verbs to complete the sentence 'PODD can ... '. Correct spellings are necessary, and are rewarded by PODD performing the actions with some animation, if he knows how! One girl who had used the program at home was very disenchanted with it but agreed to go along with a class activity after a discussion with the teacher. A few days later she was seen to be totally immersed in her group's quest to solve the PODD problem. What can be a useful and enjoyable language extension program, when played in a group, is a boring spelling game to the individual child. The social interaction of sharing the jokes and the achievements are vital to the activity of solving the problems. This might have been part of Clare's new found enthusiasm for WRITER.

A lack of keyboard skills can get in the way of progress, particularly for bright pupils. This is one result of a six-month study looking at matched groups of 10-year-olds writing on and off the computer. The collective findings of the research showed no overall performance gains for one mode of writing over the other. There was enormous variance within groups but certain points were apparent. The least able writers, Adam and Heidi, made great strides on the computer compared to their matched pair, who wrote conventionally. They wrote quantitatively more, they had fewer errors, vocabulary and sentence structure improved and their stories developed greater

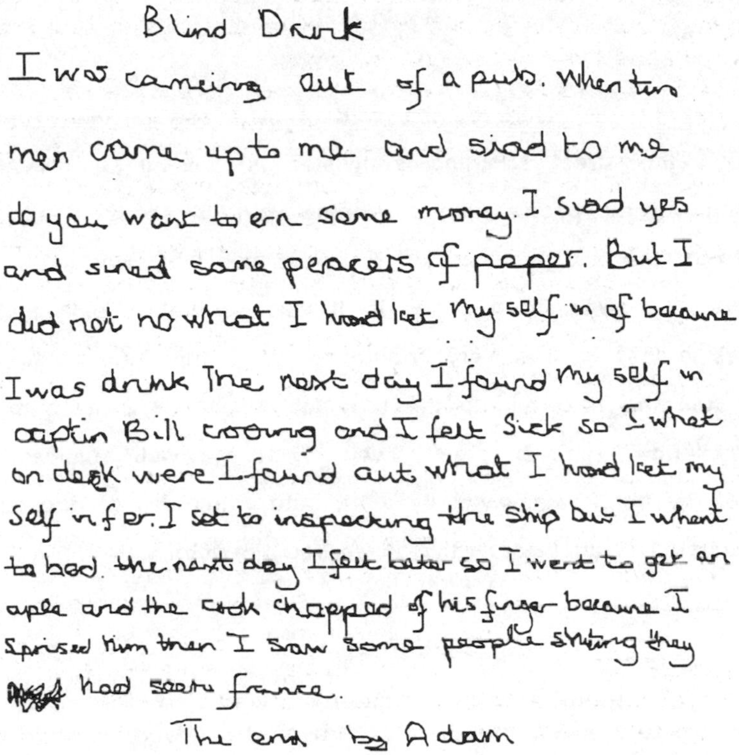

Blind Drunk

I was cameing out of a pub. When two men came up to me and siad to me do you want to ern some money. I siad yes and sined some peacers of paper. But I did not no wrat I had let my self in of because I was drunk The next day I found my self in captin Bill crooing and I felt Sick so I whet on deck were I found aut what I had let my Self in f er. I set to inspecting the ship but I whent to bed. the next day I felt bater so I went to get an aple and the cook chopped of his finger because I Sprised him then I saw some people shuting they had seen france.

The end by Adam

Figure 6.1a Adam's handwritten story about the press gang was rated by his teacher as one of the best pieces of work produced by the child that year. There are frequent errors which, coupled with the poor handwriting, make this difficult to read in places. Adam's story, although bold, lacks the variety and coherence of the computer example in figure 6.1b, written a week later.

coherence (see Adam's stories, figures 6.1a and 6.1b). This was not the case for our most able writer, Jane. She was extremely disenchanted with the machine and her stories shrank both in size and creativity.

In their study of seventh-grade students (lower secondary school in the UK), Dalton and Hannafin also found no overall difference between matched groups writing with and without the word processor. Low-achieving students, however, benefited far more from composition taught through the word processor than by conventional pen and paper methods. Additionally, informal observations showed

A wild wind.

One day in the heart of the wild west I saw a man running through the street shouting a twister is coming, a twister is coming. All the people started running wild. In about 10 seconds the town was in a panic. I tried to ask a man what was wrong but he just ran away. Then I saw it. It was 80 metres high and 20 metres across. I was very frightened so I ran into a shop to hide And the next minute the roof fell off and I said to myself these shops aren't built very well. Then the wall collapsed on top of me but I was saved by a tin bath which fell on top of me and covered me up. Later I was rescued from the debris.

THE END BY ADAM

Figure 6.1b   Adam's computer-written story about a twister shows his efforts to produce error-free text. He has improved his sentence structures, and full stops no longer appear arbitrarily. But there is more than this, because his story now has a well-defined structure.

that those children using word processors required less encouragement to revise text and were more likely to spend time on this task than the conventional writers. Low language achievers can benefit from word processing even though other types of 'special' intervention strategies have proved unsuccessful.

Why should the children with language deficits do so well, with little effect for the good writer? Our two weakest children, Adam and Heidi, were initially surprised by being able to read their own work. They felt great pride at the smartness of their printouts. There is also considerable evidence that a holistic, as opposed to a reductive skills approach to writing can be especially effective in improving the writing skills of low achievers because these learners tend to become occupied by form rather than substance. The word processor encourages this holistic approach to writing.

Jane, as a proficient pen user, had already mastered the mechanics of writing and the skills of presentation, and she was frustrated by the word processor. It slowed her down and she was no longer an expert. Her old skill was getting in the way of the new. Working alone Jane had not been bolstered by the social interaction and by the fun element of using the new machine, in contrast with our other proficient writer, Clare. Dalton and Hannafin also cite keyboard problems as a major inhibitor to work, particularly at the start of the project.

In our review of research on the evaluation of the cognitive benefits of educational computing, we expressed a worry that our conclusions were based on small-scale studies operating over a short period of time. These studies are indicative of the likely benefits of one approach or another, as here with our own evaluations of word processing. It is encouraging to see that our case study data is born out by the more extensive study of Dalton and Hannafin (1987).

Brainstorming

Initiating a story is one of the more important tasks for a teacher. Word processing facilities can be used in a number of ways to aid in this sometimes difficult task. In the following example Richard Eagles has been involved in a brainstorming session with the children and key vocabulary concerning their topic – the birth of a bird – has been jotted down. At this point the children and teacher could usefully have produced a file for all the children to use as a starting point for their story but in this case the children each typed in their own record of the words discussed which they then printed out (figure 6.2a). They then began constructing their stories about a bird hatching, on the machine. Graham and Simon chose to write about an eagle, Sarah a blue-tit and Clare a chaffinch. Clare's second and third printouts show how she progressively inserted words and ideas into her initial brainstorming (figures 6.2b–d).

At each stage the children printed out their copy. Richard Eagles described their reaction as one of receiving an offering from the computer, rather than a piece of their own work. They studied the copy, marking mistakes, inserting new words and ringing phrases to be moved. Changes were then typed in and a new copy printed. In Simon's case he has found this brainstorming technique so beneficial that he re-introduces it at the end of his third revision in order to help his completion of the story (figure 6.2e). Here, redrafting through printouts has been used to great effect by the children who have built a story, re-reading it many times until a final satisfactory draft was completed, even though ornithological detail may be a little suspect!

**hatch   egg   break   yolk   worms   insects
crack   burst   peck   sunshine   darkness
brothers   sisters   nest   walk   squash**

Figure 6.2a   Key vocabulary

**Chaffinch   hatch   egg   break,   crack,
burst   yolk   eat   worms,   insects   peck
sunshine   darkness
brothers   sisters   nest   walk   squash**

Figure 6.2b   Clare's story, copy 2

**Chaffinch   hatch   ,   dark   in   egg,   peck   to   get
out   of   egg,   sunshine   bright   when   come   out,
eat   worms,   insects
brothers   and   sisters   already   hatched,   in
nest,   learn   to   walk,
get   taught   how   to   fly**

egg   break,   burst   yolk,crack

Figure 6.2c   Clare's story, copy 3

**In   the   Chaffinches   nest   there   were   four
eggs.   All   of   the   eggs   had   hatched   except   one.
Inside   that   egg   it   was   very   dark.   Then   a
quiet tapping noise came from the egg as
the   bird   inside   tried   to   peck   his   way   out.
When   the   baby   Chaffinch   had   eventually
pecked   his   way   out   of   the   egg,   he   found   the
sunshine   very   bright   after   being   inside   the
dark   egg.   He   began   to   eat   worms   and   insects
and   as   he   walked   around   the   nest   he   found
he   had   brothers   and   sisters.   When   he   was   a**

**few weeks old he was taken to the edge of
the nest with his brothers and sisters and
taught how to fly.**

Figure 6.2d   Clare's story, the final product

**In the Golden Eagle's eerie, the mother was
waiting for her eggs to hatch. suddenly she
heard pecking from inside the eggs, then
cracks started to appear and the seven eggs
burst open. The babies were in a very
squashed nest but being as the nest was
high up on a cliff ledge the atmosphere was
very clean. The dad went to find food for
the young ones**

**insects   worms   mice
sun   sunshine   dark   bright   yolk
look   around   down   food   wood   warm
fly   return   leave   open   mouth   crowed
tread   on   everyone   else   first   time**

Figure 6.2e   Simon's story, copy 3

Sharing the writing experience

Simon and Clare were also given the task of writing a poem on the
theme of 'The Station Announcer'. After a brief discussion about the
theme, during which they jotted down a few words on paper, they
sat in front of the blank screen. The comment 'Oh, this is hard' was
followed by two minutes of mental juggling of words which eventually led to the first verse:

> Welcome to Birmingham Station,
> We hope you won't miss your train.
> But the train that is going to London,
> Will be held up because of the rain!

The emergence of verse three clearly illustrates how productive the liaison was. The tape recording of the children shows that after a short pause Simon arrived at the first two lines:

> Will everyone with a brown suitcase
> Please check the label on top

After some discussion 'brown' was changed to 'grey' using the text editing facilities. Clare, in searching for a rhyme, suggested a line ending in 'swap' which was rejected at first as the children felt that it did not keep to a reasonable story line. The next few minutes were spent working through ideas about taking the case to reception. Simon suggested that they think of a name. The name of another child in the class, Christopher Shaw, was selected because he forgot his dinner money once. Clare juggles the words mentally to make the line scan and comes up with:

> If it has on it Christopher Shaw's name

They tried this on the screen. There was a sense of freedom and experimentation by this point. Simon sought to introduce another character who had Christopher's suitcase. They discussed this second character, a man who had lost his suitcase. However, his presence in the plot is seen to be problematic and he is abandoned. The eventual last line returns to Clare's original idea and the verse is completed with:

> Then bring it to me for a swap.

How much of the text was juggled electronically and how much mentally through conversation, is not clear. The children said that they tried various words on screen and they were heard to address the screen on the tape recording. These children were fulfilling the objective articulated in the DES document *English from 5–16* (1984), by which children were to be encouraged to become involved in discussions of their own writings, assessing whether or not their writing met pre-specified goals and how such goals might be better achieved. Clare and Simon were sharing knowledge, testing ideas, discussing grammar and arguing a case for their views. Their talk was of the kind that Joan Tough (1976) stressed as being so important in learning. The two children had co-operated to great effect, and the placing of the text in the public domain on the screen appeared to facilitate this co-operation. The final product of this exercise (figure 6.3) is reproduced here as a triumph of the co-operation between two young writers and the word processor.

A fuller argument favouring the social outcomes of writing with the computer and the benefits of shared writing is presented in the next chapter. Briefly here we would like to make the point that one reason why children may be motivated to write when using the machine is that their self-image is enhanced, for example by the production of work with a well-designed, high-quality finish. It may also be enhanced by the sense of control over one's environment.

Drafting and planning

The process of learning to write creatively is fraught with contradictions. The stories that are produced should be spontaneous, but they should also be revised, with the aim of improvement. Understandably, children lose interest in their work after the first attempt, and knowledge of the need for a 'neat copy' encourages them to try to get it right first time, so as to avoid the physical difficulties and tedium of writing it out again. As a result of this, much of the spontaneity may be lost due to a 'downsliding' of concentration from high-level composing processes to 'lower-level' processes such as spelling and handwriting.

We have seen examples of children coping with very difficult problems: infants handling the keyboard, and young children using command-driven word processing packages such as VIEW. One thing to remember is that they will cope if the teacher presents the material in an appropriate way. This includes enthusiasm but also includes initially restricting the features of the word processor to be introduced to the children. For example, it is appropriate to set the program to operate in 'Insert' mode, if it has both 'Overwrite' and 'Insert' options, because this will reduce the possibilities of losing text, although more erasures will be required.

Written language is the more difficult of the two modes of language production for children to master as it makes demands that are often outside their experience, and because it is an unpractised activity for many children outside of the classroom. Word processing draws on the principle of first and second drafts, but benefits will not accrue unless the skills of revision are taught. Moreover, word processing is at its most effective as a stimulus to writing when it is a group learning and sharing activity. The computer puts writing in

The Station Announcer

Welcome to Birmingham Station,
We hope you won't miss your train.
But the train that is going to London,
Will be held up because of the rain!

The train leaving platform 11,
is sure to get there on time.
Its off on it's way to Leicester,
And it's leaving at quarter past nine.

Will everyone with a grey suitcase,
Please check the label on top.
If it has on it Christopher Shaw's name,
Then bring it to me for a swap.

I've had a request from the teacher,
From St. Werburgh's School from Derbee,
They're missing a person from their school,
And that person is called Simon Lee.

If you're after the 3.10 to Spondon,
I'm sorry to say that you've missed it.
If you're saying goodbye to a young one,
Make sure you've cuddled and kissed it.

If all you can hear is just 'chuff-chuff',
You realize its not me to blame.
I'll repeat it again in a minute,
In hope that you won't miss your train.

There's a snack bar that's on platform seven,
With Burgers and French Fries for you.
Be careful that you don't drink to much,
Or else you'll be wanting the loo!

Your partners are on platform thirteen,
Find them before you get on the train.
Make sure you remember your tickets,
Because you can't come back again.

Now its goodbye from Birmingham Station,
We hope that we'll see you again.
Don't forget to pick up your luggage
Before you leave on the train!

Figure 6.3   'The Station Announcer', a collaborative poem by Clare
and Simon.

the public domain and allows a growth in shared writing, an increasingly valued activity, but one which is quite difficult to achieve using conventional writing techniques.

One area of research we are left with concerns the evidence of transfer of training, the exchange of skills between the two writing mediums, from pen to machine and back again. We have provided anecdotal evidence of how difficult it is for adults to change their writing styles on meeting the word processor in later life. They transfer their linear writing model inappropriately to the unconstrained word processor. Salomon (1988), however, has shown that children taught writing skills such as re-drafting of text using the word processor do transfer those skills to pen and paper production. Dalton and Hannafin (1987) have also shown new of styles of writing may emerge, freer but less planned. Should we encourage this 'splurge' style of writing, or is this one of the more detrimental features of using the word processor? Does the use of programs with advanced organisers encourage off-machine planning? Do we need to teach more than one strategy of writing? This may prove difficult. As we have have been able to identify two main types of writer it would appear that students have either an in-built tendency to one style of writing or another, and that teaching has little impact on this, or there is little teaching of the approach to writing at all!

We posed the question 'What should we do with the word processor?' earlier and outlined a number of educational activities that can be based around the word processor. It can be used as an electronic worksheet for basic skills practice; for the development of advanced reading skills; for the decoding of text; to develop an understanding of story structure; and to encourage planning and information-handling skills. It can of course also be used to help children develop good writing skills and by its interactive nature put the concept of 'voice' – the flexibility of discourse – into written language. At the 1988 ITTE (Information Technology in Teacher Training) conference in Liverpool, Ian Birnbaum said that as far as information technology was concerned, given all the limits on resources, time and expertise in primary schools; he would be happy if the staff and children in his care focused exclusively on effective use of the word processor. Once the versatility of the word processor is appreciated this is a far from outrageous statement.

7 Stimulating social interaction with the computer

If only one computer is available, how should the classroom be organised for computer-based activities? One child at a time, to maximise the keyboard experience perhaps, with each individual having a few minutes of intense keyboard activity? An alternative is to have groups working together, but would the individual in such a group have sufficient opportunity for his or her own cognitive development and acquisition of skills? Grouping children together can get us over the problem of not having enough computers to place one on each desk, but perhaps if we give children the opportunity to co-operate on a task they will spend their time discussing last Saturday's football results or the latest pop record releases. And won't the more dominant boys simply elbow the girls away from the machine? Although these fears are based upon classroom realities, they are avoidable, provided that the group can be organised around a common aim. There are a number of important guidelines to be mentioned here, coming from studies of different group organisations and from studies of gender differences in the use of computers, and we shall start with the thorny issue of performance and prejudice in the use of computers by boys and by girls.

Boys and girls and computers

There is evidence that men participate in computer-based activities far more than women, and when women are portrayed in high technology publicity material it is often as the keyboard operator (cf. secretary role) with an authoritative business-suited man hovering around and pointing at the screen (cf. young executive role). Why is there this perceived disparity in the roles of the two sexes? Perhaps men are simply more able in dealing with the technology, either as a consequence of underlying cognitive structure and process, or as a consequence of educational exposure. Or is this an unjustified stereo-typical view? The stereotyping is certainly very strong, and we need to be aware of it.

Attitudes towards male and female computer users

The strength of perceived differences in men and women computer operators was demonstrated in a delightfully designed study reported by Siann et al. (1988). Almost a thousand students in tertiary education took part, first reading a short description of an imaginary person, and then completing a questionnaire seeking to determine the perceived character attributes of the individual. Attributes tapped by the questionnaire included self-reliance, sympathetic personality, personally well adjusted, ambition, approachability, competitiveness, likeability, seriousness, and so on. The description of the individual outlined a student taking a computer science course, who owned a home computer, aiming for a career in computer design, and with ambitions in the direction of management. Leisure interests were also described. Two descriptions were used, and half the participants read each of them. The only difference between the two descriptions was that one of them was about someone called Kevin while the other purported to be about Karen. In other words, the survey looked at the attitudes of students towards men and women working with computers.

The results were fascinating in that they could not easily be predicted. There were no differences between the attitudes of the male and female students completing the questionnaire; and Karen was seen as being more self-reliant, more fun to be with, more independent, more approachable, more likeable, more sympathetic, better adjusted personally, more popular, and less introverted than Kevin. The overall picture of the Kevin/Karen person was one of a competent professional with a generally positive personality, but Karen was seen as having more of these positive attributes than Kevin. If computing is a predominantly male domain, then the opposite might have been expected: Karen, for instance, might have been seen as being more aggressive in order to succeed in this alien domain, but this was not the case. The results might be explained by the type of women who enter computing being atypical of the sex stereotype, in comparison with the type of man in computer-based activities. Perhaps male computer personnel live up to a techno-masculine stereotype, while females contradict their sex stereotype. However, we can reject the idea that women in technology are stereotyped negatively, at least in the group of students sampled by the survey. This is not the general picture which emerges, unfortunately, and other work suggests that the negative stereotype is alive and well.

A 1988 survey by Lorraine Culley of the Leicester Polytechnic provides a gloomy picture of the participation of girls in computer-based activities – except in girls schools, that is. A postal survey of several hundred UK schools found signs of little interest in computing by girls. In optional activities such as computer clubs the girls accounted for less than 10 per cent of all attendees. Furthermore:

> Computer rooms in most schools were regarded as male territory and girls report being made to feel very uncomfortable by the attitudes and behaviour of boys. Several schools had recognised this problem and responded by establishing certain times as 'girls-only'. Such schemes were only partly successful however. The tendency was for the open sessions to become effectively the boys sessions and thus reduce even further the access of girls to computers. In one school the 'open' sessions were overseen by a male computer teacher, while the girls-only session was staffed by a female who had no computing expertise. (Culley, 1988, p. 4)

This suggests that girls are getting less time on the machines, and getting less expert help when they do manage to keep the boys out of the way. Culley's classroom observations picked up a tendency of boys to dominate discussion in the computer classroom, and a tendency of directing more questions to the teacher. Girls tended to sit at the back or at the sides of the room. Given that one stereotyped view of girls has them being disinterested, non-participating 'computer-phobics', it is perhaps not surprising that collaborating boys tend to take over the keyboard when working in groups.

The 'role-model' of a competent computer user is a male schoolteacher, with over 70 per cent of teachers who use computers being men. The gender disparity continues in homes where there is a microcomputer available. Just 14 per cent of girls said that it had been bought for them, whereas 85 per cent of the boys claimed it had been bought either for them or for another male in the family. Hughes, Brackenridge and Macleod (1987) found similar disparities among young working class children in Scotland, but although few girls had access to home computers, most thought that they would like to have one. Parents seem not to see the need to provide home computers for girls. Culley's survey found that teachers viewed boys as being more demanding, more interested in computing, more rewarding to teach, and as having more flair for computing. These findings possibly hold for all teaching, of course, with boys receiving more attention than girls in all classrooms from both male and female teachers. It is difficult to see how the computer demand disparity can be compatible with the questionnaire study in which Karen had more positive personality attributes than Kevin (Siann et al., 1988), unless perhaps she gained these attributes by virtue of having succeeded in a dominantly male domain. Many of us who have worked in a computer-rich environment will have strong images of the 'computer-jock' hunched over the keyboard and hacking away at his spaghetti programming. The image contains an introverted male with difficulties in relating to other people and who has an obsession for unshared knowledge. It is less easy to imagine a woman with these characteristics. Perhaps the stereotyping in the Karen/Kevin study was a result of an image of a male computer-jock being transferred to the description of Kevin. The alternative explanation is that Karen would have been attributed more positive attributes than Kevin regardless of the discipline in which she had been placed, but from the study we cannot distinguish between these alternative explanations.

In the single sex girls schools sampled by Culley a different picture emerges. The girls in these schools were enthusiastic about computing, as indicated by high levels of participation in computing options and in computer clubs. Culley concluded that the most likely reason for such a difference in the involvement of the girls between the two types of schools lay in the organisation of the teaching with and about computers.

Interactions between male and female computer users

The Hertfordshire survey of teaching practices in computer-based classrooms conducted by Jackson, Fletcher and Messer (1986) found that teachers preferred to organise mixed gender groups rather than single gender groups, but Siann and Macleod (1986) found that in mixed gender pairs the boys were socially dominant and that the girls were less motivated and also tended to be less successful in a LOGO programming exercise. When considering this in combination with the Hughes and Greenhough study (1989), which also found that girls were at a disadvantage on a LOGO exercise, we could conclude that there is a classroom management problem here, in that groups are preferred by teachers, but should we have single gender or mixed gender groups? Culley's survey suggests that girls-only groups are to be preferred if the girls are to be allowed the opportunity to develop an enthusiasm for computing. We need to examine the evidence which suggests that girls are less successful than boys when working with computers, and identify the features of social organisation which are associated with poor performance.

The interaction between gender and groups leads to conflicting conclusions. Whereas Martin Hughes and Pam Greenhough (1989) found that pairs of girls perform less well than boy–girl and boy–boy pairs, our own work has found that paired working improves performance over working alone, except for mixed pairs, which show no improvement (Underwood, McCaffrey and Underwood, 1990). Siann and Macleod (1986) also found a tendency for girls to be outperformed by boys when working in mixed pairs. There are some important differences between these studies, and so we shall describe them in some detail before attempting to resolve the apparent inconsistency.

In the tasks used by Hughes and Greenhough and by Siann and Macleod, young children attempted to move a LOGO turtle around a short track as quickly as possible. We shall concentrate on Hughes and Greenhough's more detailed study, which looked at all combinations of gender pairings. Their measures included the time to complete the task, the number of turtle moves and the number of crashes against the wall of the track. Having performed the task in a boy–boy, a boy–girl or a girl–girl pair, the children were later tested individually. The results were consistent between these testing sessions – the boys performed at the same level whoever they were working with, whereas the girls performed best when working with a boy. The girl–girl pairings performed particularly badly on this task, but it would be premature to conclude that we should encourage the formation of mixed gender groups in the computer classroom.

The differences between this study and our own study with Michelle McCaffrey, in which we found that mixed gender groups worked at a disadvantage, are to be seen in the nature of the task and in the age of the children tested. Although Hughes and Greenhough used a LOGO-type task and found poor performances from the girl–girl groups, it should first be pointed out that other studies of programming ability have found no differences between boys and girls. For example, Finlayson (1984), Webb (1984) and Light and Colbourn (1987) found that girls were as successful, if not more so, than boys. The answer here is that the LOGO-type task may not have given an estimate of programming potential so much as being a measure of spatial ability. The children may have had difficulty in relating the position of the turtle with the spatio-logical manipulations necessary to obtain the desired position. (The gender differences associated with spatial ability were also discussed by Siann et al., 1988, with much of the evidence pointing to an innate superiority in such tasks for males.) More than with the other pairings, when the girl–girl pairs crashed the turtle into the side wall of the track they tended to react emotionally and criticised each other. The way out of difficulty, in the turtle exercise, was to enter specifically correct directions to re-orient and move to a new location. There were a very limited number of correct responses to a crashed turtle, or indeed to a turtle approaching a junction. This turtle was precise, and unforgiving.

In contrast with this, the groups in the Underwood, McCaffrey and Underwood study performed a language task in which an error response caused the program to do nothing more than invite a different response. Erroneous responses did not lead to the display clouding up with unwanted letters, and so further corrective action was not needed. The program does not allow the operator to get into the equivalent mess of a turtle crashed into a wall and pointing in the wrong direction. We are suggesting two fundamental differences here – a difference between a spatial task and a language task, and a difference between what we might call 'response-constrained' and 'response-free' tasks. The subjects in the turtle task were younger than the children in our language task, and this may also have interacted with the constrained response domain to produce more emotional responses in the younger children. It does not explain, however, why it should be one particular pairing of children which showed the greatest emotionality.

The language task which showed equivalent performance for single sex pairings used the program 'Infant TRAY' and was operated by 10- to 12-year-old children. The task was to complete a paragraph of screen-displayed text which had spaces marked in place of some of the letters. One of the passages was initially shown as follows:

Jane and Gary h-- ne-er been in---e t-e s-----
k----en be--re, b-- t-e- s---- kn---e- a- t-e d--r
a-- wen- in. A-- r--n- were h--e s--n-n- s---er
c---er-. A c---- o- s-e-- w-- r----n- u-
in one c-rner o- t-e w-r- r---.

Letters were left remaining in the original display on the basis of position in the word (all first letters), position of the word in the paragraph (all letters of the first three words), and on the basis of frequency within the paragraph (the three most frequent letters were displayed). By moving the cursor to the position of one of the missing letters and tapping in a letter from the keyboard, missing letters can be guessed or estimated. If the guess is correct, then the keyboard-entered capital letter changes to lower case and remains on the screen. As for completing a crossword, the more letters there are discovered, the easier the task gets. Incorrect guesses are not punished by the appearance of something that can lead to mistaken assumptions, or which has to be removed, or which then requires some further corrective action (as in the case of a misdirected LOGO turtle, for instance), but in the case of Infant TRAY nothing would happen to the screen display. The incorrect response simply disappears when the return key is pressed to signal the end of the input. Another guess can be made immediately, or another letter can be tried elsewhere on the screen.

The program, when used in this way, can be described as using a version of the cloze task, in which every Nth letter or Nth word in a passage is deleted. One of the purposes of the Infant TRAY program, when used as it was in our study, is to encourage the development of reading skills through the interaction of different kinds of information. Orthographic and lexical information is valuable in formulating an opinion as to the missing letters of the words *WEN-* and *T-E*, and semantic information can be used to identify the partial word *S-E--* once it is discovered that the scene is a school kitchen and that the word indicates something that comes in clouds. The value of multiple sources of information becomes apparent as progress is made through the passage, and so the task can be used to help develop an appreciation of the interactive nature of decoding print. Haywood and Wray (1988) have described a number of valuable uses of this program for children of the age used in our study.

The children were first given a ten-minute session as individuals, with each attempt at a letter being noted by an observer. In the second session they worked with one other child, of either the same or opposite sex, and in the third session they again worked alone. The measures of performance were numbers of letters and words attempted, and numbers of letters and words correctly entered. For the mixed pairs there was no change in performance over the three sessions. However, for the other two groupings the measures showed the same general pattern, with the initial individual performance being lower than the performance in session two when the children worked in pairs. The improvement in session two was apparent *only* for the single sex pairs. When a boy worked with a girl there was no improvement whatsoever. When the children went back to working as individuals, in the the third session, then performance tended to drift back to that seen in the first session.

We did not attempt to direct the children to work co-operatively or otherwise, but we did make informal observations of the task-sharing organisation which emerged. There was a tendency for the single-sex pairs to work by discussion and agreement, both boys and girls, with each member of the pair contributing to the decision about which letters were good candidates, and which letters should be attempted.* In contrast, the children working in mixed pairs tended not to work by negotiation to achieve a consensus, but worked by instruction. One child would take control of the keyboard cursor controls, and their partner would give instructions as to where the cursor should be moved and when to enter the choice by pressing the return key. The instructor would be largely responsible for making the selections. There was little discussion of alternative candidate letters in the mixed pairs.

There were no effects of gender differences upon any of the measures taken in this study using the cloze language task with Infant TRAY, and this is consistent with many studies of performance using computer-based activities. The principal exception to this general conclusion is the Hughes and Greenhough (1989) experiment, in which girl–girl pairs performed rather poorly. Other studies have found that girls work as effectively as boys, for example, in the pro gramming tasks used by Finlayson (1984), by Webb (1984) and by Light and Colbourn (1987), and in Eastman and Krendl's (1987) electronic data base search task, and in the simulation exercises used by Johnson Johnson and Stanne. (1985) and by Cummings (1985). The significant feature of these studies is that the 'no-differences' results come from segregated groups or individual testing. Testing was performed without the boys and the girls interacting. Only in mixed gender pairings is the performance of girls seen to be impoverished. The LOGO turtle task which was operated by the 6- and 7-year-old children observed by Hughes and Greenhough therefore poses a problem. The differences which they found were large, and so they are difficult to dismiss. The disparities between the boys and girls in

* Following the results of the Minnesota study reported by Johnson, Johnson and Stanne (1985), and which is described in more detail later in this chapter, it is pertinent to note that the groups which co-operated were also the most successful here.

the Siann and Macleod LOGO task were not statistically reliable, but this was probably due to the use of a very small number of pairs of children.

In an early pilot investigation using the same Infant TRAY program with young children of the same age as those in the Hughes and Greenhough study, we found that mixed pairings could work co-operatively. It was a small group of less able boys who were unable to co-operate with each other. They tended to make derogatory remarks about each other's ideas, and they spent much of their time trying to gain the attention of the teacher. We have similar results working with adventure games with 7- and 8-year-olds. These observations suggest that there is an element of maturity influencing the effectiveness of group work. Immature children, while being still highly egocentric, have difficulty working together, but with maturity comes the possibility of co-operation. That co-operation is more difficult for mixed gender groups as children reach the upper end of the primary school at about the time they become more aware of sexual differentiation and gender roles.

Performance by male and female computer users

But perhaps girls are simply less able when it comes to working with computers? In their LOGO programming exercise with 6- and 7-year-old children, Hughes and Greenhough (1989) found that pairs of girls worked less successfully than pairs of boys or mixed pairs. This study is one the few to have found that girls work at a disadvantage in computer-based tasks, however, and there is good evidence to suggest that there are no gender differences in ability to use computers. Indeed, Hughes and Greenhough attribute their own findings to differences in attitudes rather than abilities.

In the evaluative study of the benefits of LOGO programming reported by Helen Finlayson (1984), a class of LOGO users was compared against non-programmers on post-programming tests of mathematical ability. Differences in performance on the mathematical tests were also analysed to look for sex differences. Although the 11-year-old boys spent more of their free time than girls using the classroom computers, there was no difference between them in their post-test performance. The boys often chose to use the computers rather than be involved in other activities during their free time, and the girls tended to avoid the machines except at set times, even when the boys were not present. The boys spent half as much time again as the girls using the computers, yet the girls performed just as well in the pencil and paper tests which were sensitive to the LOGO programming exercises.

The gender differences observed by Culley (1988), it is important to note, are not *generally* associated with ability with computing concepts, for we have described a long series of studies which has found no gender differences on computer-based learning and programming tasks. The results which suggest that girls are less able, with LOGO programming tasks, are an exception to this generalisation. Girls perform at the same level as boys in a variety of computer-related tasks, and are also less likely to hold stereotypical attitudes about gender differences in ability. This conclusion about attitudes comes from the Eastman and Krendl study (1987), in which children in a middle school science class learned how to access an electronic encyclopedia and collect materials to support their writing projects. In addition, their attitudes to their own relationship with computers were determined with a questionnaire before and after the electronic search exercise. The study found no differences in success of computer operation between the boys and the girls, but there were differences in attitudes. In particular, the boys were more likely to think that computers were for boys and that boys are more able when working with computers. The girls were less likely to hold stereotypical views, and, encouragingly, when the attitude questionnaire was presented *after* the exercise there were no differences in the attitudes of the boys and the girls towards gender roles. Experience had removed the stereotypical attitude, at least in the short term.

The weight of evidence goes against the notion of girls being less able with computer-based tasks, and we suggest that the safest conclusion is that the differences with the turtle were due either to the constrained nature of the available responses ('correctness' was very constrained) or to the task's providing measures more representative of spatial ability than of LOGO programming ability.

Classroom organisation

With one computer on each desk, it may seem that the only problem is to select the software that meets the teacher's educational goal and matches the student's academic ability. Until our schools have one microcomputer for each pupil, group work will be the norm. We currently have far more children in our classrooms than we have computers: this has been described as the loaves and fishes problem applied to classroom computers. We could try arguing for greater provision, but is it desirable to have pupils working individually? The questions asked here are whether individual work is preferable to group work, and what organisations of groups can be advocated on the basis of empirical research.

If we can generalise from the survey of UK classroom practice made in Hertfordshire, the majority of primary teachers use micro-computers for group work. Jackson, Fletcher and Messer (1986) reported that 42 per cent of teachers only used small groups, in comparison with less than 1 per cent preferring individual work when using classroom computers (this figure represents one teacher out of 197 questioned). The remaining teachers used both methods, with most of their work being done with groups. Individual computer use was mainly for drill-and-practice programs. When teachers have the choice, group work is generally preferred for the use of activities based around data handling, games, problem-solving and open-ended programs. When deciding upon the organisation of the groups one popular criterion was gender, with 81 per cent of teachers preferring mixed gender groups.

The value of group discussion

Some of the teachers in the Hertfordshire survey mentioned the benefits of group interaction during computer-based activities, and most of them encouraged their pupils to talk, to reach group decisions and to take turns at the keyboard. This role of language in groups as an aid to individual understanding is supported in another analysis (Cummings, 1985). The use of a computer-based simulation game, used by both groups of boys and groups of girls, was associated with predominance of task-associated discussion. Only 27 per cent of the discussions were categorised as being social in nature. Task-related discussion between children coming to grips with their understandings is confirmed in the Maple Leaf transcript (see chapter 2) from a group of three primary school children engaged in a microcomputer data base building task. In that example the importance of efficient questioning can be seen to be appreciated through the discussion of alternatives. Classroom data base use has been shown to foster the development of the cognitive abilities such as categorisation (Underwood, 1986), and at least part of this development of cognitive skill comes through group discussion and shared understanding.

Working in pairs at the word processor, even at the error correction stage of writing, can be very beneficial. We observed that our group involved in shared writing learned very quickly from each other. When one child observed a 'new' action by another a frequent cry of 'How do you do that?' went up and was readily answered by the other child. 'You've got to delete it now' was one of many comments which showed co-operation and close examination of the text. This is a significant statement. In the first place one child is carefully monitoring the actions of another and secondly the child being helped is willing to tolerate these intrusions. The word processor in this case allows the child to cope with peer guidance, for while it is not acceptable to make mistakes with a pencil because you are in the top class, it is quite acceptable and even amusing to make 'keyboard' errors. These children not only tolerated but appeared glad of the help of the 'spectator' child when working at the keyboard to the extent that one child was able briefly to take command of the keyboard from the writer, to facilitate error correction, without a murmur of objection from the writer.

Word processing promotes co-operation. 'Tell me when to stop' was one comment captured on tape. Another was 'You big "nana brain". Look what you've done!' to which the response was a giggled 'Oops!'. There appeared to be no threat to self-image here. Similar critical comments on a pen and paper exercise would be a reflection on their handwriting or thinking skills and would be intolerable. This was not only true for our primary school children for it is also true for adults. Blaming the keyboard or having poor keyboard skills is not an ego-threatening position.

We also looked at young children (5- and 6-year-olds) children using data bases both in groups and in a one-to-one relationship of child, computer and adult helper. The enthusiasm noted by the teacher under the first regime evaporated in the second situation when the adult was working with an individual child. Our co-operating teacher commented that her young charges required the stimulation and interest of the other children to maintain their own interest. Activities with the adult were seen as work. Teachers habitually make distinctions between 'play' and 'real work', and it would appear that these 5- and 6-year-olds had already learnt that distinction. The comments from this study raise a number of educational issues: one is the deep prejudice against play in the classroom which is understood and accepted by even very young children; a second is the assumption that work cannot be fun; and the third is that play cannot have extrinsic goals.

The value of group work

We may not be able to have one computer on every child's desk for economic reasons, but there are sound educational reasons for saying that we *should not* have one computer on every desk. The research evidence is very clear in this matter – children work better in groups.

Our conclusion about the effectiveness of group work can be demonstrated by describing one particular study in some detail. It is a thorough experiment, and has enormous implications for classroom management both with and without computers. The experiment was conducted by Roger Johnson, David Johnson and Mary Beth Stanne (1985) at the University of Minnesota, and extends their earlier work on the advantages of co-operating groups in a variety of classroom activities (e.g., Johnson and Johnson, 1975). The study shows the benefits of computer-based activities for the acquisition of cognitive skills, but its main value is in demonstrating the effectiveness of one particular classroom organisation that involves groups of co-operating individuals.

The Minnesota study observed groups of 11- to 13-year-old children who worked in a geography class with a computer simulation game involving map reading and navigation. The simulation allowed the children to direct a sailing ship to a new continent and back, using the sun, stars, ocean depth, climate and trade winds for navigation. The purpose of the voyage was to search for gold, and measures of success included navigational accuracy and the amount of gold collected. Not only did the students need to keep track of where they had been, and where they were, but they also had to take account of their supplies of food and water, and handle problems caused by storms and by pirates. The exercise lasted over a ten-day period, and achievement measures were recorded daily from worksheets and at the end of the exercise with a final test.

A typical class session would involve children being given material to read, perhaps concerning the determination of latitude from the positions of the stars. Following a planning session which would require them to make use of this new information, they would decide upon their course of action and enter their decisions with the simulation program and observe the results. They would also be given further information about such factors as wind direction and current positions of the stars. They would then leave the computer, and plan their next action. Not only does this classroom organisation have a group of children working on one computer successfully, but they are using the machine as an occasional instrument as required. They come to the computer to use it for a specific purpose, and most of their work is done with other materials and by discussion.

The children's verbal interactions were observed during task activities, and they also completed questionnaires about their perceptions of the task. Three kinds of groups were compared, with each group having about four members. The children either helped each other and shared the credit for their achievements, in a *co-operative* group, or they worked together but were evaluated against each other, in a *competitive* group. In the third kind of group they were assessed *individually* but were not in overt competition with other group members.

Children in each group had access to the computer for equal amounts of time, and the teachers were first given extensive training in the organisation of co-operative, competitive and individualistic learning. In a co-operative group, the children were instructed to ensure that each group member acquired the map reading and navigational skills necessary for the task, and told that grade points would be awarded on the basis of group achievement. Their grade was allocated on the basis of the average of the scores of the four children in their group, and a bonus was also allocated on the basis of an average of all the co-operating groups. These steps made explicit the importance for the individual of achievement by every colleague, and so each child had incentives to keep their colleagues up to standard and not to let their team-mates down as a result of their own weak work. The four children in each group were given different roles during the simulation (captain, navigator, meteorologist and quartermaster) and these roles were rotated between group members during the exercise. Once a skill had been acquired, therefore, it was in the interests of the individual to pass it on to other group members, for the grade to be achieved in the exercise was based upon group rather than individual achievement.

In the competitive groups the children were instructed to compete to find out who was the best in their group. A class chart was pinned up so that they could all see who was winning. These children were given sub-goals to find who in the 'group' could land first and who would be the first to acquire gold, and they were encouraged to compare their own performance with that of the other children in their group. These children were motivated to acquire skills, but not to communicate them to other group members.

The children who were given what were called 'individualistic goal structures' completed the simulation task in groups with minimal co-operation or competition. These children were told to do their own work without interacting with other children, and feedback about their success with the daily worksheets was given to the children privately. There was no cause for these children to help others or to compete with them.

We can say then that the children in this experiment worked with each other, or against each other, or independently of each other.

The measures of achievement included the number of worksheet questions correctly completed, factual recognition test items, new problem-solving test items, and of course, the amount of gold accumulated. The results were clear-cut: children in the co-operative group achieved more than the children in the other two groups. All of the measures of performance showed this pattern of results, and for this reason alone we should consider organising classroom activities around the co-operating group in which children are encouraged to help each other to achieve common goals.

Verbal interactions were recorded during performance of the simulation task, and it was the co-operating children who made more statements about the nature of the task and about the management of task activities, than children in either of the other two groups. Co-operators also made fewer social statements – comments about topics unrelated to the task – and also called upon the teacher less often. Less than 1 per cent of the co-operator comments were addressed to the teacher, in comparison with 19 per cent from the competitors and 12 per cent from the individuals. The co-operators had become autonomous – they were responsible for their own learning – and the measures of performance tell us that this is associated with effective learning.

The results from the Minnesota study are striking: co-operating children performed more accurately during the course of the exercise, and performed better on a final test. Their discussions were more concerned with the performance and management of the task, and they called upon the teacher less often. Children who performed the task as individuals tended to perform at a similar level to the competitive groups. In the co-operative groups the learners were responsible not only for their own individual performance but also for the performance of their colleagues. It seems that group activities are not only a solution to the problem of what to do with a small number of classroom computers, but also that co-operative groups actually provide a desirable form of organisation. These children completed the exercise both knowing more and being more able to solve new problems.

Some educators have expressed concern over the amount of discussion that takes place when children work in groups. Too much talking is thought to get in the way of learning. However, the analysis of verbal interactions reassures and informs us that, with the appropriate group organisation, discussion not only becomes task-oriented but that it is also associated with improved performance. Discussions in the competitive groups were much more likely to be social comments which were unrelated to the exercise, but co-operators discussed the task itself.

The importance of discussion and explanation was also empha-sised in Fletcher's (1985) comparison of group and individual work on a microcomputer-based mathematical problem-solving task. Silent individuals were compared with groups of three children who were encouraged to talk to each other and reach a group decision before declaring their solutions. In three out of four tasks the groups required fewer decisions in order to reach their solutions, and spent more time considering their decisions. In a third experimental condi-tion children worked alone, but were instructed to talk aloud while making their decisions, describing their reasons for the decisions reached. Individuals who performed in this 'concurrent verbalisa-tion' condition resembled the groups rather than the silent indivi-duals, and Fletcher concluded that group facilitation effects are partly a product of cognitive processes associated with explaining one's reasoning. The greater number of task statements and manage-ment statements made by the children in the co-operating groups, in the Johnson et al. experiment, may be an indication of these explana-tory processes being encouraged by the incentive to see achievement in other members of the group.

Not all of the evidence supports the view that group work results in improved performance, with Light and Colbourn (1987) reporting no advantages for groups in a microPROLOG programming task when compared with the performance of individuals. The absence of group facilitation effects may be associated with the specific task used in this study, or with the opportunity afforded to the 'indivi-duals' to interact with other members of the class during the pro-gramming exercise.

Gender differences in classroom groups: some conclusions

The three types of groups investigated by Johnson, Johnson and Stanne (1985) revealed some interesting differences between the boys and the girls who participated, and this allows us to make some specific recommendations about classroom organisations.

In relation to our earlier comments about boys having more suc-cess with spatial tasks such as the navigation simulation used here, we can first note that in all three classroom groups the boys per-formed best on the factual recognition and problem-solving tests which were administered at the end of the exercise. Some performance differences were already known to the participants – sociometric scales indicated that the boys were perceived as being 'best at computers' and as being most able to influence other group members.

Differences between the three groups existed mainly because the girls were uneasy in the competitive groups. Girls in the competitive groups completed fewer of the class worksheet items during the exercise, and also accumulated less gold in the simulation. These disparities in task performance were also reflected in the children's attitudes. After the exercise the girls in the competitive groups liked computers less than did the boys. In the co-operative and individualistic groups there was a slight tendency for computers to be liked by girls more than by boys. Although this was not a statistically reliable reversal of trend, it does go towards emphasising the antipathy that the girls had to the competitive groups. A similar statement can be made about attitudes towards geography at the end of the study. In comparison with the boys, girls in the competitive group tended to dislike geography, while girls in the other groups tended to like geography more.

After the ten-day exercise the girls in the competitive groups also had the impression that they had received less academic and personal support from the teachers, in comparison with the impressions gained by the boys, and they also declared they had less confidence than the boys in their ability to work with computers. The girls were also less motivated when in this group structure. An attitude question which asked about task persistence found that girls had more persistence than boys, when in the co-operating or the individualistic groups, but the reverse was the case for children in the competitive groups. Competition encouraged task persistence for boys. The interaction was due to a combination of boys becoming less persistent in co-operating and individualistic groups, and girls becoming less persistent in the competitive groups.

From the point of view of our discussion of stereotyping of gender roles in the use of computers, it is interesting to note that compared with the boys, the girls considered that computers were less of a male domain. This supports a result from Lorraine Culley's (1988) survey of the participation of girls in computer-based activities, but only to a certain extent. That survey found that girls tended to view the computer as a male domain, and that enthusiasm only appeared in single sex schools, whereas the Minnesota study (Johnson, Johnson and Stanne, 1985) found that girls (in mixed groups) tended to like computers more than did the boys, and had the impression of a male-dominant domain less than did the boys. If task persistence can be taken as a measure of enthusiasm, then the girls in the Minnesota study were more enthusiastic than the boys, unlike the girls in Culley's survey. The apparent disagreement in these results may be due to the nature of the classroom organisation in the schools surveyed by Culley. Her results are consistent with those from the competitive groups, and may be an indication of the way in which many of our classrooms are organised, or at least the way they are *perceived* to be organised by the children involved. Unless teachers take steps to avoid competition in the classroom then girls will not only achieve less than they can when co-operating, but they will also develop more negative attitudes towards their interactions with computers than they would if given experiences in groups co-operating in computer-based tasks.

Co-operating groups achieve more than other organisations, according to the Minnesota experiment with mixed groups, but in our cloze task with Infant TRAY it was the mixed groups which performed the poorest (Underwood, McCaffrey and Underwood, 1990). There is no real inconsistency here, because our mixed pairs could not be described as being co-operative. We informally observed the mixed pairs to operate by instruction rather than consensus. In contrast, the successful pairs, which happened to be both types of single sex groups, were more co-operative and tended to engage in more discussion about the task. The problem facing the mixed pairs was that they did not discuss the task, and so group performance was limited by the ability of the poorest member, rather than being raised to that of the more able member. A different picture may have emerged had we organised our groups around the principles of co-operation advocated by Johnson, Johnson and Stanne, but certainly some measure needs to be taken to encourage cross-gender discussion and negotiation if mixed gender groups are to be seen working successfully.

Here we are advocating the benefits of co-operative learning, but how easy is it to get learners to co-operate? We had seen a number of undergraduates working on group writing projects express their discomfort with the task because collective writing violates their perceptions of what is academically respectable. They feel that only individually produced and original work is of value – warnings about plagiarism having been carefully noted. Outside of the classroom, however, co-operation is the norm: witness the activities taking place in the playground.

Some learners find it difficult *not* to co-operate, as we have found with computer-based mathematical games, for example. One such family of programs, designed to give practice with arithmetic operations, is based on the pencil and paper game of noughts and crosses (tic-tac-toe). In the program version of the game the screen consists of an ordered table of numbers (1–99), below which are the representations of two or three die, depending upon the level of difficulty selected. Each dice provides a random number. The goal is to cover four numbers in a line; the numbers may be in a horizontal, vertical or diagonal line. To cover a number each player in turn is presented with a set of two or three random numbers by the die, and from which a product must be calculated by the player, to match one of the numbers in the table. The game is easily understood and can be played using very basic arithmetic skills. For example, given the numbers 4 2 3 we can cover the number 9, using addition. From the point of view of game tactics it may be better to cover a different square, however, and successive multiplication allows us to cover the number 24.

There are several points that can be made about the value of such games, but it is an observation of both children and teachers playing them that is important here. Although these are designed as competitive games, it is fascinating to watch how more able mathematicians and strategists find it difficult to stop themselves from helping less able partners. Help may occur in the form of simple encouragement, by pointing out that there is actually a number that could be covered by that particular dice roll, but help also comes in the form of comments such as 'Is that really the best number to cover?' and 'You could really stop me if you cover the number on the left'. We were amused to hear one teacher's plaintive cry of 'Oh look, I've stopped myself from winning!' after one such altruistic act. Of course, the competitive edge can be very sharp when evenly matched and adept players are pitted against each other.

The desire to co-operate is never too far from the surface, but most learners do not see it as part of the educational process. Johnson's team deliberately encouraged co-operation by the design of the task, and this is how teachers can encourage it for themselves. One of our post-graduate students working with mixed-age and mixed-ability groupings was disappointed with the work that he was achieving with Infant TRAY. He had created a group of 6-, 7- and 8-year-old boys, with the 7-year-old being a slow learner with few reading skills. When first using the program the eldest boy dominated, with some input from the youngest, who was bright and confident. After discussing the problem with the 8-year-old group leader, and suggesting that he acted more as the teacher than as the problem-solver, the student sent the group to work again at the computer. Progress was slow at first, but gradually through comments like 'Let John type the next bit in' and 'What do you think the next word is, John?' the elder boy drew the 7-year-old into the activity. This succeeded in integrating him into the group, slowly at first but with growing confidence, and he was installed as the keyboard operator while the youngest boy pointed out the appropriate keys. The student felt that all of the children gained from their co-operative experience. Certainly, the less able boy gained self-confidence from being able to work with the group. As with many peer-group experiences, the main gains were by the 'child-teacher' who was extremely proud of his achievement in completing the task, and also in the fact that he was able to claim that 'John can read some words now'.

The evidence from both educational research and from informal classroom observations shows that co-operative learning can have many benefits. It seems odd that education should remain the bastion of competition and individualism.

Child teachers and teacher–learners

One of the changes that has been apparent in all our classroom experiences of using the computer as a tool has been the subtle shift in the social order or power structure in the classroom. This is apparent in a number of different ways. Our colleague Richard Eagles certainly felt this and found himself at one point actively drawn into the creative process by the children in his word processing classes. Whitehead (1985) has pointed out that children learn to write shopping lists and party invitations because they have models to emulate, and that potentially the most powerful and least developed model writer for children is their own class teacher. Teachers should show that they value writing and how to write by being transparently involved in the activity. Writing with and alongside children can be very natural with a word processor. Similar shifts in teacher–pupil relations – to the co-worker status – have been noted by LOGO users, by Daiute for word processing and by the ITMA group in problem-solving in mathematics with the machine.

Old habits die hard, however, and we should not expect new working relationships to be forged simply because a computer is on the workbench. Richard Eagles describes one child's view of the role of the word processor, in which the computer was thought to be as much an aid to the teacher as to himself: 'If a child puts a piece of writing on it,' he said, 'the teacher could go back and find the mistakes'. This is consistent with most areas of school work in which children offer work to the teacher for correction. Their involvement is to respond to the teacher's remarks rather than to evaluate their own writing.

Our work with individual children showed they were keen to use the editing facilities of the word processor but that they tended to use a very restricted set of actions. Once they had found a means of correcting a mistake which worked they were unlikely to search for a more elegant method. Observations of a number of student teachers and teachers using the word processor confirm this pattern of development. If, however, either children or adults work together on a piece of writing, or have adjacent machines, then new tricks are readily passed on. What we are seeing here is the power of group learning which has also been seen in the rapid learning of new video games. Turkle (1984) has commented on the distress of parents at the immersion of children in the 'games culture' but here we see that powerful co-learning culture being used to enhance writing.

In a number of data base studies, which we have described in earlier chapters, there was a gradual shift in the nature of interactions as the project continued. For example, teachers were actively involved in teaching about the computer and about using the data base at the outset of the project, but there was a gradual reduction of this didactic role as the children's skills increased. Teachers commented on their changing role from authority figure to facilitator as the children grasped the elements of 'computer speak'. By the third or fourth session with the machine, some teachers were operating a deliberate policy of withdrawal to allow the children to discuss and make decisions without them.

To discuss interactions in terms of the relationship between teacher and pupil over-simplifies the wealth of relationships that has been established in these studies. One of the more encouraging outcomes is the willingness, and the competence, of children to take on roles of responsibility, caring and sharing. The production of a programme of work by one class of 8-year-olds for another has already been discussed. Interestingly, the teacher judged that, in teaching their peers, the children came to a better understanding of the material in question and actually retained factual knowledge that had been excluded from the data base – a reflection that is supported by other research on peer-group teaching. She argued that, of three parallel classes, only those not involved with the computer developed negative attitudes to the project as a whole. The two computer user groups retained sufficient enthusiasm to search the library for further information once the formal project was over.

The most invigorating observation that arises out of these studies is the dynamic nature of the interactions in which the computer plays a full part, as recorded in the Maple Leaf transcript (chapter 2). Perhaps the most encouraging development in this was the appearance of the children's questioning of their own questions – they came to understand what was a good question through evaluation, and were willing to discuss the values of alternative questions co-operatively. They have also come to realise that the 'goodness' of the question may vary with the task it is to serve. In the Maple Leaf transcript and in other discussions outlined here, such as that on 'biting and stinging' from the insect project described in chapter 4, there was evidence of the teacher stimulating the children to take an active part in the discourse. This was achieved in a number of ways; for example, by the use of 'distancing' questions or by offering suggestions or speculations congruent to the context of the study. All lessons structured around an enquiry have this potential, but it is because the use of information processing packages stimulates enquiry-type activities that the opportunity for these beneficial aspects of discourse can be encouraged.

Shared experiences and autonomous learning

Lepper (1985) has commented upon the motivating aspects of computer use, and has pointed to the opportunities for an education that capitalises upon them. The sense of fun and play when writing at the computer was exhibited by Graham sternly telling the cursor to 'get up this time', to the amusement of his partner, followed by 'Now we're in business' when he got it right. There was a sense in which they were working together against the computer. Daiute (1985) has noted that 'it's fun for children to feel smarter than something that pretends to be smart – and they learn quickly that computers are only machines that carry out people's instructions'. Papert refers to this sense of mastery over one's environment as a powerful motivator when children LOGO program, and we have found the same growth in self-esteem, with consequent improvement in cognitive development when children work with data bases.

Self-esteem may develop because children feel at the centre of their worlds. Teachers have commented on both the thrill children receive on seeing their own names on the screen and, indeed, have recorded problems of management because of the over-stimulation of the children. Motivation in such situations is due to the sense of positive power which comes from the ownership of a skill or of knowledge and is very closely aligned to self-esteem. In one of our example schools a high level of motivation was essential for the successful completion of the task. In this school computing facilities were particularly poor and children had to put their own data into the machine in any, and every, free moment. That children were willing to work unsupervised over lunch-times or before and after school is indicative both of the spirit and self-discipline they brought to the project.

Girls are at risk of not participating in the use of computers in our classrooms. There is currently low participation, except in girls-only schools, and classroom experiments have shown that this is not a product of ability differences. Girls are at least as able as boys in computer-based activities, including computer programming. Boys tend to think that computers are part of a male domain, and boys enjoy competitive social structures – so the research tells us. Social competition is what is turning girls away from computing: the important work of Johnson, Johnson and Stanne (1985) demonstrates very convincingly that girls not only perform better when in co-operative rather than competitive groups, but that they can develop negative attitudes to the computer and the curriculum when working competitively. The implications of this research are quite straight-forward.

Group work performed with computers should be organised around the basis of what Johnson et al. described as the co-operative learning group. In these groups children become responsible for their own learning and for the learning of their colleagues. Knowledge becomes shared rather than private. Far from the girls performing better in these groups at the expense of the boys, it must be pointed out that children as a whole perform better in co-operative rather than competitive groups. Their on-task performance measures are better, they perform better in post-task tests, they solve more new problems, and their group discussions are more likely to be task related. These groups learn more effectively than competitive groups, but it is the girls in particular who are disadvantaged by working in competitive organisations. Computer-based class work provides us with the opportunity of encouraging autonomous learners who can discuss their learning experiences and share them as teacher-learners. The gains for cognitive development are demonstrable, and educators have a responsibility to ensure that the gains are made equitably, and this does not mean simply ensuring that children have the same length of time on the keyboard.

8 Evaluation and innovation

The goal of introducing software into the classroom must be to assist with the intellectual development of its user. One approach to the consumer's question of 'What software?' is to look first for any proven benefits, and then to select those packages which will meet the perceived educational goal. This was basically the approach taken in chapter 2, in which we examined the evidence concerning the effects of LOGO programming, the use of problem-solving and simulation packages, and the use of data base information-handling packages. We shall continue to exclude software that is introduced for child-minding purposes, and for the purpose of rewarding other activities, and restrict our discussion to educational packages.

We have considered the research evidence which allows us to recommend educational computing. There is good reason to select the computer-based curriculum, and the question which this raises concerns the specific software which might meet educational needs. One criterion to be discussed here is that of software that will engage the user's mind. It is one thing to know what educational goals will be achieved if the software is used, and it is another to know *whether* it will be used. Software must motivate the learner.

The second issue to be aired in this chapter is that of the evaluation of educational outcomes. We have already touched upon this in chapter 2, of course, for the research studies reviewed there presented results in terms of the intellectual gains made by classroom computer users. Research can take routes that are not always available in classroom practice, however, and it can avoid issues of current concern. In addition to the evaluation of potential software and its likely benefits in the classroom, the educator is also in a position of evaluating the individuals who have the opportunity of learning from these computer experiences. Here we shall be considering the distinctions between product and process evaluation, between individual and collaborative work, and between linear and non-linear work. Each of these distinctions poses its own problems for the educator required to assess a piece of computer-based work.

Identifying effective educational software: learner-control is the key

Can we now describe the characteristics of computer software that will lead to desirable educational outcomes? The answer to this question is a qualified yes. It is a truism to say that activities that motivate children also lead to successful learning, and that motivation is strongly linked to the child's involvement in the learning process. Classroom software that motivates children will therefore produce successful learning, and will involve children in learning. This statement begs the question, however, for we need to know far more about the nature of that involvement and about the type of learning which is taking place. In reviewing the insights into this question that current research provides, we will relate the styles of computer programs to established theories of learning. We shall start by summarising these established educational benefits, before moving to a classification of software which may help us to anticipate its probable usefulness in advance of empirical testing.

There have been a number of reviews critical of the use of LOGO programming, and, despite the enthusiasm of Seymour Papert and his international band of followers, LOGO cannot be said to have left a widespread mark on educational practice. Surveys of the use of software indicate a popularity for drill-and-practice, and a neglect of open-ended tools such as programming, word processing and data base packages. The LOGO movement has certainly generated plenty of interest, and few primary school and mathematics teachers will be unaware of it; so why is it not in extensive use? If anything, interest is beginning to wane. The British LOGO User's Group (BLUG) is retracting its activities, and when we asked a hacker-colleague for advice on a LOGO issue recently, he replied that he thought LOGO was the picture on Batman's chest! Advocates of LOGO recommend it on the basis of a number of desirable properties: that it requires rigorous thinking; that it provides an environment for the exploration of mathematical concepts; that it fosters the heuristic approach to problem-solving; that it emphasises the importance of debugging during the development of solutions; and that it gives an awareness of the process of problem-solving. Is LOGO losing its popularity because it does not fulfil these claims, as might be suggested by the early negative reviews? Apparently not, because there have been a number of evaluations which suggest that LOGO *does* foster the development of problem-solving and mathematical thinking.

It is unfortunate that classroom teachers sometimes reject the results of experimental studies in education on the basis that experiments call for artificial conditions of testing that cannot be repeated in the conventional classroom. The misfortune is that educators are neglecting valuable information: experiments do tell us the specific conditions under which an educational manipulation can be seen to have an effect upon children's thinking. There are a number of experimental evaluations of LOGO which show positive effects, but LOGO is not being ignored because of the *method* of evaluation. Intensive case studies are a popular alternative for educators who prefer not to think about experiments, and Robert Lawler's (1985) detailed description provides all the evidence which should be required to convince a teacher who is trained to appreciate case studies. Lawler's daughter Miriam acquired debugging skills with LOGO, and transferred them to other activities, and in a second case study Lawler (1986) later described how his son Robby developed heuristic problem-solving approaches with LOGO.

To discover the more specific benefits we need to consider the empirical data, and here too there are examples of LOGO debugging skills being transferred to other problem-solving tasks, and of the experience of angles and variables necessary for turtle graphics providing positive transfer to other tasks involving mathematical operations. We have no reason to suppose that LOGO does not reach its targets, so why is it not being used extensively in all classrooms which have microcomputers?

One of the principal reasons for the limited impact of LOGO in our classrooms, we suggest, is that it requires intensive involvement on the part of the users – both the students and the teachers. Programming skills take time in their acquisition, and it is notable that the successful evaluations we have described here were those that had children working for extended periods of time on their LOGO exercises. Re-scheduling of classroom activities to accommodate this innovation may be seen as a cost which is not justified by the educational benefits. Perhaps teachers believe that the gains made with LOGO could be made just as effectively with non-LOGO exercises which do not require classroom reorganisation. If LOGO is seen as a vehicle for teaching a restricted curriculum of angles or scale, then there is every justification for this view. But LOGO is much more than this, and the belief seems implausible given the range of intellectual gains which are made in LOGO classes. Acquisition of programming skills by teachers, to the extent where help can be provided to enthusiastic young programmers, may also be seen as providing a poor return on the time and effort required. This is unfortunate, for when groups of co-learners, including children and teachers, jointly acquire skills, we have seen that learning is particularly effective. A current lack of skill should not keep a good learner down, but of course it can be very difficult for teachers to accept this new role of co-learner.

With the costs associated with the introduction of LOGO, it is perhaps not surprising that those research reports that find no positive effects of programming experiences are the ones that are remembered. There exist a number of convincing reports of the effectiveness of this activity, however, and we suggest that LOGO is worth a second look.

While there is a decrease in the amount of interest being shown in LOGO at the present time, there is an increasing appreciation of the value of information handling with data bases and spreadsheets. The evidence of their educational effectiveness is again two-fold, with both case studies and classroom experiments demonstrating effects upon thinking skills. The specific benefits associated with the use of data bases can be seen in the quality of questioning which is produced after the exercise, and in the conceptual development evident in categorisation skills (Ennals, 1984; Underwood, 1986, 1989). Classroom computers can be shown to have positive effects upon children's cognitive development by a number of evaluation techniques, but the approach we shall consider next is to attempt to predict what would be an effective software package, on the basis of a number of its features.

Classifying educational software

Numerous classifications of educational software have been produced over the past decade and a half, and that offered by Kemmis (1977) and his colleagues is a useful starting point for our discussions. They described four educational paradigms into which educational software could be placed. These are:

- the instructional paradigm, which includes programmed learning and drill and practice;
- the revelatory paradigm, in which the learner makes discoveries using simulations;
- the conjectural paradigm, using the computer to build and evaluate models; and

- the emancipatory paradigm, in which the computer is used as a tool to manipulate numbers or text or for information handling, so freeing the user to concentrate on the learning experience.

These cannot be considered to be mutually exclusive categories, because we showed in chapters 4 and 5 that information-handling packages, while emancipatory, may also promote hypothesis testing and model building.

These four paradigms can be clearly related to Gagné's (1970) four conditions of learning, which are, together with their computer-based applications:

- intellectual learning, which includes learning, practising and testing rules or concepts [for example, drill-and-practice programs];
- cognitive learning, which includes problem-solving using previously learnt rules [for example, adventure games and some simulations];
- verbal (and, in the case of computers, visual) information learning, which includes learning from hearing or reading (or seeing) about a subject [for example, demonstration programs including some simulations]; and
- motor skill learning, which includes developing and testing perceptual/motor skills [for example, arcade games].

Analysis of classifications such as this reveals that a number of criteria are either explicitly or implicitly employed in their development. For example, in differentiating between revelatory programs and drill-and-practice programs, Kemmis has highlighted the active nature of the learning process of the former and the passivity of the latter. Emancipatory programs and conjectural programs, on the other hand, are user-directed and in the case of emancipatory programs such as word processing the goal has to come from the user rather than being defined within the software.

Describing and categorising software is a useful starting point but it becomes pointless if we cannot go further and say how those different categories of programs will affect learning and motivation. A clear consensus exists amongst practitioners in educational computing, if not among the teaching fraternity in general, about the relative merits of these four types of programs in the Kemmis classification. We join the many workers who have decried the proliferation of small drill-and-practice programs in our schools. These have been used at the expense of programs which the user is encouraged to 'think with' or 'think about'. Are we justified in our rejection of certain uses of the computer? Are past or current learning theories of any use in helping us here to go beyond description towards a predictive evaluation of the software we use with children?

Bloom (1956), in the taxonomy of educational objectives in the cognitive domain, proposed a hierarchy of cognitive skills development starting with knowing and understanding facts and concepts, and moving to the ability to apply knowledge and evaluate outcomes. The application of this hierarchy into schools led to concern about the concentration of our education system on 'knowing' rather than higher-order skills such as 'applying'. This in turn influenced the introduction of educational innovations such as the Nuffield Science curriculum. One of the concerns, on both sides of the Atlantic, is a reversal of this trend and a re-focusing on practice rather than application skills with the introduction of classroom computers.

A great deal of research has been undertaken in developing theories of intrinsic motivation underlying cognition. The principle of control being with the user is a notion which is central to Papert's (1981) explanation of why LOGO is such an effective learning medium. It is also central in Turkle's (1984) explanation of the compulsive involvement of some children and adults with arcade games and programming. In drill-and-practice software the computer is in the driving seat – setting the questions and evaluating the outcomes – but when users build models or type-in text they are directing the computer because they are setting the goals. Krathwohl, Bloom and Masia (1956), in their taxonomy of objectives for Bloom's affective domain, considered the development of positive attitudes towards an activity. Attitudinal change is mirrored in behavioural changes, as first the learner shows a willingness to attend to events, and it is shown later as the active seeking out or participation in an activity.

Jerome Bruner (1966), in *Towards a Theory of Instruction*, argues that positive attitudes to learning are encouraged by the complexity and challenge of the task at hand. Complexity encourages curiosity, and perceptual curiosity in turn generates a state of high arousal or excitement which is relieved by exploration of the stimulus. Bruner's challenge is the drive to achieve competence at a task, the need to have mastery over the environment through understanding of its complexity.

Intuitively, it is not difficult to relate the need for mastery over the environment or for a reduction in arousal through exploration of a stimulus, to the high levels of motivation observed in boys playing arcade games. Indeed, Malone (1981) found that motivation when playing computer games was highly correlated with challenge as defined by a clear goal, or by the keeping of a score, and to the ability of the program to stimulate curiosity. Curiosity is created by providing an optimal level of informational complexity, and the optimal level will depend upon the individual's current state of arousal or excitement. For an individual who is currently bored, it may take very little to happen in the world or on the computer screen before curiosity is aroused. For Malone, the use of graphics and sound, or the introduction of a random element, led to perceptual curiosity and to a motivation to explore the world simulated in the computer game. Incomplete information or showing the game player how much they know, and therefore how much they do not know about a subject, so motivating them to find out more, led to cognitive curiosity.

In the model shown in figure 8.1 Wishart and Canter (1988) have formalised the relationships between those factors which may influence user motivation and involvement in the education process with learning outcomes. This 'mapping sentence' is an interesting formalisation of the inter-relationships between influential factors and learning outcomes in the education process. It is built upon investigations into the drawing power of arcade games. Schaffer (1981) identified five dimensions influencing attitudes to these games. These were complexity, type of fantasy, user involvement and control, loudness and novelty. For Bobko, Bobko and Davis (1984), complexity became dimensionality, fantasy related to level of violence and there was a collective factor of graphic quality. These together confirm Malone's findings of the need for challenge, fantasy and curiosity in computer games, but perhaps also in educational software more generally.

Jocelyn Wishart's (1989) extensive classroom investigation set out to test the behavioural effects of a number of the possible alternative models indicated in the 'mapping sentence' in figure 8.1. In particular, she was interested in the influence of the factors of control, complexity and challenge, both individually and in combination, on attitudes and on learning outcomes. To do this she developed six versions of a simulation called VESTA, a program designed to make children aware of fire hazards and safety procedures in the home by presenting scenarios, possible solutions and outcomes involving fires. Each of the six versions of the program either did, or did not, present the user with challenge, control or complexity, as shown in table 8.1.

Control was provided by allowing the children a choice of routes through the program. In VESTA 1 and 2 there was no choice path and these two versions were electronic blackboards with or without graphics. The presence of graphics added Wishart's factor of com-

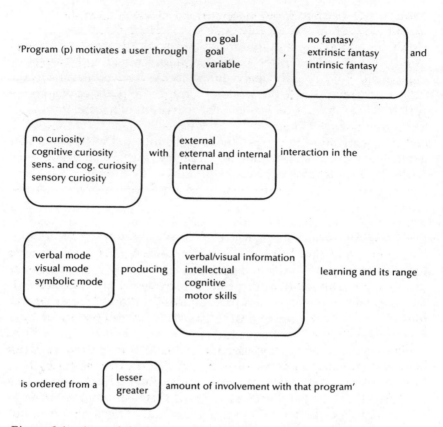

Figure 8.1 A model of motivation, involvement and learning resulting from the use of educational software. (After Wishart and Canter, 1988)

plexity. A score ticking over on the screen provided the challenge in VESTA 5 and 6. The 'mapping sentence' for VESTA 6 might be as follows:

VESTA 6 motivates a user through {setting a goal}, in a simulation {intrinsic fantasy} and generating {sensory and cognitive curiosity} with {external and internal} interaction in the {verbal and visual modes} producing {intellectual and cognitive} learning and its range is ordered from a {greater} amount of involvement with that program.

Although one might argue with Wishart's terminology, she has clearly defined the factors she investigated. In a careful randomised

Table 8.1   Cognitive factors present in the six versions of VESTA

Version	Choice of routes (Control)	Graphics (Complexity)	High score table (Challenge)
1	No	No	No
2	No	Yes	No
3	Yes	No	No
4	Yes	Yes	No
5	Yes	No	Yes
6	Yes	Yes	Yes

Source: Wishart (1989)

design, she tested the programs on 300 school children (54 per cent boys) aged from 6 to 12 years. The children were first tested on their knowledge of fires and then, working in pairs, played one version of the VESTA game twice. They were then re-tested. After this knowledge test, the pairs tried a different version of the VESTA game and their attitudes to the two versions of the game were assessed by a short questionnaire.

The results of the investigation showed that factual learning increased significantly when the children had control over the game, that is VESTA 3 produced far better results than VESTA 1 or 2. This increase in learning was further enhanced by the addition of complexity (graphics – VESTA 4) and challenge (scoring – VESTA 5) but these two factors alone (VESTA 1 and 2) produced limited learning.

Those versions of VESTA which led to knowledge gains were also more popular with the children. They liked programs that gave them control, particularly when linked with challenge or complexity or both. The children felt more involved with VESTA 4, control and complexity (graphics), than with VESTA 5, control and challenge (scoring), which was viewed by the children as more difficult and therefore less involving. Interestingly, however, the children learnt more when using version 5 of the game. That is, as perceived difficulty increased, this resulted in more effective learning, even though the children felt less at ease with this version. VESTA 1 and 2, although seen as conceptually simple, were undesirable because they were boring, and the children were aware that they were not maintaining concentration. They simply did not want to work with those programs again. This is an important statement and belies the belief of many teachers that children will work at anything if it is on the computer. Children can be very discriminating, and this selectivity applies as much to educational software as it does to arcade games and non-computer activities.

Wishart's study of VESTA may also throw light on the differential gains by children in our own studies of the development of classificatory ability both on and off the computer. In chapter 2 we described a comparison of different types of program and their effects upon children's questioning in the twenty questions game (Underwood, 1989). There were three types of program used in this investigation – the instructional drill-and-practice game LOGIBLOCKS 2, the conjectural open-ended problem-solving program THINKLINKS, and the emancipatory information-handling programs SEEK and FACTFILE. Although all children showed improved classificatory skills after using these programs, the gains were most robust for those children using the information-handling packages and least for those using the drill-and-practice programs. Indeed children using the LOGI-BLOCKS 2 game performed no better than children working away from the computer, but for the other two types of program the computer groups out-performed pencil and paper groups.

These differences between groups of children using the three computer programs are consistent with those described in Wishart's study, in that skills gains increased with the degree of control the children had over the program. However, isolating the influence of the factors of challenge and complexity is more problematic. Only one of the programs had an element of competition built in, and that was LOGIBLOCKS 2 – the least successful of the programs. The children appeared to develop their own challenge in the other two programs. In THINKLINKS they argued vociferously that their ordering of the lists was the best and in the information-handling sessions the challenge appeared to be to get the computer to release their information. That is, with the data bases they saw the formalisation of the question as a challenge. The relative failure of the LOGIBLOCKS 2 program cannot be ascribed to lack of motivation. The children were very keen to play and never turned down a chance to be involved.

Complexity as defined in terms of graphic quality of the programs was largely irrelevant in this comparison. Only LOGIBLOCKS 2 had recognisable graphics and they were very simple. Complexity here might be better described by the number of choice points or pathways a child could follow through the program and this was far greater when working with the data bases. Giving a choice of route is associated with increasing control, in Wishart's description.

The study of arcade and computer games has certainly increased our understanding of motivation and involvement but much of this work relates to the behaviour of adolescent boys. The key questions are whether we are to expect similar patterns of behaviour by adults or young girls, and whether the same patterns of behaviour will occur for the non-arcade types of software. If the answers suggest that motivation and involvement can be generated only with an arcade format, then must we turn all computer-based education into an arcade game?

Wishart's study is important because it re-emphasises the central importance of learner-control in effective learning. Such control is found not only in programs structured as arcade games, but is also inherent in tool-type programs such as word processing, LOGO programming and in data bases, which are each highly rated by children (Smith and Keep, 1986; Robinson and Uhlig, 1988; Wishart and Canter, 1988). Indeed, it is the level of involvement with programs that predicts children's positive views of any one piece of software.

The notion of scaffolding (Wood, Bruner and Ross, 1976) implies that children prosper in an educational environment which, while providing conflict, has a firm history of successful outcomes. Developing minds thrive upon challenges to their working assumptions which also meet with resolved outcomes. This appears to be what is happening in VESTA 5 which, although the children found it difficult, produced such a good learning curve. Software, even if it provides children with control, challenge and complexity, however, will not involve the children if it has a poor ratio of success to failure. Such a poor ratio accounted for the children's low opinion of the simulation SHOPPING in Wishart and Canter's study, and, in our own experience, for the disillusionment some children feel with generally well-thought-of adventure games and problem-solving programs.

Adventure games pose interesting problems for teachers. While many students are highly motivated by such programs, often to the point of addiction, other users, whether young or old, find them boring and a total waste of time. The feelings of frustration that arise in a classroom when adventure gaming is going wrong are tangible and disturbing. We have seen many bright and hopeful trainee teachers, fired with enthusiasm for games such as FLOWERS OF CRYSTAL or MARTELLO TOWERS, in near tears as they force reluctant, demotivated children on to the computer to complete a game that is the central focus of a term's topic work. Disillusioned that their all-powerful motivating agent has flopped they are in despair two or three weeks into a teaching practice. Some continue the project with ever mounting resistance from a significant portion of the class, while others abandon the project and resolve never to use the machine again.

If we look at a typical adventure game problem we can see why they can be such a classroom flop. In DREAD DRAGON DROOM the children have to cross a river by way of a set of stepping stones. A successful crossing is achieved by placing a set of randomly generated numbers, in the correct numerical sequence, one number sitting on each of the stones (figure 8.2). To complete this game successfully the children first have to realise that this is a simple number pattern game testing their understanding of the sequence of numbers from one to ninety-nine. The following set of nine numbers, generated in the order presented, would have to be placed on the stones:

Random numbers:　44　23　99　70　9　15　81　37　59

The numbers appear on the screen one at a time, and must be allocated to the stepping stones as they appear. The difficulty is in allocating a number to a position in the sequence without knowing what other numbers will subsequently be presented by the program.

Those children who do not recognise the problem have three options at this point: they can have a go and see what happens; they can call on help from the teacher or from their peers; or they can basically give up. Which strategy they employ will depend on a number of factors. Often intelligent guessing is the only way forward until information has been collected but for some this is not an easy path to take. A most harrowing example of this was provided by the reactions of an amiable and intelligent 18-year-old, who, when asked to suggest a first move in a more advanced problem-solving task responded extremely emotionally. The members of the class, who were a small and close-knit group, were deeply shocked but eventually the student recovered enough to speak. Her comment was 'I can't do it! I'd have to guess.' This was agreed but she replied, 'Guessing is wrong. You must know the right answer.' What we as educators and parents have done to that young lady gives us pause for serious thought.

For players who have identified the problem this is not a difficult task although a problem could arise if they are counting tens, twenties, thirties etc. from stone one, as this would put the first random number 44 on the fourth stone. The number 37 would then have to be placed out of sequence, probably on stone six if the same strategy is employed, or on stone five if the players view 59 as being almost sixty and modify their strategy (figure 8.2b). For the players who reach this incorrect solution, whether by chance input or by use of an appropriate strategy which fails to produce success, the response is the same: 'would you like another try?'. Feedback is minimal, as is often the case with such games, and the teacher or the peer group

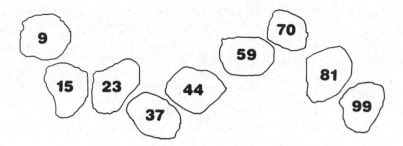

Figure 8.2a   The correct solution to the stepping stones problem, using the random numbers given in the text.

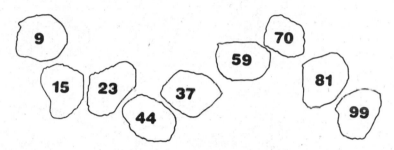

Figure 8.2b   An incorrect solution to the stepping stones problem. Numbers are in reversed positions as a result of the tens/twenties strategy and the early occurrence of number 44.

plays a vital role here in identifying and declaring what was appropriate and productive in the players' actions, and what was not.

We have already talked about children's expectations of fair play when working with the computer. Turkle discusses this at some length from observations of young children playing tic-tac-toe with MERLIN, a computer game 'who' must cheat because 'he' wins so often! This expectation can lead to rejection of an adventure game if the children feel they are making appropriate moves and not being rewarded. The fact that a 'bad' sequence of numbers in which close bunching occurs, for example the sequence

Random numbers: 44   23   99   70   9   15   21   37   59

prevents even the best strategist winning, is viewed as amusing by some children and as an injustice by others. The children who are particularly vulnerable here are those who expect to get everything right, and for whom the collecting of ticks or gold stars is the *raison d'être* for being in school. Indeed, this approach to life is carried into adulthood, and a case in point is provided by a mathematician colleague who was seen to hit the computer after her third failure with this problem. The small but very real chance that less able peers may succeed by answering the computer's randomness with their own random inputs just compounds the problem. Where a bad bounce of a ball on the football field is viewed as bad luck and accepted by most people, a bad run of numbers making logical strategies redundant is simply not on. It is a wise teacher who can both accept this 'unfairness' and instill in children an acceptance and understanding of what is happening or even present an air of amusement at the computer's devious behaviour.

We can now reflect on these observations in the light of Snow and Yallow's (1982) discussions of the relationship between teaching style, ability levels and learning outcomes. Their review shows that paced learning with carefully structured steps removes individual differences in ability, while discovery learning emphasises those differences. The VESTA programs and our own information-handling packages, although they both involve discovery learning to a greater or lesser degree, also have clearly defined steps that the user should follow (albeit with choice points), and these packages allow most children to learn. The steps within an adventure game or many mathematical problem-solving games may be less obvious particularly to less able users, and learning may not take place as the child becomes increasingly demotivated. The provision of appropriate steps, whether large or small, is the key role of the teacher. The computer does not make teachers redundant but emphasises their roles as interventionists when the success/failure ratio becomes critical. They provide the scaffolding that supports the child when a problem becomes overwhelming and therefore uninteresting.

Past experience with the specific type of problem is also a major factor in the successful introduction of a new activity. In his book *How Children Think and Learn*, David Wood (1988) has explained that for many of the failures that children have in solving problems, such as those in the classic Piagetian tradition, and with which older children and adults have no difficulty, the problem is with their lack of experience. They are indeed 'learner problem-solvers' who lack the store of previous examples of a problem to call upon and which are available to the more experienced. The influence of experience can be seen in 'gaming classrooms' and in computer clubs as children rush from the completion of one game into another.

As more boys than girls have access to computers both in the classroom and at home there is often a gender difference in the rate of success and therefore in the enthusiasm for adventure games. This may account for boys having a greater willingness to try a novel problem or a novel program than girls, although the girl's reticence may also be linked to the need to be sure of success.

The question of gender differences remains, however. Many girls do not get involved in arcade games. Malone may have the answer here when he says that challenge, that is the goals set in any game, must be personally meaningful. Killing giants, rescuing princesses or starting an inter-galactic battle may not be of any great interest to the majority of girls or indeed to some boys. This does not mean that game software designed for girls should be based around the Miss World beauty contest – a bright idea of one male-dominated software house! Indeed it might be that co-operative activities rather than competitive games hold more interest for girls. The work of Johnson, Johnson and Stanne (1985) certainly suggests that co-operative computer activities lead to more positive attitudes towards computing as well as to greater educational gains. Our own experience of adolescent computer awareness classes shows that, while the boys are keen to play games, many girls want activities which are pursued in the world beyond the classroom and the arcade hall, such as word processing. What is meaningful may be different across the sexes but identifying with the goal of the program remains a major motivating force in individual involvement with any task.

If we return now to our original question of 'Can we identify the characteristics of computer software that will lead to desirable educational outcomes?' we find that software that gives learners control is most likely to be successful. Coupled with this control, the learner needs to be challenged, and to have a clear and personally meaningful goal to aim for, whether it is answering a question using a data base or gaining the highest score on an arcade game.

There are caveats, however. Children need to be successful, not all the time, but enough of the time to generate a good self-image and raise self-esteem. This will not be achieved if the child has no idea of how to start the task at hand or indeed if the task cannot be identified. What is a challenge for one child is a daunting uphill struggle for another. Many of the best regarded programs in use in our schools adopt an approach based upon discovery learning, but in a classroom which normally adopts a more passive or didactic style, the introduction of any discovery program will simply lead to confusion. With the introduction of a new style of teaching the children will not be able to meet what they see as the teacher's expectations of 'getting things right, in the prescribed manner' with the more 'explorative' approaches required for many adventure games. The open-endedness of many tool programs such as data bases can be similarly disturbing in a classroom where all the t's are crossed and the i's dotted! The change to more active learning on the part of the children must pervade all class activities – it cannot be compartmentalised and brought out for the odd jolly jaunt with the computer.

Evaluating outcomes

We have been presenting an argument for active learning in the classroom and we have highlighted the impact of such a learning/teaching style on classroom organisation. There are, however, other management issues, the most demanding of which are concerned with assessment and evaluation. Key questions here are:

- How should we assess or evaluate the outcomes of work with programs that emphasise the processes of thinking rather than facts or final solutions?
- What is a final solution when learners are working in media that invite them to return and encourage further editing?
- How do we give individual assessment grades when the work is collaborative?

Summative and formative evaluation

We can start with the first question by considering the criteria for evaluating 10-year-old Tamma's solution to the problem of designing a mouse trap (figure 8.3). This is a problem generated with THINK-LINKS, a program designed to encourage lateral thinking.

What are the criteria for assessing Tamma's piece of work? Functionality perhaps, but the questions set by the program are often fanciful. For example, a child might be asked to capture a bear in the super-market using five specified objects. Should the criterion be the use of all the materials provided? But recognising redundancy is a skill to be cultivated and not easily acquired, as the least able in this class working with THINKLINKS showed. If not inclusivity, then novelty perhaps? But should we applaud an inefficient solution? Or are we looking for neatness and good handwriting? The answer will probably lie with the teacher's own objectives in using the program: functionality will be praised by some but not by others.

Similar problems occur when using data bases. Should we reward

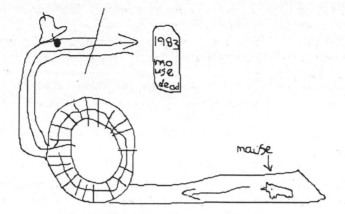

"**The mouse runs along the wood round
the wheel up the road ring the bell.
Swot the mouse grave ready.**"

Figure 8.3   An example of children's work using the THINKLINKS program. *Problem*: Design a mousetrap. By Tamma, aged 10 years ('low ability').

children who use all the search, sort and graphical tools at their disposal, or those who ask good questions and achieve relevant and useful answers. For the IT teacher the computing skills will be paramount while for the historian the search for meaning may be the goal.

Even here we are discussing summative evaluation, the end products of the learning experience, rather than formative evaluation of the process of learning. The LOGO case study described by Hoyles, Sutherland and Evans (1986) shows how we can be misled by an end-product evaluation. It reports the work of pairs of children over an extended period of time. While most pairs in the class had both successes and setbacks, two boys continuously produced exciting visual patterns using recursive procedures. Further analysis showed, however, that the complex patterns of one week varied little in structure from those of previous weeks, even though the patterns were often visually dramatically different. The boys were 'handle-turning' by manipulating variables in a procedure. Even more disturbing, they had borrowed the initial procedure was being manipulated from a neighbouring group in their first week of the project. Summative evaluations of their work marked them out as being highly successful, but more careful evaluation of the processes they were operating revealed two children stuck in their own procedural loop, trapped by initial success and now unwilling or unable to experiment.

The debate concerning formative and summative evaluation has a long history in education, and is by no means confined to the computer-based classroom. While many of us prescribe formative evaluation, we practise summative procedures. It is so much easier to give an end of the week test than to monitor progress over time. Even the attainment targets for the DES National Curriculum in the UK, although they take more frequent snap-shots of progress, are essentially driven by the end product rather than being an analysis of the path upon which the child has travelled. Placing computers into the classroom should increase the pressure for process analysis, although this may not be so if we confine ourselves to IT skills acquisition. A tick-list of whether or not learners can use a certain facility in a word processor is no less product-driven for being skills-oriented, than are earlier knowledge-driven assessment procedures.

Several years ago we were privileged to watch a group of 14-year-old Finnish girls using PC PAINT for their first time, in an IT classroom in Turku. The girls were members of a well-established design class, and their term's work was to be based around appliqué techniques. The lesson which we observed started with an introduction to the paint package and the mouse/pointer facility, and then the girls were asked to produce one or more designs for appliquéd cushion covers. Despite their computing inexperience, and after a brief period of trial and error, the girls rapidly filled their screens with designs. Although anyone can produce a recognisable design or a typed letter or a musical tune with these comprehensive packages, even when they are inept with traditional brush, pen or musical instrument, those with skills will have them amplified through the medium.

Watching the class in Turku we were particularly taken by one girl's vibrant design of a wild tulip which attracted the attention compulsively. As we watched, the beautiful image disappeared under the 'paint fill' command, but we were more upset than the designer. Talented as she was, she felt less attached to her creation than we did. She knew that she could produce another design equally as good, and she was excited about the new medium which she was exploring. She had discovered that 'paint fill' can have a dramatic, and at first sight unpredictable effect. The screen was swamped with colour because she had not created closed shapes.

The outline of her tulip was not fully joined up, a trivial matter when drawing by hand, but catastrophic when using computer graphics. This was a first lesson in how different the medium was from her pencil and paper world. She had also learnt the need to 'save' (capture) her images, not when they were complete, but stage by stage when each satisfactory addition had been made. Conceptually this is like block-printing. Painting with the computer can be very like programming, with progress being made towards an end product using modules, procedures, or part-pictures.

There are two reasons for mentioning the design class. First, if we had not been watching the process of creation we would have been disappointed with the work finally produced by this student. Summative evaluation would have been inappropriate, however. Watching her at work had given us an understanding of her artistic talent, the weakness of her IT skills and an appreciation of her drive to learn. She represented the antithesis of the pattern producers in the study by Hoyles, Sutherland and Evans (1985), who were driven by product rather than exploration.

A computer-based spiral curriculum?

A second reason for recounting our experience is that it raises the question of when is a piece of work finished. This is a long-standing problem in education. Is the story finished when the bell goes for the next class, or will it need a correction session and fair copy before it is complete? Should we stop now on this painting or continue editing it until the class ends formally? Good writers, painters and scientists know when a thing is done. One of the most difficult abilities to develop is that of parsimony – an economy of style, the pause, the nothingness that makes a thing complete.

IT complicates these decisions on completeness. In one sense it gives us freedom, because with easy editing facilities it removes time-constraints and allows us to return again and again to our story, painting or circuit design. In chapter 6 we described how children, writing with pencil and paper, rejected late thoughts or new material for a text because insertions meant they would have to re-write the passage. These children quickly realised that this was not the case when using a word processor. Insertions could take place at any time during the writing process and so second thoughts were no longer something to be stifled. They were no longer more trouble than they were worth, but rather they were seen as improvements to the developing text. With judicious saving of the file we can return afresh to the incomplete text or picture, but even more emancipating is the fact that we can step back in time and return to a point in development three or four stages back from where we are today. This is a facility not available even to the painter at his easel.

The innovatory quality here is that the linearity of production of much of our work off the computer – the idea that we must start at the beginning and go on to the end – is no longer true when working with computer tools. We can start in the middle if we wish, or with a number of small beginnings which will eventually be fashioned together. This modular approach to work is an essential part of LOGO programming, but it can also be seen when a child develops a procedure, to take an example from control technology, for controlling model traffic lights which at some later date can be re-used in a larger project such as a suburban traffic simulation. An expressive phrase or paragraph may be plucked out of earlier work and act as a stimulus for new work. A data file from one year may be added to or changed by subsequent classes, thereby providing continuity through the years. Heppell (1989) has expressed a concern that we have not fully appreciated the significance of this non-linearity of computer-based work. In particular, he has argued that we have not yet developed an appropriate language for its use. We still talk as if we are working with pen technology, and with texts being finished or originals or pre-planned, but these terms are less useful when working in a technology-rich learning environment, because they prevent us from using the freedom provided by the medium.

The facility to return to work, to re-use, to build upon and to modify previously produced material is a major benefit of this emancipating technology. It is not just labour-saving in the conventional sense of time or physical effort, for it allows all learners to build upon a store of past experiences and ideas. This is an ability which good learners have in abundance, according to Wood (1988). The reworking of ideas and knowledge is an essential part of Bruner's (1966) spiral curriculum. Whereas linear curriculum models forge limited links between pieces of knowledge, engendering attitudes of completion and closure, in the spiral curriculum knowledge has multiple links and is constantly growing in an associative network and is therefore more readily available to use.

When Bork (1984) commented that LOGO is stifling and that the cry from one sixth grade class (lower secondary school in the UK) at the start of a LOGO project is likely to be 'Oh no! Not another triangle!' he has missed the point of the exercise. The point is not to repeat but to build upon past experiences. The problem in many half-hearted LOGO classrooms is that the teachers themselves rarely

develop skills beyond simple shape production and they are therefore unable to facilitate further exploration.

Evaluating individuals in groups

The problems of assessment and evaluation in a technology-active
classroom are not just due to the non-linearity of procedures, and not
just to the need to focus upon the process rather than the product.
There is a third challenge created by the nature of the goals which
can be set in these classrooms. Instead of asking children to write
individual stories we can ask them to produce newspapers and
multi-media presentations involving graphics, sound and text.
Instead of asking children to produce work for presentation to the
teacher, we can ask them to produce a resource, a data file perhaps,
to be used by other children. We might even ask them to produce a
learning pack for their peers.

These new goals are too great for any one child to meet, and co-
operative work is essential if we are to take the opportunities on
offer with classroom computers. This poses very real problems in
assessment, not only because of the nature of the interactions with
the media themselves, but also because of the attribution of worth.
Take, for example, the work from an undergraduate group reproduced in figure 8.4. The group was composed of inexperienced
computer users taking basic training in IT skills. These skills are
taught through workshops and are designed to give students competence in any area of IT. In this case it was word processing and
desk-top publishing (DTP).

The example is the front page of a newsheet produced by the students, and distributed to a local council housing estate in the Sinfin
area of Derby. The students were fulfilling a commission from the
local city council to design a newsheet to inform residents of new
environmental improvements and, just as importantly, to encourage
the residents to participate actively in the decision-making procedures concerning their estate. The task was quite daunting. This was
an example of writing for a 'real' audience and involved a print-run
of 700 copies. It also involved careful negotiation with the local housing office responsible for the estate, for political bias and offence is
easily achieved if the information is not precise and if the flavour of
the document is not neutral.

The question here is how to assess the students' progress and
achievements when the product is the work of a collaborating group.
We know that the newsheet was a success because people on the

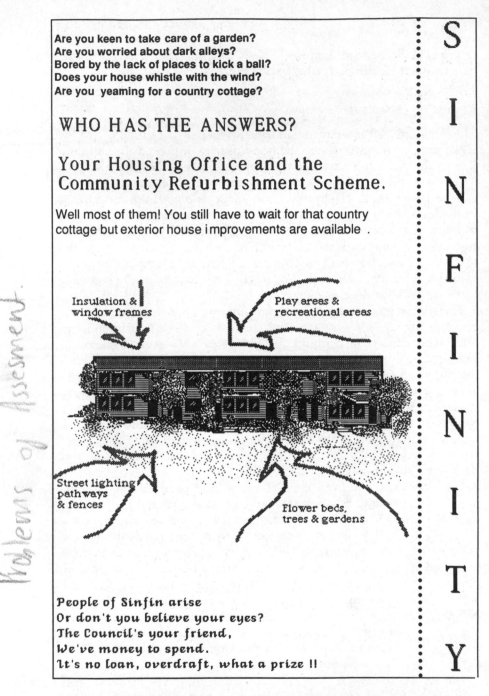

Handwritten note in left margin: *Problems of Assesment*

Text within the figure:

Are you keen to take care of a garden?
Are you worried about dark alleys?
Bored by the lack of places to kick a ball?
Does your house whistle with the wind?
Are you yearning for a country cottage?

WHO HAS THE ANSWERS?

Your Housing Office and the Community Refurbishment Scheme.

Well most of them! You still have to wait for that country cottage but exterior house improvements are available .

Insulation & window frames

Play areas & recreational areas

Street lighting pathways & fences

Flower beds, trees & gardens

People of Sinfin arise
Or don't you believe your eyes?
The Council's your friend,
We've money to spend.
It's no loan, overdraft, what a prize !!

S I N F I N I T Y

Figure 8.4   The front page of a DTP newsheet produced for housing estate residents. The purpose of the newsheet was to inform residents of an environmental refurbishment scheme, and to encourage their participation.

estate went to the local housing office to make comments about the information contained in it, but how do we apportion marks between the participants? How do we equate the work done on layout with the production of text articles? The idea for the front page picture came from one member of the group, was produced by two others, and a fourth added the all-important text arrows that gave meaning to the graphics. Is the top summary, a key message in the newsheet, any more important than the limerick at the bottom? As this was an IT skills class, is the creativity of limerick production relevant at all?

In this case, with clear IT objectives, assessment did not seem to be a major problem. This was a pass/fail situation for the students and at the end of term students were asked to word process an individual report on their own progress through the workshop. This was a report which, they knew, would be placed on record. The production of the word processed report (that is, summative evaluation) confirmed that they had acquired basic IT skills, whatever the students claimed for themselves in it. The students were often quite ruthless about their own progress but they did pinpoint attitudinal changes and the IT and social skills that they had acquired.

What was not identified in the evaluations were the changes in the students' thinking, or the conceptual level that they had reached. Sheingold (1981) found that teachers' comments on LOGO were focused on social outcomes such as interactions, and on the development of self-esteem, rather than on what the children had learnt. To some extent our case study work with data bases agrees with this conclusion, although we found teachers keen to identify IT skills acquired, if not intellectual skills. It is only by identifying areas of conflict and monitoring resolutions that we can follow the intellectual progress made by learners. We showed clear examples of this in the 'Road-traffic', 'Insect', and 'Ourselves' projects. It is by watching the resolution of conflict in problems such as the use of the Boolean 'AND' that growth can be seen. To do this, however, teachers need to recognize potential conflict points. For data bases, just as in the LOGO classroom, teachers need to develop their own expertise to act as both facilitators and evaluators of a project. In our DTP project, teachers' comments from observations were added to the students' reports, and these comments focused on points of conflict met by students.

For most academic work self-assessment is not an acceptable option. How then can we cope with the problem of the assessment of a single product from a group of co-learners? Johnson, Johnson and Stanne (1985) maximised learning by making group members collectively responsible for the product. Assessment was shared. This is summative evaluation again.

Heppell (1989) argued for a technological solution in which the computer would keep a log of the investigative strategies of the learners. This is not the skills 'tick-list' of the National Curriculum so much as being the monitoring of an on-going process. This method of logging could go some way to forcing us to focus on process, although the logged data would still need very time-consuming evaluation.

Educational computing: invasion and revolution

At the outset our discussion of educational computing asked whether any good will come of the introduction of information technology into our classrooms. There has been an invasion, but will it result in a revolution? Will computer-based education result in changes in classroom practice and qualitative benefits for the development of children's minds, or is this misguided romanticism? We started our attempt at answering this question by looking at evaluations of the potential for change. What benefits *can* be seen when learning activities are based around the classroom computer? Should we view this technology as an amplifier of our own skills, or is it more than this? Although it is undoubtedly an amplifier, as a lever is for our personal strength, we would argue that the computer allows children and teachers to enter successfully areas of activities in which they had previously felt unsure. There should be qualitative as well as quantitative change. The computer is more than an amplifier. For example, the poor writer may produce good text and the non-musician can produce identifiable music. The computer can act as a catalyst to cognitive development, and many of our discussions have reviewed research which has demonstrated the intellectual gains which can be made when computers are used as open-ended tools.

Although we recognise the necessity of the development of automatic sub-skills through practice, there is opportunity for their development in more generally productive packages such as those involving programming, the exploration and development of simulations, word processing, and information handling. Computer-based education should not mean drill-and-practice programs. The evidence leads to the straightforward conclusion that children's powers of thinking are developed when these packages are introduced. Research based upon classroom experiments and upon the case study approach points to improvements in problem-solving, hypothesis testing, and questioning, as well as in specific curriculum skills. These improvements can be seen in comparison with smaller improvements in the children who do not engage in the computer-based activities.

Extensive descriptions of tool-like packages have formed a major part of our discussions. They are based upon classroom observation, and indicate some of the pitfalls to be avoided, as well as some of the intellectual gains that can be made. Another pitfall, and one only touched upon here, concerns the participation of girls in computer-based activities. The small number of classroom computers leads us to expect an increase in the amount of group work. Indeed, it is to be advocated. There is research which suggests that certain types of groups can advance educational progress. These are groups based upon co-operative principles and in which learners become responsible for each other's learning. These types of co-operative groups are beneficial to girls in particular, whereas competitive groups tend to inhibit their participation, their attitudes and their education. There is a danger here, and the re-organisation of the classroom to accommodate group work should be done with this potential pitfall in mind.

Consideration of the use of educational computing leads to questions of the re-organisation of classroom activities. They are not a case of old activities dressed as new, and they require a re-thinking of educational goals. They also require a consideration of the questions of evaluation raised in the present chapter – which software package to use, and how should the educational gains be assessed. The answer to the first question is relatively straightforward. The successful programs are those that put control into the hands of the user, but this is a different question to that of the educational benefits which might accrue, and the two issues need to be considered separately. Our second concern with evaluation is with the assessment of individual children working as part of a group. The assessment of processes rather than products, and of non-linear work which does not have a beginning and an end, are also issues here. These are issues which we are compelled to consider when we move towards a computer-based curriculum, and they require us to reconsider our educational goals.

Just as we are encouraging children to face challenges and clarify their thinking through the use of classroom computers, so we should welcome this opportunity to clarify our own thinking about the nature of education.

References

Amarel, M. (1984). Classrooms and computers as instructional settings. *Theory into Practice*, **22**, 260–6.

Barker, R. G. (1968). *Ecological Psychology*. Stanford, California: Stanford University Press.

Becker, H. (1982). *Microcomputers in the Classroom: Dreams and Realities*. Report no. 319. Baltimore, MD: Johns Hopkins University, Center for the Social Organisation of Schools.

Bleach, P. (1986). *The Use of Microcomputers in Primary Schools*. Reading and Language Information Centre, Reading: University of Reading.

Bloom, B. (1956). *A Taxonomy of Educational Objectives: Cognitive Domain*. New York: Mackay.

Bobko, P., Bobko, D. and Davis, M. (1984). A multidimensional scaling of video games. *Human Factors*, **26**, 477–82.

Bork, A. (1984). Computers and the future: education. *Computers in Education*, **8**, 1–4.

Bransford, J. D. (1979). *Human Cognition: Learning, Understanding and Remembering*. Belmont, California: Wadsworth.

Brosey, M. K. and Shneiderman, B. (1978). Two experimental comparisons of relational and hierarchical database models. *International Journal of Man–Machine Studies*, **10**, 625–37.

Bruner, J. S. (1966). *Towards a Theory of Instruction*. Cambridge, Mass.: Harvard University Press.

Bruner, J. S. (1971). *The Relevance of Education*. New York: Horton.

Bruner, J. S. (1983). *Child's Talk: Learning to Use Language*. Oxford: Oxford University Press.

Bruner, J. S., Goodnow, J. J. and Austin, G. A. (1956). *A Study of Thinking*. New York: John Wiley.

Bullock Report (1975). *A Language for Life*. London: HMSO.

Burns, H. (1984). Computer–assisted pre–writing activities: Harmonics for invention. In R. Shostak (ed.), *Computers in Composition Instruction*, Eugene, Oregon: ICCE Publications.

Carroll, J. M. (1982). Learning, using and designing command paradigms. *Human Learning*, **1**, 31–62.

Chandler, D. (1984). *Young Learners and the Microcomputer*. Milton Keynes: Open University Press.

Chatterton, J. L. (1984). Evaluating CAL in the classroom. In I. Reid and J. Rushton (eds), *Teachers, Computers and the Classroom*, Manchester: Manchester University Press.

Clark, R. E. (1983). Reconsidering research on learning from media. *Review of Educational Research*, 4, 445–59.

Clark, R. E. (1984). Learning from computers: Theoretical problems. Paper presented at American Educational Research Association, April, New Orleans.

Clements, D. H. and Gullo, D. F. (1984). Effects of computer programming on young children's cognition. *Journal of Educational Psychology*, 76, 1051–8.

Cockcroft Report. (1982). *Mathematics Counts*. London: HMSO.

Collins, A. M. and Quillian, M. R. (1969). Retrieval time from semantic memory. *Journal of Verbal Learning and Verbal Behavior*, 8, 240–7.

Culley, L. (1988). Girls, boys and computers, *Educational Studies*, 14, 3–8.

Cummings, R. (1985). Small group discussions and the microcomputer. *Journal of Computer Assisted Learning*, 1, 149–58.

Daiute, C. (1985). *Writing and Computers*. Reading, Mass.: Addison–Wesley.

Dalton, D. W. and Hannafin, M. J. (1987). The effects of word processing on written composition. *Journal of Educational Research*, 80, 338–42.

Dede, C. (1986). Computers in schools: educational and social implications. In T. Forester (ed.), *The Information Technology Revolution*. Oxford: Basil Blackwell.

DES (Department of Education and Science) (1984), *English from 5–16*. London: HMSO.

DES (Department of Education and Science) (1985) *Science from 5–16*. London: HMSO.

Dillon, J. T. (1982). The multidisciplinary study of questioning. *Journal of Educational Psychology*, 74, 147–65.

Dixon, P. and Judd, W. (1977). A comparison of CMI and lecture mode for teaching basic statistics. *Journal of Computer Based Instruction*, 4, 22–5.

Donaldson, M. (1978). *Children's Minds*. London, Fontana.

Durding, B. M., Becker, C. A. and Gould, J. D. (1977). Data organisation. *Human Factors*, 19, 1–14.

Eastman, S. T. and Krendl, K. (1987). Computers and gender: differential effects of electronic search on students' achievement and attitudes. *Journal of Research and Development in Education*, 20, 41–8.

Eaton, S. and Olson, J. (1986). 'Doing computers?' The micro in the elementary curriculum. *Journal of Curriculum Studies*, 18, 342–4.

Einstein, A. (1957). Foreword. In M. Jammer (ed.), *Concepts of Space*, Cambridge, Mass.: Harvard University Press.

Ennals, R. (1984). MicroProlog and classroom historical research. In I. Reid and J. Rushton (eds), *Teachers, Computers and the Classroom*, Manchester: Manchester University Press.

Eyre, R. (1989). Using your Concept keyboard to support extended language activities. *Microscope*, 27, 14–15.

Finlayson, H. M. (1984). The transfer of mathematical problem solving skills from LOGO experience. Research paper no. 238, Department of Artificial Intelligence, University of Edinburgh.

Fischer, G. (1983). Word processing: will it make all kids love to write? *Instructor*, **92**, 87–8.

Fitter, M. (1979). Towards more 'natural' interactive systems. *International Journal of Man–Machine Studies*, **11**, 339–50.

Fletcher, B. (1985). Group and individual learning of junior school children on a microcomputer–based task: social or cognitive facilitation?, *Educational Review*, **37**, 251–61.

Gagné, R. M. (1970). *The Conditions of Learning*. New York: Holt, Rinehart and Winston.

Galloway, J. P. (1989). Students' use of analogies of computing concepts in computer literacy education. In J. H. Collins, N. Estes, W. D. Gatts and D. Walker (eds), *The Sixth International Conference on Technology and Education*, volume 2. Edinburgh: CEP.

Gardner, A. D. (1984). CAL and in-service teacher training. *British Journal of Educational Technology*, **15**, 173–86.

Goff, P. (1985). The textbook in the year 2000. In J. Ewing, (ed.), (Reading and the New Technologies,) London: Heinemann.

Goodyear, P. (1985). Computer-assisted learning, computer-based guidance and the teaching of educational research methods. *British Journal of Educational Research*, **11**, 291–300.

Goor, T. L., Melmed, A. and Ferris, E. (1981). Student use of computers in schools. Fast Response Survey System. US Department of Education, no. 12, March.

Graves, D. H. (1979). What children show us about revision. *Language Arts*, **56**, 312–19.

Graves, D. H. (1983). *Writing: Teachers and Children at Work*. London: Heinemann.

Harrison, C. (1981). The textbook as an endangered species: the implications of the economic decline and technological advance on the place of reading in learning. *Oxford Review of Education*, **7**, 231–40.

Haywood, S. and Wray, D. (1988). Using Tray, a text reconstruction program with top infants. *Educational Review*, **40**, 29–39.

Heywood, G. and Norman, P. (1988). Problems of educational innovation: the primary teacher's response to using the microcomputer. *Journal of Computer Assisted Learning*, **4**, 34–43.

Heppell, S. (1989). Today's students, tomorrow's schools, next decade's technology; Defining the issues and seeking solutions for teacher education. Paper read at the CAL '89 Conference held at the University of Surrey, Guildford.

Holt, J. (1969). *How Children Fail*. Harmondsworth, Middlesex: Penguin.

Homa, D. (1984). On the nature of categories. In G. H. Bower (ed.), *The Psychology of Learning and Motivation*, New York: Academic Press.

Hoyles, C., Sutherland, R. and Evans, J. (1985). Using LOGO in the mathematics classroom. What are the implications for pupil devised goals. *Computers in Education,* **12,** 61–73.

Hughes, M. (1986). *Children and Number: Difficulties in Learning Mathematics.* Oxford: Basil Blackwell.

Hughes, M., Brackenridge, A. and Macleod, H. (1987). Children's ideas about computers. In J. C. Rutkowska and C. Crook (eds), *Computers, Cognition and Development,* Chichester: John Wiley.

Hughes, M. and Greenhough, P. (1989). Gender and social interaction in early LOGO use. In J. H. Collins, N. Estes, W. D. Gattis and D. Walker (eds), *The Sixth International Conference on Technology and Education,* volume 1, Edinburgh: CEP.

Hughes, M. and Macleod, H. (1986). Using LOGO with very young children. In R. W. Lawler, B. Du Boulay, M. Hughes and H. Macleod (eds), *Cognition and Computers: Studies in Learning,* Chichester: Ellis Horwood.

Ihde, D. A. (1975). A phenomenology of man–machine relations. In R. Feinberg and E. Rosemont (eds), *Work, Technology and Education,* Urbana, Illinois: University of Illinois Press.

Jackson, A., Fletcher, B. and Messer, D. J. (1986). A survey of microcomputer use and provision in primary schools. *Journal of Computer Assisted Learning,* **2,** 45–55.

Johnson, D. W. and Johnson, R. T. (1975). *Learning Together and Alone: Co-operation, Competition and Individualisation.* Englewood Cliffs, New Jersey: Prentice-Hall.

Johnson, R. T., Johnson, D. W. and Stanne, M. B. (1985). Effects of co-operative, competitive, and individualistic goal structures on computer-assisted instruction. *Journal of Educational Psychology,* **77,** 668–77.

Jones, R. (1980). *Microcomputers: Their Use in Primary Schools.* London: Council for Educational Technology.

Kemmis, S.. Atkin, R. & Wright, E. (1977). *How Do Students Learn?* Working papers on CAL. Norwich: Centre for Applied Research in Education, University of East Anglia.

Kidd, M. E. and Holmes, G. (1984). CAL evaluation: A cautionary word. *Computers in Education,* **8,** 77–84.

Kingman Report (1988). *The Teaching of English.* London: HMSO.

Klahr, D. and Carver, S. M. (1988). Cognitive objectives in a LOGO debugging curriculum: instruction, learning and transfer. *Cognitive Psychology,* **20,** 362–404.

Krathwohl, D. R., Bloom, B. S. and Masia, B. B. (1956). *A Taxonomy of Educational Objectives: Affective Domain.* New York: Mackay

Labbett, B. (1985). Creating the classroom space to handle information. *Cambridge Journal of Education,* **15,** 88–91.

Lampert, M. (1986). Knowing, doing and teaching multiplication. *Cognition and Instruction,* **3,** 305–42.

Lawler, R. W. (1985). *Computer Experience and Cognitive Development.* Chichester: Ellis Horwood.

Lawler, R. W. (1986). Natural learning: people, computers and everyday number knowledge. In R. W. Lawler, B. Du Boulay, M. Hughes and H. Macleod (eds), *Cognition and Computers: Studies in Learning*, Chichester: Ellis Horwood.

Lepper, M. R. (1985). Microcomputers in education: motivational and social issues. *American Psychologist*, **40**, 1–18.

Levin, J. A., Boruta, M. J. and Vasconcellos M. T. (1983). Microcomputer-based writing: A writer's assistant. In A. C. Wilkinson (ed.), *Classroom Computers and Cognitive Science*, New York: Academic Press.

Light, P. H. and Colbourn, C. J. (1987). The role of social processes in children's microcomputer use. In W. A. Kent and R. Lewis (eds), *Computer Assisted Learning in the Social Sciences and Humanities*. Oxford: Basil Blackwell.

Longworth, N. (1981). We're moving into the information society. What shall we teach children? *Computer Education*, **38**, 17–19.

Lunzer, E. and Gardner, K. (1979). *The Effective Use of Reading*. London: Heinemann.

Malone, T. W. (1981). Toward a theory of intrinsically motivating instruction. *Cognitive Science*, **4**, 333–69.

Martlew, M. (1983). An introduction. In M. Martlew (ed.), *The Psychology of Written Language: A Developmental Approach*, Chichester: John Wiley.

Maxted, D. (1987). Word processing and special needs. *Educational Computing*, **8** (4), 25–6.

Mersich, D. (1982). Advances in CAL. *Canadian Data Systsems*, **14**, 37.

Miller, G. A., Galanter, E. and Pribram, K. H. (1960). *Plans and the Structure of Behavior*. New York: Holt, Rinehart and Winston.

Mosher, J. and Hornsby, J. R. (1966). On asking questions. In J. S. Bruner, R. R. Olver and P. M. Greenfield (eds), *Studies in Cognitive Growth*, New York: Wiley.

Nold, E. W. (1981) Revising. In C. H. Frederiksen and J. F. Dominic (eds), *Writing: Process Development and Communication*, Hillsdale, N.J. Erlbaum.

Olsen, D. and Bruner, J. S. (1974). Learning through experience and learning through media. In D. Hawkridge (ed.), *New Information Technology*, London: Croom Helm.

Opacic, P. and Roberts, A. (1985). CAL implementation. In I. Reid and J. Rushton (eds), *Teachers, Computers and the Classroom*. Manchester: Manchester University Press.

O'Shea, T. (1982). A self-improving quadratic tutor. In D. Sleeman and J. S. Brown (eds), *Intelligent Tutoring Systems*. New York: Academic Press.

Papert, S. (1981). *Mindstorms: Children, Computers and Powerful Ideas*. Brighton: Harvester Press.

Papert, S., Watt, D., DiSessa, A. and Weir, S. (1979). *An Assessment and Documentation of a Children's Computer Laboratory*. Final report of the Brookline LOGO Project, Brookline, Massachusetts.

Pea, R. D. and Kurland, D. M. (1983). *LOGO Programming and the Development of Planning Skills*. Technical report no. 16, Center for Children and Technology, Bank Street College, New York.

Pea, R. D. and Kurland, D. M. (1984). On the cognitive effects of learning computer programming. *New Ideas in Psychology*, **2**, 137–68.

Perera, K. (1984). *Children's Writing and Reading: Analysing Classroom Language*. Oxford: Basil Blackwell.

Piaget, J. (1952). *The Origins of Intelligence in Children*. New York: International Universities Press.

Preece, J. and Jones, A. (1985). Training teachers to select educational computer software: Results of a formative evaluation of an Open University pack. *Journal of Educational Technology*, **16**, 9–20.

Reason, J. (1979). Actions not as planned: The price of automatisation. In G. Underwood and R. Stevens (eds), *Aspects of Consciousness*, volume 1: *Psychological Issues*. London: Academic Press.

Reisner, P. (1981). Human factors studies of database query languages: a survey and assessment. *Computing Surveys*, **13**, 13–31.

Ridgway, J., Benzie, D. Burkhardt, H., Coupland, J., Field, G., Fraser, R. and Phillips, R. (1984). Investigating CAL?*Computers in Education*, **8**, 85–92.

Robinson, B. (1988). Data from words. *Educational Computing*, **9** (3), 25–6.

Robinson, M. A. and Uhlig, G. E. (1988). The effects of guided discovery LOGO instruction on mathematical readiness, visual-motor integration, and attendance of first grade students. *Journal of Human Behavior and Learning*, **5**, 1–13.

Rosch, E. H. (1975). Cognitive representations of semantic categories. *Journal of Experimental Psychology: General*, **104**, 192–233.

Rosson, M. B. (1984). Effects of experience on learning, using and evaluating a text editor. *Human Factors*, **26**, 463–75.

Rubin, A. (1983). The computer confronts the language arts: Cans and shoulds for education. In A. C. Wilkinson (ed.), *Classroom Computers and Cognitive Science*, New York: Academic Press.

Rushby, J. (1979). *A Introduction to Educational Computing*. London: Croom Helm.

Salomon, G. (1988). Artificial intelligence and natural wisdom: How cultural artifacts can cultivate the mind. Keynote address presented at the 24th International Congress of Psychology, Sydney, Australia.

Scardamalia, M. and Bereiter, C. (1983). The development of evaluative, diagnostic, and remedial capabilities in children's composing. In M. Martlew (ed.), *The Psychology of Written Language: A Developmental Approach*. Chichester: John Wiley.

Schools Council (1981). *Information Skills in the Secondary Curriculum*. London: HMSO.

Schaffer, E. M. (1981). Predictors of successful arcade machines. Proceedings of the Human Factors Society 25th Annual Meeting, pp.390–4.

Sharples, M. (1985). *Cognition, Computers and Writing*. Chichester: Ellis Horwood.

Sheingold, K. (1981). *Issues Related to the Implementation of Computer Technology in Schools: A Cross Sectional Study*. Report presented to NIEC. Washington, DC, February 1981.

Shepard, R. N. (1967). On subjectively optimum selections among multi-attribute alternatives. In M. W. Shelley and G. L. Bryan (eds), *Human Judgements and Optimality,* New York: John Wiley.

Shortliffe, E. H. (1976). *MYCIN: Computer-Based Medical Consultations.* New York: Elsevier.

Siann, G., Durndell, A., Macleod, H. and Glissov, P. (1988). Stereotyping in relation to the gender gap in participation in computing. *Educational Research,* **30,** 98–103.

Siann, G. and Macleod, H. (1986). Computers and children of primary school age: issues and questions. *British Journal of Educational Technology,* **17,** 133–44.

Sigel, I. E. and Saunders, R. (1979). An inquiry into inquiry: Question seeking as an instructional model. In L. Katz (ed.) *Current Topics and Early Childhood Education,* volume 2, Norwood, N.J.: Ablex.

Simon, T. (1987). Claims for LOGO – What should we believe and why? In J. C. Rutkowska and C. Crook (eds), *Computers, Cognition and Development.* Chichester, John Wiley.

Simon, T., McShane, J. and Radley, S. (1987). Learning with microcomputers: training primary school children on a problem solving program. *Journal of Applied Cognitive Psychology,* **1,** 35–44.

Smith, D. and Keep, R. (1986). Children's opinions of educational software. *Educational Research,* **28,** 83–8.

Snow, R. E. and Yallow, E. (1982). Education and intelligence. In R. Sternberg (ed.), *Handbook of Human Intelligence,* Cambridge: Cambridge University Press.

Spavold, J. (1989). Children and databases: an analysis of data entry and query formulation, *Journal of Computer Assisted Learning,* **5,** 145–60.

Spavold, J., Underwood, J. and Newman, I. (1989). The design of relational data files for local history research.

Statz, J. (1973). The development of computer programming and problem-solving abilities among ten-year-olds learning LOGO. Unpublished PhD thesis, Syracuse University, New York.

Suppes, P. (1966). The uses of computers in education. *Scientific American,* **215,** 207–20.

Tough, J. (1976). *Listening to Children Talking.* London: Ward Lock.

Turkle, S. (1984). *The Second Self – Computers and the Human Spirit.* London: Granada.

Turner, I. F., Scullion, L. T. and Whyte, J. (1984). Relationship between reading proficiency and two types of classificatory ability. *Journal of Research in Reading,* **7,** 123–34.

Underwood, G. (1978). Attentional selectivity and behavioural control. In G. Underwood (ed.), *Strategies of Information Processing.* London: Academic Press.

Underwood, G. (1982). Attention and awareness in cognitive and motor skills. In G. Underwood (ed.), *Aspects of Consciousness 3: Awareness, and Self-Awareness.* London: Academic Press.

Underwood, G. and Briggs, P. (1984). The development of word recognition processes. *British Journal of Psychology*, **75**, 243–55.

Underwood, G., McCaffrey, M. and Underwood, J. (1990). Gender differ ences in a co-operative computer-based language task. *Educational Research*, **32**, 16–21.

Underwood, G. and Underwood, J. D. (1986). Cognitive processes in reading and spelling. In A. Cashdan (ed.), *Literacy: Teaching and Learning Language Skills*. Oxford: Basil Blackwell.

Underwood, G. and Underwood, J. (1987a). The computer in education: A force for change? In F. Blackler and D. Oborne (eds), *Information Technology and People: Designing for the Future*. Leicester: British Psychological Society.

Underwood, J. (1983). Analysing command language paradigms in software for computer assisted learning. *Human Learning*, **2**, 7–16.

Underwood, J. (1986). The role of the computer in developing children's classificatory abilities. *Computers in Education*, **10**, 175–80.

Underwood, J. (1988). An investigation of teacher intents and classroom outcomes in the use of information-handling packages. *Computers in Education*, **12**, 91–100.

Underwood, J. (1989). The effectiveness of computer based learning in developing children's classificatory abilities. In R. King and J. Collins (eds), Amsterdam, Elsevier.

Underwood, J., Spavold, J. and Underwood, G. (1989). Novice use of a relational database.

Underwood, J. and Underwood, G. (1987b). Data organisation and retrieval by children. *British Journal of Educational Psychology*, **57**, 313–29.

Underwood, J. and Underwood, G. (1989). Teacher attitudes to the use of computers in school. In J. H. Collins, N. Estes, W. D. Gattis and D. Walker (eds), *The Sixth International Conference on Technology and Education*, volume 2, Edinburgh: CEP.

Vygotsky, L. S. (1978). *Mind in Society: The Development of Higher Psychological Processes*. Cambridge, Mass.: Harvard University Press.

Wason, P. C. and Johnson-Laird, P. N. (1972). *The Psychology of Reasoning*. London: Batsford.

Webb, N. M. (1984). Microcomputer learning in small groups: cognitive requirements and group processes, *Jurnal of Educational Psychology*, **76**, 1076–88.

Welford, R. (1989). Introductory analysis in the Social Sciences using small-scale databases. *Journal of Computer Assisted Learning*, **5**, 95–102.

Whitehead, M. (1985). On learning to write – recent research and developmental writing. *Curriculum*, **6**, 12–19.

Whitmarsh, E. (1988). Handwriting held in high regard. *The Independent*, 10 March, p. 15.

Wishart, E. (1988). Using a TTNS electronic mailbox in a junior class: a case study. *Reading*, **22**, 144–51.

Wishart, J. (1989). Cognitive factors related to the user involvement with computers and their effects upon learning from an educational computer game. Paper read at the CAL '89 Conference University of Surrey, Guildford.

Wishart, J. and Canter, D. (1988). Variations in user involvement with educational software. *Computers in Education*, **12**, 365–79.

Wood, D. J. (1988). *How Children Think and Learn*. Oxford: Basil Blackwell.

Wood, D. J., Bruner, J. S., and Ross, G. (1976). The role of tutoring in problem solving. *Journal of Child Psychology and Psychiatry*, **17**, 89–100.

Wood, H. A. and Wood, D. J. (1983). Questioning the pre-school child. *Educational Review*, **35**, 149–62.

Wood, J. D. (1984). The Resources and Potential of Current U.K. Commercial Organisations Supplying Educational Software for the Microcomputer. Report for the Economic and Social Research Council, London.

Woodruff, E. (1984). Computers and the composition process. In R. Shostak (ed.), *Computers in Composition Instruction*, Eugene, Oregon: ICCE Publications.

Name index

Subject index